Eight Myths that
Convict the Innocent

FALSE
JUSTICE

Jim Petro
Former Attorney General of Ohio
and Nancy Petro

PUBLISHING

New York

© 2010 by Jim Petro and Nancy Petro

Published by Kaplan Publishing, a division of Kaplan, Inc.
395 Hudson Street
New York, NY 10014

Library of Congress Cataloging-in-Publication Data has been applied for.

Printed in the United States of America.

10 9 8 7 6 5 4 3 2 1

ISBN-13: 978-1-60714-467-0

Kaplan Publishing books are available at special quantity discounts to use for sales
promotions, employee premiums, or educational purposes. For more information
or to purchase books, please call the Simon & Schuster special sales department at
866-506-1949.

False Justice is dedicated to
Ohio Inmate #A246292
and all innocent persons in prison today

and to

the countless men and women in our justice system
who are committed to not just winning the contest,
but to pursuing truth and true justice.

CONTENTS

PROLOGUE

Our system of criminal justice is best described as a search for truth.[1]

—U.S. Attorney General Janet Reno

AS ATTORNEY GENERAL OF OHIO, I was responsible for the largest law office in the state and the oversight of 35,000 active civil and criminal legal cases at a time. Yet I was totally unaware of the extent of wrongful criminal conviction—convicting the innocent—in America. One cornerstone of my service was nation-leading utilization of DNA technology. I advocated capturing the DNA of all convicted criminals. During my administration (2003–07), Ohio added 210,000 criminal DNA profiles to the national database, known as the Combined DNA Index System, or CODIS. This effort immediately identified prime suspects and solved hundreds of cases in Ohio and, no doubt, in other states as our DNA matched crime scene evidence in CODIS. But DNA also proved the innocence of some who were imprisoned for major felony crimes that they had not committed.

Prompted by my belief in the certainty of DNA, I made the decision in September 2005 to advocate as attorney general on behalf of a man convicted and imprisoned for murder and rape. The case had been accepted by the Innocence Project, the nonprofit legal clinic that pioneered the use of DNA to prove wrongful conviction. It was a politically risky but ultimately rewarding decision. The absolute innocence of Clarence Elkins—a family man with no prior criminal record—who was wrongfully convicted and sentenced to life in prison, introduced me to a national nightmare.

At the time, I was unaware of the factors that contribute to wrongful conviction. I did not know then that I was the first state attorney general in the country to intervene in an Innocence Project case, or that intervention by an attorney general was "unheard of," in the words of Louis Bilionis, dean of the University of Cincinnati College of Law.[2]

I did recognize that it was highly unusual for a state attorney general to go head-to-head in public debate with an elected county prosecutor over the guilt or innocence of a convicted murderer and rapist. But this was what was required when the authorities in this case refused for more than a year to recognize what DNA test results revealed about Clarence Elkins: He was an innocent man.

The thought of innocent people wrongfully imprisoned haunted my wife, Nancy, and me. We became determined to learn more. What we discovered was disturbing, and we committed to try to do something about it. Both of my worlds—law and politics—gave birth to the concept and mission of this project, and we knew that this book must engage both of them to achieve its purpose. A lifetime in public service has taught us that significant institutional change usually cannot occur before conventional wisdom changes.

When Nancy and I looked deeper into wrongful criminal conviction, we discovered that many of our questions had already been answered. Nevertheless, this information, which was the life work of many gifted people in diverse fields, is largely unknown to Americans in general and even to many professionals in our criminal justice system.

DNA-proven exonerations and extensive analysis of what went wrong in these wrongful convictions have consistently revealed the same six common contributors to flawed verdicts since the nation's first widely publicized exoneration for murder, the Boorn case in Vermont in 1819: false confessions, the use of "snitches," bad lawyering, unreliable science, government misconduct, and mistaken eyewitness testimony. Much is now known about how these contributors undermine accuracy in verdicts and what can be done to diminish their destructive impact. Many reforms currently being debated in legislatures and in other jurisdictions throughout the United States can significantly reduce conviction error.

However, Nancy and I recognized that the contributors to wrongful conviction are protected, bolstered, and empowered by common misunderstandings about our criminal justice system, and that, until these misconceptions are corrected, reforms will be hard won. *False Justice* seeks to identify and challenge eight myths that undermine efforts to improve accuracy and fairness in American criminal justice. Our intent is to speak not only to professionals in the justice system but to all Americans, because the voting public holds the ultimate power to change and improve the system, whether we recognize it or not—another overriding message of this book.

False Justice reveals, through case example, research, and opinion, why these common beliefs are dead wrong and are destructive to finding truth and justice.

MYTH 1: Everyone in prison claims innocence. In fact, guilt is usually clear and undisputed either because the criminal was caught in the act, left substantial evidence, or made the decision to take a plea. While taking a plea does not ensure guilt, often a combination of the above reveals the soundness of the defendant's decision to plead rather than go to trial. Lauren McGarity, a mediator, conflict resolution expert, and educator who has worked with hundreds of Ohio inmates for ten years, dispels this myth for us in *False Justice*.

MYTH 2: Our system almost never convicts an innocent person. We mined and shared the research and opinion of both conservatives and liberals, and we have concluded that the 253 persons exonerated of serious felonies to date, June 2010, by DNA technology (which was first employed in criminal forensics in the U.S. in the late 1980s) must be the tip of the iceberg, a phrase commonly mentioned in our research. Following the Elkins experience, Nancy and I suspected that there are a substantial number of innocent people in our prisons, but we had to revise our thinking upward throughout this project. Estimates have ranged from, conservatively, about one thousand to as many as tens of thousands of innocent people in American prisons today. We believe—and research and logic suggest—that our system convicts innocent persons far more frequently than most imagine and that most Americans, if more fully informed, would consider this a national travesty.

MYTH 3: Only guilty people confess. Stephen Boorn confessed to a murder in Manchester, Vermont, even though there was no trace of evidence, including a body. Boorn is not alone. *False Justice* explores what prompted Christopher Ochoa and others falsely accused of murder to incriminate themselves. We explore why the Miranda warning failed in these cases to provide intended protections.

MYTH 4: Wrongful convictions are the result of innocent human error. As a former prosecutor and as attorney general, I was disappointed to learn that misconduct by police and prosecutors has contributed to many wrong verdicts. Prosecutorial misconduct was a factor in thirty-three of the first seventy-four DNA exonerations (44.6 percent) and police misconduct was present in thirty-seven, or exactly half of those cases.[3] This book challenges thinking on what tactics are proper and what fairly should and should not be dismissed as "human error."

MYTH 5: An eyewitness is the best evidence. Mistaken eyewitness testimony, a contributor in 75 percent of wrongful convictions, was the prevailing contributor to the wrongful conviction of Clarence Elkins, Michael Green, and others included in the book. *False Justice* shares highlights of what we now know about memory and how this has shaped legislative and procedural reforms that will enable more accurate capture of eyewitness testimony.

MYTH 6: Conviction errors get corrected on appeal. The long, difficult, and expensive struggle to reverse a conviction is demonstrated in the Boorn, Elkins, Green, and Gillispie cases. Our appeals process addresses only certain errors that may have occurred in preparation of the case or in the courtroom. Post-conviction relief is difficult to attain in a system that properly seeks finality in the criminal process. The other route to correcting a conviction error is through new evidence, which, as indicated in the Elkins and Gillispie cases, must meet specific requirements that are very difficult to achieve.

MYTH 7: It dishonors the victim to question a conviction. *False Justice* reveals that, contrary to popular opinion, only a minority of convicted persons claim innocence and represent cases that are worthy of post-conviction DNA analysis. Prosecutors who oppose access to post-conviction DNA evidence, which could conclusively prove guilt or innocence, frequently claim that this would dishonor the victim. Public safety requires that we abandon this myth or understand that by allowing the real perpetrators to escape justice, we contribute to an increase in crime and victims. How does *that* honor victims?

MYTH 8: If the justice system has problems, the pros will fix them. While most men and women who work in the criminal justice system are well meaning, committed, and deserving of our respect, they typically do not have the authority, resources, perspective, time, or inclination to change the system. *False Justice* recommends reforms achieved through legislation, policy, and court opinion. However, these will not occur with any urgency until conventional wisdom catches up with the truths revealed in this DNA age. Therefore, it will take us—everyday American citizens—not the pros, to accelerate this process. By abandoning myths and advocating reforms, we will not only stop the destruction that comes with wrongful conviction but will also make the United States safer.

WHEN I RETURNED TO PRIVATE PRACTICE in 2007, I joined the Innocence Project and a group of Ohio legislators in an effort to draft, introduce into legislation, and advocate reforms that require the preservation of crime scene evidence, access to crime scene evidence for post-conviction DNA testing, best procedural practices for capturing eyewitness testimony, the electronic recording of custodial interrogations, and the taking of DNA samples from those arrested for felony crimes. These improved practices are gradually gaining acceptance but have met with resistance from some prosecutors and law enforcement officers not only in Ohio but nationwide. *False Justice* seeks to challenge this resistance.

A special note about the death penalty: Efforts to quantify the extent of error in criminal conviction are of great interest to those who advocate for or against the death penalty. Clearly, if it is established that the justice system makes frequent conviction errors, death penalty opponents gain the strong argument that executions are too irreversible for an error-prone system. Conversely, establishing the reliability of the justice system is equally important for advocates of the death penalty. Debates surrounding the innocence movement sometimes overlap debates on the death penalty, and advocates on both sides of these issues are quotable experts. The death penalty is a subject in and of itself and is beyond the scope of *False Justice*, which focuses instead on understanding the extent of wrongful conviction, the contributors to conviction error, the reforms that minimize error, and the necessity of effective citizen involvement in this issue. *False Justice* provides the professional position, credentials, and general philosophical stance on the death penalty for some persons quoted in the book—including me—to provide context.

On a personal note, Nancy and I have been married for nearly thirty-eight years. Our shared understanding of the politics of institutional change led to this book's concept and thesis. Researching and writing *False Justice* has been a shared effort. We hope that by the grace of God, *False Justice* will help correct common misunderstandings with a critically important message: True justice is "a search for truth," requiring constant vigilance, and is ultimately the responsibility of every citizen.

—Jim Petro
Attorney General of Ohio (2003–07)

PART I

Failed Justice

"The duty of the prosecutor is to seek justice, not merely to convict."

—ABA Standards of Criminal Justice:
Prosecution Function 2d Def. Function § 3-1.2(c),
The Prosecution Function, standard 3-1.2(c)
(American Bar Association 3d.ed.)

CHAPTER 1

The Devil Cheats Justice

A N UNEXPLAINED MURDER changes a small town irreversibly. In a major city, the daily media parade of tragedies—the fires, the accidents, and the murders—is numbing. The victims and their shocked families are strangers, which makes it easier to put their sad stories out of mind. But in a small town (not a suburb, but a complete community in a sea of countryside), a murder is much more personal.

"I don't even lock my doors or close my windows at night," is often volunteered as proud testimony to the benefits of living in a small town—until the discovery of an unspeakable act of savage violence, which has somehow occurred, with no living witness. A bereft family member and stunned safety officials can barely take in the brutality, the senseless loss, and the disheartening truth: They have arrived on the scene way too late. Stomach-turning revulsion and grief are mocked by delicate curtains waving gently in the breeze of open windows.

Within hours, the town is transformed. Everyone is talking about the murder. Even though the victim is not especially prominent, she is nevertheless "one of us." The shock of the crime is accompanied by the frightening recognition that the killer may also be "one of us." Fear is palpable. No security system or shiny new locks on doors and windows bring even a hint of the sense of security once taken for granted. The entire town is on edge.

If the crime remains unsolved, life returns very gradually to normal, but to a changed normal. The town will never be the same.

If a suspect is caught, indicted, and brought to trial, everyone in town focuses on the next step. They expect justice, meaning a conviction. If the alleged perpetrator is a local, people begin to recall little things: offhand remarks, unsettling relationships, odd behaviors. Yes, in retrospect, they should have known.

One person experiences unique anxiety. The elected county prosecutor, who has never prosecuted a capital case, feels growing pressure not to blow it—not to overlook anything, not to miss or mishandle evidence, not to get trumped by the defense attorney, who has come to town for the duration of the trial. Wisely, the county prosecutor takes the advice of colleagues and asks for assistance from the Office of the Ohio Attorney General. That is when, as attorney general, I would turn to Chief Deputy for Criminal Justice Jim Canepa. He, or one of his staff prosecutors, would carefully review the files, drive to the small town, and prosecute the case before the trial judge in the county courthouse, with the county prosecutor sitting by his side.

Canepa's boyish appearance and casual style often mask his professional talents in early discussions with defense attorneys. He is known for his playful banter and quick, funny comebacks, which put most folks at ease and even off guard. But when focused in a courtroom, that mental quickness is an advantage in the unpredictable verbal exchanges with witnesses, attorneys, and judges. Lean and athletic looking, Canepa comes to trial prepared and confident just short of cocky. But he speaks with a down-to-earth, eye-to-eye delivery, as if he is talking confidentially to you and you alone, that connects immediately with just about everyone, including jurors. His manner in court may appear to be laid back—another attribute that charms his audience—but Canepa knows exactly what to do in a capital case. He is a prosecutor's prosecutor.

That is why in the small-town murder case that resulted in the conviction of Clarence Elkins, it was unusual when I asked Jim Canepa to apply his considerable advocacy skills *on behalf of* the imprisoned man convicted of murder and rape. Seven and a half years after he was convicted and sent to prison, DNA analysis had excluded Clarence Elkins from the crime scene of two rapes and a murder. Canepa looked into the matter at my request, and we came to the shared conclusion that Elkins was innocent. But the jurisdiction's elected county prosecutor and common pleas judge refused to respond to our concerns about evidence of an error that had imprisoned an innocent man and let a guilty one go free.

I asked Canepa to discuss the case with the county prosecutor. Repeatedly, she was too busy to talk to him—too busy to even schedule an appointment. Understandably, discussions of exonerating convicted felons are not a top priority for busy prosecutors. They often believe that conviction by a jury is a final decision. Especially after the protracted appeal process, revisiting jury verdicts could needlessly tie up the justice system. Second-guessing a verdict is also risky for prosecutors who are elected by a public that has no sympathy for criminals.

Frustrated, Canepa decided to try another tactic to press a meeting with the prosecutor: He drove 125 miles to Akron. But once again, she was too busy to see to him.

Nevertheless, the trip was not a total waste. Our frustrated attempts to work with the prosecutor's office suggested an unusual lack of professional courtesy toward the Office of the Attorney General. If Canepa had started the day with any reservation about the merits of this assignment, he at least no longer had any doubts.

THAT FATEFUL SUNDAY, June 7, 1998, started out sleepy as most Sundays did—until Melinda Elkins spotted an officer in SWAT gear, gun drawn, running just outside the large picture window of her mobile home.

Then all hell broke loose.

In the bewildering moments that followed, Melinda struggled to absorb multiple jolts of incomprehensible news in the midst of total chaos. Her eventual testimony in court would detail a nightmare.

Melinda hadn't realized that officers of the Carroll County Sheriff's Department had surged onto the Elkins's property, four acres in Magnolia, Ohio, acquired for the house that she and her husband, Clarence, hoped to build someday. Clarence had heard something, though, and stepped out the back door.

Within an instant, a sheriff's deputy was at the front door. He directed Melinda and her younger son to a porch, where Melinda could not see what was going on outside on the other side of the home. There, Clarence was running toward their older son, fifteen, who was handcuffed on the ground, surrounded by officers with their guns pointed at him.

As the deputy ushered Melinda and her son onto the porch, he asked, "Are you Clarence Elkins's girlfriend?"

"No, I am his wife,"[1] answered Melinda, bewildered. She and Clarence had been married for seventeen years.

Then he told the boy to go back inside so that the young teenager would not hear what he was about to say.

"What is your mother's name?" the sheriff's deputy asked Melinda.

"Judith Johnson," she said, begging him to tell her what was wrong. Was her mother okay?

"No," he answered. Then he told her the awful truth. In an instant, she learned that her mother had been murdered, her niece had been sexually assaulted, and Clarence had been named as the attacker.[2] The crimes had taken place sometime earlier that morning at her mother's home in Barberton, nearly an hour's drive away.

"I was hysterical," Melinda recalled. "My mind was going back and forth between my mom being killed and them saying it was Clarence."[3]

By this time, the Barberton police had also arrived on the scene.

Realizing that they had cuffed the wrong person, officers began to take the cuffs off Clarence's son. Hearing his mother screaming, the teenager jumped up with one cuff still dangling from his wrist and ran into the home to find her. He knew why she was crying. When the officers had cuffed him and laid him out on the ground, they told him that they were arresting him for the murder of Judith Johnson. His grandmother.

The officers then rushed to cuff Clarence Elkins, who was as confused as the rest of his family about what was happening.

Melinda called her relatives on both sides of the family. The news had already gotten to some of them, which confirmed what Melinda did not want to believe.

She immediately consented to having their property searched that morning. Two detectives spent hours meticulously looking for evidence in the Elkinses' mobile home and their two cars. Detective Jim Weese of the Barberton police asked Melinda to sit down in the kitchen, where he proceeded to read the shocked woman her rights. That she would be treated with suspicion was another part of the nightmare.

Clarence's brother, having heard through the family phone calls what was happening, came by just as the police were taking Clarence away. Clarence trusted the police and the system. He indicated to his brother from the police car that everything would be okay.[4] His brother stayed with Melinda and the boys and watched incredulously as the police did their work. As the detectives were leaving, he overheard Charlie Snyder, an agent from the Ohio Bureau of Criminal Identification and Investigation (BCI), say to another detective, "We don't have anything here."[5]

While the investigation of the Elkinses' property was taking place, Clarence was undergoing questioning at the Barberton police station. He never resisted, and cooperated when a detective asked to scrape his fingernails and photograph his hands for evidence.[6] Clarence knew that he was innocent and trusted that he would be home that evening. Instead, he slept in the Summit County Jail that night. He would not be back in his own bed for nearly eight years.

Not a shred of evidence at the crime scene connected Clarence Elkins to the crimes. Judy Johnson's small home was searched for hours by detectives, who collected a broken fingernail, buttons, and Johnson's denture, which had been knocked out of her mouth by the sheer violence of the crime.

The most important evidence submitted to the BCI was secured in two envelopes and included a black hair collected from Mrs. Johnson's rectum, fingernails found at the scene, and hair fragments collected in the rape kit of Clarence's six-year-old niece.[7]

Ten months later, on May 20, 1999, the trial began with Judge John Adams presiding in the Summit County Court of Common Pleas. Clarence was represented by attorneys Lawrence Whitney and Jeffrey Haupt, while Summit County assistant prosecuting attorneys Rebecca Doherty and Michael Carroll represented the state.

Over the course of the next two weeks, the jury heard from 48 witnesses on behalf of the state and the defense. The state presented 139 exhibits of evidence.[8] Detective Matthew Hudak of the Barberton Police Department described the evidence items, numbered consecutively. None of these items implicated Clarence Elkins. In fact, the jury heard testimony that Elkins's DNA did not match that of the crime scene evidence. However, they also heard the six-year-old victim name her uncle Clarence as the perpetrator.

The case was sent to the jury on June 3rd. Clarence Elkins was found guilty on the counts of murder and attempted aggravated murder, three counts of rape (one involving Judith Johnson and two involving the niece), and felonious assault.[9] His parents, five brothers, Melinda, and the Elkinses' sons were devastated.

The sentencing hearing on June 18, 1999, began with Judge Adams's declaration of Clarence as a sexual predator. Clarence began his unwavering claim of innocence by refusing to sign the document that referred to him as being among the most violent of sexual criminal offenders.[10]

April, Melinda's sister, spoke directly to Clarence, expressing the family's anger. "I hope that you plead for your life every day in prison the way my mother and daughter begged you to spare them. You deserve to be raped every day of your life."[11] She then asked the judge to consider the fact that she would never see her mother again and that therefore "it would only be fair that he have no means of contact with his mother for the remainder of his sentence."[12]

A transcript of a recorded statement by the young victim, now seven years old, was also read. "You shouldn't get a second chance because my grandma didn't get a second chance," she said. "You left me all alone and broke my heart, and now I am feeling empty. At one time I loved you, but now I hate you...I can't believe that you turned out to be a...bad person."[13]

Before sentencing, Clarence addressed those in attendance. "I would like to tell everyone, let everyone know, I am an innocent man. I feel this justice system here has failed, very much so," he said. "I would like to thank my God, my family and friends for all their support. That's all."[14]

CHAPTER 2

A Haunting Doubt

CLARENCE ELKINS WAS sentenced to fifteen years to life for murder, ten years for attempted aggravated murder, ten years for one count of rape of Judith Johnson, and two life sentences for the rape of the young girl with force. The sentences were to be served consecutively.[1]

His first parole hearing would be in 2054, when he would be ninety-one years old.[2]

It has been said that God does not give anyone more than she can bear. Melinda Elkins had lost her mother and now her husband. Because she believed that her husband was innocent, she no longer had the support of her sister, her grandmother, and many of her friends. She would somehow have to raise her two sons without Clarence or her family. She may not have known her own strength, and she certainly never could have anticipated the road ahead, but if there were ever a person who could bear the burdens of these multiple injustices, it was Melinda Elkins.

HOW COULD AN INNOCENT man with no prior criminal record be convicted of crimes of this magnitude? Clarence Elkins was convicted almost exclusively on the testimony of his six-year-old niece. She had been knocked unconscious and left for dead by her brutal attacker, but she regained consciousness and found her grandmother on the living room floor. The little girl knew that her grandmother was dead.

Confused about what to do, the girl looked out the window and saw her grandmother's phone, which must have been thrown by the intruder to prevent any calls for help. She went outside, retrieved the phone, and tried to call a family friend, but no one picked up. The girl left a frantic voicemail message: "Somebody killed my mammaw."[3]

She then walked down the street to the home where three playmates— sisters ages six, seven, and eight—lived. When Tonia Brasiel, the girls' mother, opened the door, she found a distraught little girl covered in blood. Nearly a year later at trial, the girl would be unable to recall her words at this critical moment, but Tonia Brasiel testified that she had said, "My Uncle Clarence killed my grandma."[4]

Despite the child's obvious injuries, Brasiel did not call police or an ambulance. Instead, while the girl waited patiently outside, Brasiel took thirty minutes or more to get her three daughters together and then pile all four girls into her car. She drove to the victim's home, a few blocks away. April testified at trial that after a few stuttering attempts to explain what had happened, her daughter cried, "Mammaw is dead laying in front of the couch, and Clarence stabbed her."[5]

April woke her husband, who immediately sped off in his car to his mother-in-law's house while April called the police. When the officer arrived, he insisted that her daughter go to Barberton Hospital, where it was determined that she had been beaten and raped vaginally and anally. Later that day, she was transferred to Akron Children's Hospital. There she underwent surgery to repair injuries from the rapes.[6]

She returned home from the hospital the same day. Her grandmother's best friend and her husband arrived at the home just as the girl was being carried inside by her father. Later in the evening, the woman visited with her after she had been tucked into bed.

"I *think* it sounded like him," the little girl said, revealing her uncertainty about indentifying Clarence.

The woman probed, "You're not sure, honey?" Because everyone had been saying that Clarence had done this, it was a troubling surprise when the child briskly shook her head no.[7]

Yet, testifying at trial ten months later, the girl was certain that Uncle Clarence was the man she had seen in the dark home that terrifying night. In the months leading up to the trial, she had said this many times to her parents, to the police, and to psychologists. Her entire family, except her

Aunt Melinda, believed that Clarence killed her grandmother, and they were angry with Melinda for siding with him.

Witnesses for the prosecution included many detectives and law enforcement officers who testified in great detail about evidence that ultimately proved the obvious—brutal crimes had been committed—but the jury must not have noticed that they failed to connect any evidence to Elkins.

Friends of Judy Johnson said that Judy feared Clarence and that the two did not get along. The prosecution sought to imply that Clarence was motivated by anger at his mother-in-law for interfering in his marriage.

Tonia Brasiel, the neighbor who drove the victim home after the crime, testified that the girl said not only that her Uncle Clarence had killed her grandma but also that "her and her grandma tried to grab a knife, but he already had one."[8] Yet no knife was recovered, and no evidence supported this allegation.

Judy Johnson's best friend testified for the defense regarding the girl's expression of uncertainty about the perpetrator after she'd returned from the hospital the evening of the crime, but her testimony was overshadowed by the eyewitness identification of Clarence at trial.

Clarence took the stand in his own defense. He and Melinda had been out separately with friends on the Saturday night before the crime. Clarence's friends were his alibis for the evening hours, and Melinda was his alibi for the early Sunday morning hours. The state lawyers, however, minimized the impact of alibis by implying that Clarence had time to secretly leave home in the early morning hours, drive to the crime scene *nearly an hour away*, commit the crimes, drive back home, and be back in his bed a few hours later. How a person could do this without leaving a trace of evidence—murder weapon, fingerprints, bloody clothing—anywhere did not raise reasonable doubt with the jury.

As for the forensic evidence left at the crime, an analysis report prepared by a DNA laboratory called LabCorp, dated May 4, 1999, about a month before the trial, excluded Clarence Elkins from the DNA in the hairs collected from both victims' rape kits.[9] (*Excluded* is the common term to express the fact that the DNA of this evidence did not match the DNA of the defendant, Clarence Elkins.)

Summit County prosecutors and the Barberton detectives apparently did not consider this a troubling inconsistency in their case against Elkins, and Clarence's defense lawyers did not convince the jury of this either. Neither the defense nor the prosecution tested the other DNA evidence, such as the scrapings from under Mrs. Johnson's fingernails, even though there obviously had been a violent struggle.

Three years after the trial, Brent Turvey, a forensic scientist and author of the book *Criminal Profiling: An Introduction to Behavioral Evidence Analysis*, at the request of Clarence's defense team, reviewed the DNA analysis report from LabCorp. He concluded that, according to this report, the black hair collected from Mrs. Johnson was "consistent with the genetic materials originating from the child, Judith Johnson, or someone maternally related to them." Simply stated, this hair may have come from one of the victims or one of their family members. Clarence Elkins was completely excluded.

Furthermore, Turvey determined that the hair in the rape kit did not come from either victim and that it did not come from Clarence Elkins. Turvey reported, "…this DNA evidence alone completely excludes Clarence Elkins, pointing to another offender."

Turvey concluded, "Given the overwhelming DNA evidence, the undisputed fact that *no* physical evidence associates Clarence Elkins with the crime scene or the crime, and the proven tenuousness of eyewitness ID (especially that of a frightened 6-year-old child), this examiner is at a loss as to why Mr. Elkins has been convicted of any crime related to this case."[10]

MELINDA ELKINS WAS determined to find justice for Clarence, her mother, and the young rape victim, but she could not have imagined what this would require. For starters, she did not even have time to grieve. Melinda lost her job as a customer service representative for a national company before her mother had been buried. When she called into work after her three days permitted for bereavement, she was stunned to learn that she could no longer go to her office in Canton but would have to drive much farther to Cleveland. She didn't have a reliable car for that long of a commute, and she couldn't spare the travel time with all of her responsibilities at home. She asked her supervisor to reconsider and said that she would call back in a couple of days to get the decision on the office question.

Melinda learned that during her absence, the police had gone to her workplace, rummaged through her desk, and let it be known that she was a suspect. Ultimately, Melinda was let go on June 5 for missing more than three days of work. Her mother was buried on June 12.[11]

Melinda had no choice but to sell the Elkins's mobile home and four acres of land, netting only $2,800. She barely scraped by, even when kind people rented a small modular home to her for $300 a month.[12]

But through it all, she never lost focus on the case. Melinda's perseverance would be essential. Clarence's appeal to the Summit County Court of Appeals was denied on September 27, 2000. In November, Elkins's attorneys sought review in the Ohio Supreme Court. However, on February 7, 2001, the high court declined jurisdiction: It would not review the case.[13]

For more than two years, Melinda engaged in the frustrating work of a detective, exploring leads that only eliminated suspects from a list of possible perpetrators, which she had compiled. Her lawyers told her there was nothing left to do to help Clarence. As she explored possible options, she learned of Martin Yant, a local investigative journalist who had written about wrongful conviction and had subsequently become a licensed private investigator.

Melinda sent Yant an email with the subject line "Curious." She told him about Clarence's wrongful conviction and then got to the subject of her curiosity: Did Yant think that anything could be done now that the appeals process had been exhausted and her attorneys said they could do no more?

AFTER GRADUATING FROM Georgetown University, Martin Yant had pursued a career in newspaper reporting. Now in his mid-fifties, the sandy-haired, physically fit Yant still had the soul of an old-school investigative reporter. He never forgot a lesson he'd learned while still an aspiring journalist: "When your mother tells you she loves you, check it out."

It was a natural step for Yant to apply the skills he had honed as an award-winning investigative reporter and author to his second career as a licensed private investigator. The one difference between Yant and other PIs was that he never carried a gun. One lasting boyhood memory was of a neighbor's three-year-old child finding a handgun in her home and accidentally shooting her brother; Yant would have nothing to do with a gun for the rest of his life. Judging from the one time that his knock on the door of a "person of interest" resulted in a shotgun being pointed at his face, he also reasoned that, even if he did carry a gun, he probably wouldn't have it drawn at the right moment anyway.

Fortunately, Yant survived that unsettling moment. By the time Melinda contacted him, he had assisted in seven wrongful conviction cases that led to exoneration. He had also written a book that was an important contribution to the emerging study of wrongful conviction, *Presumed Guilty: When Innocent People Are Wrongly Convicted*.

Yant responded to Melinda with information that few laypersons outside the justice system fully understand. He told her that there are two tracks available in a wrongful conviction case. The appeals process, familiar to most people, can address only information and processes that were part of the trial. However, a track called "post-conviction actions" addresses new information that challenges the judgment of conviction. Federal and state laws govern post-conviction relief. For example, in Ohio, these actions must be taken within 180 days of the time stamp on the trial transcript. The exception is new evidence, which does not have the time limitation but needs to meet other requirements to be viable.

Melinda decided to hire Martin Yant to assist in finding the "new evidence" that could cast light on the person who killed her mother. One of the first things that Yant instructed Melinda to do was the one most intimidating to her: reconcile with her sister, April.

On November 10, 2001, Yant accompanied Melinda on an unannounced visit to her sister's home. The two had not seen each other since Clarence's sentencing two years earlier. Before then, April and Melinda had been very close. Summoning her courage, Melinda walked up to the door with Yant. April's husband, David, responded to her knock and opened the door partially. When he saw who it was, he closed the door leaving it slightly ajar. A few seconds later, April opened the door, and the two sisters collapsed into each other's arms in an emotional reunion. They set aside their differences about Clarence and finally consoled each other over the loss of their mother.[14]

YANT WOULD ALWAYS remember this as one of the most moving events of his life. He excused himself to give April and Melinda some time alone. He introduced himself to the victim, now nine years old, who had been standing back in the adjacent living room. The two sat down on the sofa and began to chat. Yant asked the all-important question, "Are you sure it was your Uncle Clarence who killed your grandmother?"

"I was never really sure," she replied without hesitation, "and I'm less sure now."[15]

It was as if she had been carrying a heavy burden that she could finally put down. Experienced as he was with the fallibility of eyewitness testimony, Yant was not surprised. He knew that children had additional vulnerabilities as witnesses. For example, children seek adult approval and therefore are very susceptible to suggestion and manipulation, whether intended by authorities or not. She had been attacked in the dark of night and had been knocked unconscious. She had suffered a severe blow to the head and had been deprived of oxygen when her attacker tried to strangle her. How so many had put full credibility in her identification was one of the mysteries in this case.

Over the next weeks, she shared her doubt with her mother and Aunt Melinda. She said that right after the crimes, she had tried to tell the people working for the prosecution that she wasn't sure about Uncle Clarence. They told her not to feel bad about saying that it was her uncle. "We've got all of this other evidence," they said. "*You're* not going to put him in prison."[16]

This led to the first real opportunity for the Elkins team. In May 2002, nearly four years after the crime, the girl formally recanted her testimony identifying her uncle as the perpetrator. On July 30, Clarence's lawyers submitted a motion to Summit County Common Pleas Judge John Adams—the same judge who had sentenced Elkins—and they supplemented it on August 9, 2002, with a twenty-point affidavit in which she detailed her account of the crime, her initial identification of her uncle, her subsequent doubts, the pressure she had felt to stick with this identification, and her eventual confirmation that he was not the man who had killed her grandma and assaulted her. The motion sought to have the judge grant Elkins an evidentiary hearing or a new trial.[17]

A hearing on the motion was held on July 30, 2002, before Judge Adams. Summit County prosecutors claimed that the young witness had been coached on her new position and that a thirty-minute hypnosis session had contributed to her change of testimony.

Martin Yant later recalled that the hypnosis session had been a brief attempt of five to ten minutes to see if anything could be revealed about the perpetrator. The hypnotist, Dr. Bruce Goldsmith, a clinical psychologist, was well respected and often used by law enforcement. In fact, according to Yant, the Supreme Court of Ohio included guidelines on the use of hypnosis in its 1988 decision to overturn a conviction for a double murder—in large part due to Goldsmith's testimony regarding the proper use of hypnosis with witnesses, without suggestive questioning, in criminal cases. The wrongfully convicted Dale Johnston was released after serving seven years in prison, and the true perpetrators of the gruesome crime were arrested and convicted. A key witness in the original trial that produced the wrongful conviction had been subjected to suggestive questioning while under hypnosis. In the Elkins case, Goldsmith quickly determined that the girl's memory *of her testimony* had compromised *her original memory.* Therefore he cut the hypnosis session short with the girl.[18]

Mike Carroll had called Goldsmith after the session. Yant recalled, years later, that Goldsmith had told Carroll about the short session, emphasizing that no suggestive questions were asked. That didn't stop Carroll from telling the press the next morning that the hypnosis had altered the victim's memory. Elkins's attorney, Elizabeth Kelley, said that the hypnosis only confirmed that four years earlier, authorities had manipulated the young child's memory and testimony in the first place.[19]

Judge Adams did not see validity in the new testimony. On December 9, 2002, he granted the state's motion to dismiss, declaring that her "recent recantation lacks credibility." Believing the prosecutors' arguments, he wrote in his fifty-four-page ruling, "The Court is of the opinion that the child-victim told the truth originally and her change of mind is the result of influence from her family and others who have an interest in the success of this Petition."[20]

CHAPTER 3

Relentless Pursuit

ALTHOUGH DISAPPOINTED, Melinda remained undaunted and showed remarkable resilience by redoubling her efforts. Carrying mounting debt, she launched a website, www.freeclarence.com, in September 2003. The site featured a 1996 Elkins family photo with Clarence, Melinda, and their young boys dressed in casual clothes. All smiling into the camera's eye, they were the typical American family, with no clue that their lives would soon be turned upside down and would never return to the normalcy of this snapshot. Below the family photo, an image of the stark, foreboding face of Lebanon Correctional Facility communicated their new reality. Also on the home page: a case history that began on June 4, 1999, the day after the jury had received the case. Clarence was convicted of murder, attempted aggravated murder, three counts of rape, and felonious assault. Melinda shared the haunting tale of a wrongful conviction.

The story was compelling—and effective. The website would eventually generate about $40,000 in donations for Clarence's defense. It trickled in especially after the case was aired on television in the United States and in reruns all over the world.[1]

Meanwhile, Melinda had been working on her list of suspects and was focusing on a younger man. Elkins's attorney would indicate in a petition for a new trial that this alternative suspect had a "bizarre infatuation" with her mother "even though she was 30 years older." Mrs. Johnson, age fifty-seven at the time and in poor health, "had repeatedly rejected him" when he asked to take her out.[2]

The transcripts from the hearing before Judge Adams on the petition for a new trial reveal what Yant and Melinda had discovered about this new suspect. The man had "suffered a head injury as a child" and was "on anti-psychotic medication." He had been "evicted by a landlord when he had been caught molesting their ten-year-old daughter." As a juvenile, he was convicted of rape with a foreign object, the same form of assault used in the attacks on Mrs. Johnson and her granddaughter.[3]

After the murder, at least three people indicated that the man "had scratches on his face, neck, and arms, which he said came from a night 'with a wild woman.'" He had been observed "acting extremely nervously" at the reception following Johnson's funeral[4] and "admitted to investigator Yant that he had been in Judy Johnson's neighborhood the night of the murder.[5]

Melinda's suspect rented from Mrs. Johnson's friend, and she was very suspicious of her tenant's odd behavior. Melinda asked the man to provide his DNA to prove his innocence. He refused, but Yant had an idea. He asked his associate private investigator, an attractive woman, to go to the suspect's favorite bar, engage him in conversation, and try to get his DNA on a bottle or cigarette butt. The first time they tried this, on a Saturday night, Yant and Melinda waited outside in the car. The tension was killing Melinda as the clock clicked slowly on. Finally, she said, "I've got to go in there!"

People in town knew Melinda, and perhaps some in the bar put two and two together when they saw her walk in the door. Melinda left after a while and returned to the car. The suspect never showed up that night, but Yant got a call soon thereafter from a police detective asking him how to get in touch with the suspect. Shortly after that, the suspect volunteered to give his DNA, explaining that he wanted to prove his innocence.[6]

Melinda had learned a new tactic to reach the goal she and Yant had set to get the DNA of the most promising on their list of suspects. She began to frequent the bars of the area's less savory neighborhoods in order to interact enough to get a suspect's DNA on a cigarette butt, beer bottle, or drinking glass.[7]

However, testing of the top suspect who had finally volunteered DNA—and any other suspects—would have to wait. The defense team wanted to utilize the new technology of Y-STR DNA, an analysis of the Y chromosome present only in males. First, however, Melinda and Clarence's family needed to raise an estimated $30,000 to $50,000 to pay not only for Y-STR DNA testing of the suspect and of Clarence but also Y-STR testing of the crime evidence.[8]

MELINDA'S INVESTIGATIVE instincts had impressed Martin Yant, the seasoned detective. She made the kind of observations that professional investigators would call "profiling." In her view, the prosecution had exaggerated the discord between Melinda and Clarence as well as the animosity between Clarence and her mother. This theory that hostility between two adults led to violence did not synch with the rape of a child. Melinda surmised that the perpetrator was likely a pedophile.

Working on many leads at a time, Melinda was always alert to any possible connection to the case. These efforts had been rewarded on April 28, 2002, when an article in the *Akron Beacon Journal* reported that Earl Mann, convicted of raping three young girls, had received the minimum sentence—seven years—due to prosecutorial error. Since Mann was in prison for robbery, the seven years would be added to his current sentence. The article mentioned that Mann was the common-law husband of Tonia Brasiel. The mention of that name took Melinda's breath away. Brasiel was her mother's neighbor, the person Clarence's niece had turned to in the early morning hours of her grandmother's murder. It was Tonia Brasiel who let a bloodied child wait on her porch for a half hour or more before taking her to her home. It was Brasiel who neglected to call the police or an ambulance when the girl told her of her grandmother's murder. And it was Brasiel who later testified that the girl had identified Clarence as the murderer and rapist.

Tonia Brasiel's three young daughters—the girl's playmates whenever she visited her grandmother—were Mann's three rape victims.

The revelations in the *Beacon Journal* might explain Brasiel's odd behavior the morning of the murder and her testimony about the struggle with a knife that had never been found. Had she stalled that morning and lied in her testimony to protect Mann? The circumstances of Melinda's mother's death might now have a frightening logic. Earl Mann, who had a long violent criminal record, was now also classified as one of the worst of sexual offenders in Ohio: a sexual predator. His victims had been little girls. Could it be that Melinda's mother died trying to protect her visiting granddaughter from this predator?

Still, the younger man who had been rebuffed by her mother remained at the top of Melinda's list of suspects, and she needed to rule him in or out.

WHILE TRYING TO PULL together financial resources and investigating leads, Melinda was busy on other fronts. Not only was she a self-trained detective, she also learned to utilize the media to gain attention and support for her cause. Throughout this ordeal, she found ways to keep the case in the public eye. She held vigils on the anniversary of her mother's murder; she led marches in front of the prosecutor's office;[9] she even got on national television.

CBS News's *48 Hours* devoted a segment to the Elkins case on September 13, 2003, which gave Clarence the opportunity to repeat to the nation, "I'm not a violent person. I did not do this crime. I'm totally and completely innocent."[10] Two months later, the A&E show *American Justice* also focused on the Elkins case, with appearances by Clarence and Melinda Elkins, Prosecutor Michael Caroll, Martin Yant, and others. Melinda knew that keeping the case in front of the public could only help her cause. And publicity kept desperately needed donations flowing to freeclarence.com.

Timing in 2004 began to work in Melinda's favor. She learned of an opportunity to get pro bono legal assistance. Melinda contacted Mark Godsey, cofounder of the Ohio Innocence Project/Rosenthal Institute for Justice at the University of Cincinnati, a litigation organization dedicated to using DNA technology to exonerate the wrongfully convicted. The Ohio Innocence Project is an affiliate of the Innocence Project of the Benjamin N. Cardozo School of Law at Yeshiva University in New York City. Founded by Barry Scheck and Peter Neufeld, pioneers in the use of DNA technology to prove innocence, the Innocence Project is now a national organization that also seeks to advocate criminal justice reform to prevent wrongful conviction.

Because the Elkins case had depended nearly exclusively on eyewitness testimony of a child, and because DNA evidence from the crime scene still existed, Godsey put the case on a fast track to acceptance by the young legal clinic.

Over the next year and a half, Godsey and twenty University of Cincinnati law students would achieve several breakthroughs in the case. However, they would also endure crushing disappointments, as the justice system denied their motions to grant Elkins a new trial.

Initially, the Innocence team requested and received from the Ninth District Court of Appeals, without objection from the prosecutor's office, the crime scene evidence. In January 2004, Mark Godsey convinced Orchid

Cellmark labs to perform the Y-STR DNA testing of the prime suspect, of Clarence, and of the crime scene evidence, at a 50 percent discount through the laboratory's pro bono program. Even with the discount, however, the cost came to more than $20,000.[11]

The lab results brought mixed blessings. According to the report, the odds were 94.5 percent that the male DNA profile found in the victim's underwear and on the vaginal swab from Judy Johnson's rape kit were from the same male. Only one male Caucasian in eighteen would have a DNA profile with these four male chromosome markers. The odds were 99.87 percent that the DNA evidence found on Mrs. Johnson's fingernail and on the girl's panties were from the same man. Clarence Elkins was excluded, but Melinda's prime suspect was also excluded.[12]

The Innocence Project lawyers again petitioned for a new trial. On March 23, 2005, Judge Judy Hunter presided over a hearing. Orchid Cellmark forensic scientists testified that the Y-chromosome DNA findings, while not as specific as nuclear DNA, nevertheless conclusively excluded Clarence Elkins. Godsey and one of Elkins's lawyers, Jana DeLoach, argued that this new evidence met the standards for a new trial.

The state responded that DNA evidence excluding Elkins had been presented in the original trial, and the jury had found him guilty anyway, based on the eyewitness testimony of the victim. Elkins's attorneys argued that this DNA was more conclusive than what had been available at trial, and that if the new findings had been introduced then, the jurors would have reached a different verdict.[13]

The Elkins team felt that the hearing had gone well, and they waited with confidence for the judge's decision.

Nearly four months later, however, Judge Hunter denied the motion, just as Judge Adams had two years before. She sided with the prosecutors, writing that the evidence of another man's DNA at the crime scene was "insufficient to support the need for a new trial," and concurred with the state's argument that since DNA had not linked Elkins to the case originally, it should not be a factor in excluding him: "The jury found Defendant [Elkins] guilty beyond a reasonable doubt; and this Court hereby finds that, even if a jury had this new Y-STR DNA evidence, it would not be sufficient to change the outcome of the trial."[14]

The unexpected ruling jarred the Innocence Project team. Devastated, Melinda experienced one of the darkest moments since her mother's death. Martin Yant understood that she was discouraged. One day, while he was in the area working on another case, the detective paid Melinda a visit. To offer encouragement, Yant shared a maxim that had proved itself in many of his cases: "Melinda," he said, "it is always darkest before the dawn."[15]

JUDGE HUNTER'S RULING knocked Melinda back to square one. She would have to do what all of the police investigators and the justice system had failed to do. She would have to find, with irrefutable evidence, her mother's killer.

Fortunately, Martin Yant's prediction was about to come true.

With the younger man ruled out as a suspect, Melinda turned her full attention to obtaining Earl Mann's DNA. Only by matching it to the samples taken at the crime scene would her husband be freed. She wrote to Mann in prison, again and again, under an assumed name, posing as an interested pen pal. Hopefully, he would write back—and, in the process, leave his DNA on the envelope.[16] But Earl Mann did not take the bait.

Then, in that summer of 2005, Melinda learned of an amazing coincidence: Mann had been transferred to Clarence's prison and, incredibly, to the same cellblock. The odds of this happening were long, and Melinda did not know if the assignment was permanent. She urged Clarence to find an opportunity to get Mann's DNA as soon as possible.

This was risky for Clarence. He worried about getting caught either by Mann or the prison guards. However, he patiently waited and watched, and one day a perfect opportunity came. Clarence walked into a room and noticed Mann smoking a cigarette. Here was his chance! Mann put out his cigarette, stood up, and walked out of the room. Making sure that no one was watching, Clarence picked up the butt with a napkin and placed it in a plastic sandwich bag. He hid it in his study Bible until he could mail it to his attorney.

Once again, the Elkins family was forced to incur the expense of more DNA analysis. This time, the lab results did not disappoint: They had a match! Ironically, Clarence had been living in close proximity to the perpetrator of the crimes that were stealing his life away. But would the Summit County elected officials acknowledge the error? After being rebuffed so many times, the Elkins team worried that even this definitive evidence would be dismissed. Mark Godsey knew that the next move was critical, and he had an out-of-the-box thought. What if he could gain the support of someone who could not easily be ignored by the Summit County prosecutor? What if he could get a very unlikely political ally? It was a long shot, but in Godsey's line of work, what wasn't?

CHAPTER 4

Political Genes

I HAVE OFTEN FELT THAT people who seek elected office fall into one of two camps: public servants and politicians. Public servants are inspired by the work; that is, the opportunity to drive an agenda in public office and perform exemplary public service. Politicians, on the other hand, relish the process—the competition of political campaigns, the quest for political power, the opportunity to speak and be heard. In truth, all successful elected public officials have at least some aptitude in both essentials of public life, and the best of the best are highly skilled at both. The media loathes the thoughtful delivery of the former (sometimes referred to as "wonkish") and loves the crisp, well-delivered sound bites of the latter (sometimes referred to as "exciting").

As a lifelong Republican with many years in elected public office, I like to think that I can give a decent speech and that I am a skilled political strategist, but my political reputation was built on attributes often viewed as less exciting: good judgment, honesty (sometimes to a fault), and capable public management. As a lawyer, I cared most about fair resolution and justice. As an elected public official, my goal was to be innovative, to increase productivity while cutting costs, and, in targeted objectives, to bring transformational improvement. While these things rarely, if ever, get media attention, I received fair treatment by Ohio's press most of the time and won nearly all newspaper endorsements in my fifteen elections—although the word "wonkish" occasionally reared its ugly head.

Public service is in my genes. My father, an attorney and an elected justice of the peace, served as the Republican ward leader for forty years in our hometown, Brooklyn, Ohio, a blue-collar suburb of Cleveland. Teaching me the duties of partisan politics as soon as I could walk, my father took me with him door to door, distributing political literature in our precinct before every election.

Later, I felt great pride as I pulled my red wagon filled with campaign literature to the Good Shepherd Lutheran Church in November 1956. I was eight years old, and it was the first time that I worked the polls. I handed out political flyers from the moment school was out until the polls closed, in a last-minute effort to gain votes for Republican candidates.

That evening, my mother, father, older brother, Bill, and I gathered around our small black-and-white television to learn the results. It was a spectacular night for Republicans. Dwight D. Eisenhower was re-elected president; C. William O'Neal became the new governor of Ohio, and Paul Herbert, lieutenant governor; Bill Saxbe was elected attorney general; Jim Rhodes (who would join the short list of four-term governors in U.S. history) beat Joe Ferguson for auditor of state; Ted W. Brown was re-elected secretary of state; and Roger Tracy was re-elected state treasurer. Nearly all of my candidates had won! We had done it! And it felt so easy.

But I soon learned that the grace of election victories falls to the other side just as dramatically. Two years later, the Republicans lost the governor's race and the posts of lieutenant governor, attorney general, and treasurer, as well as a U.S. Senate seat. These defeats were followed in another two years with the Republicans' loss of the presidency to John F. Kennedy.

Years later, I could rattle off the statewide office results of every Ohio election since 1958. For most people, it was just forgotten trivia, but for me it was a political history inextricably tied to family memories that were always colored by a nostalgic, unabashed pride in the Republican Party, our state, and our nation.

Only a fraction of my public high school classmates went directly to college after graduation. Most in this small industrial town opted instead for local jobs, marriage, and starting a family close to family—the continuation of a good life that was satisfying if not extravagant.

The academic rigors I found at Denison University in Granville, Ohio, were a shock even with the preparation I had received in the small college prep classes I'd taken in high school. I just was not accustomed to the scholastic intensity and the intellectual vigor that my classmates brought to every course. I majored in history and eventually found my academic footing, even sound achievement, with the help of professors who loved to teach and were accessible to students—a hallmark of the school. Denison taught me far more than how to study. My brother, Bill, also an attorney, said that my four years there had worked me over like a pumice stone. I emerged with the rough edges polished significantly; a transformation had occurred that went beyond mere maturity.

Even while balancing academics, the demands of being the varsity heavyweight wrestler in Denison's strong wrestling program, and commitments to numerous campus organizations, I was drawn to politics. Bill, who was nine years older, got me involved in a statewide political race, Ohio Attorney General Bill Saxbe's 1968 U.S. Senate election campaign. I shared the duties of advance work (preparing the logistics and maximizing the impact of Saxbe's public appearances) with another young political neophyte, Mike Oxley. Neither of us could foresee then that Oxley would one day become one of the most powerful members of the U.S. Congress or that he would leave a legacy known globally as the Sarbanes-Oxley Act, which changed the rules of governance and financial reporting for publicly traded corporations.

After graduating from Denison in 1970, I went directly to study law at Case Western Reserve University School of Law in Cleveland. Following my first year in law school, I spent the summer working on Capitol Hill in Washington, D.C., after snagging a staff job with Senator Saxbe.

Returning to Case Western, I worked as a dorm resident and served as Saxbe's representative at Ohio events when the senator could not attend personally. Working the two part-time jobs, I paid my way through the last two years of law school.

In my second year at Case, my formal legal education was augmented with another practical experience. I got involved in an uphill political campaign for mayor of Cleveland. My brother, Bill, was handling finance for Ralph Perk, the Republican county auditor, and told me the campaign staff could use some help. I soon found myself spending more time on the campaign than on law school.

Perk was not expected to win this election, his second attempt to become mayor in Democrat-rich Cleveland. But a surprise was in store in the 1971 mayor's race. For years, Ralph Perk had been building a coalition of the city's ethnic groups. Dozens of ethnic neighborhoods in Cleveland were home to those who had the common cause of pride in and allegiance to their roots, with family members remaining in former homelands such as the many captive nations of Eastern Europe, then controlled by the Soviet Communists. These hardworking people raised their children to speak both English and the language of their former homeland. They made certain that their children would never forget their ethnic heritage and never surrender hope for these nations to gain their freedom. Nonetheless, these people were now proud Americans. They valued their U.S. citizenship as much as, if not more than, many who were born into citizenship. Every one of them considered voting a sacred privilege. And in 1971 they voted for Ralph Perk.

No one was more surprised than Perk when he won. Under the charter then in force in Cleveland, the newly elected mayor took office the Wednesday after the first Tuesday following Election Day. Eight days after winning, Ralph Perk moved into the mayor's office. My brother became secretary to the mayor, the equivalent of chief deputy, and I worked full-time organizing the office, hiring personnel, and assisting in the logistics of establishing a new administration.

By then, I had reconnected with a Denison classmate, Nancy Bero, and urged her to move to Cleveland. After graduating, she had gone to Annapolis, Maryland, to teach school. Perk needed an administrative assistant to handle the volumes of mail that were coming in every day, and Nancy was a good writer. At my urging, she took the job.

I helped Nancy find an apartment not far from my apartment near the law school. Hers was on the third floor, in a building with a woefully small elevator. Her parents and I helped carry her things up those three flights. In the midst of unpacked boxes, we had a delicious early supper of fried chicken, baked beans, and potato salad that her mother had prepared. I learned later that Nancy's father told her that any man who shows up on moving day is a good man.

Nancy didn't know anyone in Cleveland, and I invited her out for dinner the next night. She paid me back with a homemade dinner the next night. I reciprocated the next night. As it turned out, we rarely missed a dinner together for the next thirty-seven years (and counting). We were married in December 1972.

After law school, Nancy and I traveled for three weeks around the country and Ohio before deciding upon a place to settle. I had a few offers from private law firms, but the one I found most intriguing was a public-sector opportunity with Franklin County prosecutor George Smith, in the state capital of Columbus. Typically, a new lawyer with the prosecutor's office would cut his or her teeth on juvenile cases for a couple of years before moving up to prosecuting adult felonies. Breaking that tradition, Smith offered me the opportunity to immediately prosecute major adult felonies. It was an inducement I couldn't refuse.

Of course, being a member of the bar is a prerequisite for trying a case in court. After learning that I had passed the bar exam, I was sworn into the Ohio bar on a Saturday about a week later. On the following Monday, I was in a courtroom prosecuting a rape case.

CHAPTER 5

Advocating for a Victim

R APE CASES WERE NOT popular among the assistant prosecutors. Often "she said, he said" affairs, they were tough to win. The office had lost several prior rape cases, and no one minded giving this one to the new guy. The case involved an Ohio State University coed who lived in one of the many rental homes near campus. She was out on her front porch one warm evening during a campus event. A young man walked over and struck up a casual conversation. She didn't know him but assumed that he was another OSU student. He eventually said that he was thirsty and asked whether she had anything to drink. Without thinking about the risk, she invited him in for some water. He noticed an open bottle of wine in the refrigerator and asked whether he could have some. She agreed and poured him a small glass.

Then he raped her.

She testified that she had fought him, screamed, and yelled, *"No! No! No!"*

He said that she "wanted it." He was so confident that he had even returned to her home the night after the rape, which enabled the identification leading to his arrest.

It was a tough case because the young woman had willingly engaged in conversation, had invited the young man in, and had poured him a glass of wine. In the 1970s, rape victims were often reluctant to come forward. It would not be unusual for them to be grilled about their behavior, their clothing, and anything else that might convince a jury that they shared guilt by "asking for it." This attitude has diminished but still is a factor in unreported rapes.

The jury might wonder why this young white coed had opened her home to someone she did not know: a young African American. At the time of the

trial, November 1973, many of the nation's college students and recent graduates had been challenged to confront their stereotypical views on race. Pro-
tests over the war in Vietnam were often accompanied by other challenges
to the status quo, resulting in campus disruptions and emotional, opinion-
exchanging campus-wide dialogues.

The victim told me, and testified in court, that after a casual, short conversation with this random person whom she thought was a fellow student,
she didn't want to seem like a racist when he asked her for something to
drink. Ten years earlier, a young woman may not have invited a stranger in,
regardless of his race. But in 1973, she barely questioned it; it was the right
thing to do.

The fact that the perpetrator returned to the scene the next day to see
her again was difficult to explain. Did he really believe that this was "a relationship"? Was the difference in the two accounts of what happened truly a
matter of conflicting interpretations?

I met with the victim. She was still very shaken, frightened, and both
angry and deeply saddened. It was almost as if she were in grief. An act of
kindness had been answered with brutal violation. Her trust and innocence
had been stolen, and she would never be the same. There was no question in
my mind that she was the victim of a violent crime and that we had the true
perpetrator.

The testimony part of the trial lasted two days and was very intense for
everyone, including me. I prepared at night and was so focused in my first
experience as a courtroom prosecutor that I developed a throbbing headache
during each trial session. The judge adjourned on the evening of the second
day. Closing arguments before the jury were scheduled for the next morning.

The final argument weighed heavily on me that night. I wanted justice
for the victim and felt that the final argument could be the deciding factor
for the jury. I could not imagine the added insult if the jury were to come
back with a verdict of not guilty. Yet I knew that this happened with cases
that were stronger than this one. I worked on the closing argument and then
practiced it out loud. Nancy served as my jury.

The next day, I was nervous—not about speaking in front of the jury but
about the outcome. I gave the argument and was satisfied with my effort.

The jury came through, delivering a guilty verdict. The victim trembled with emotion and anxiety, but, as the outcome settled in, she slowly calmed down and breathed more easily. I felt that she would be able to move on. She would not be afraid that her attacker would return any time soon.

The defendant, now a convicted rapist, was shocked. He was later sentenced and would ultimately serve three years in prison. I wondered whether he still genuinely believed that he had not committed a crime.

This was the beginning of my career in law and politics. Seeking justice and pursuing public service had always been important to my family and seemed worthy career objectives. Nancy and I moved back to Cleveland, my home, and I took a job as assistant director of law with the City of Cleveland. We bought our first home in the western suburb of Rocky River, where I served as legal counsel for the Division of Police. I joined my brother and father in forming a new law firm, which gave me the flexibility to serve on the city council when a vacancy occurred. I was appointed to the vacant council seat in 1977 and elected without opposition later that year. Two years later, I was elected director of law in Rocky River and learned from another mentor, Mayor Earl Martin, that capable public management, excellent city services, and good government matter in a community.

In 1977 and 1979, two events changed our lives: the births of our son, John, and daughter, Corbin. When I was elected to the legislature in 1981, the children were one and a half and three and a half years old. Often I was at my legislative office in Columbus three or four days a week, but for the children—who were asleep when I left and returned—it seemed longer. One Thursday, six-year-old John asked me on the phone, "Are you coming home tonight?"

"I'm sorry, honey," I said, "I can't be home until tomorrow."

"Daddy, I don't think I can take it anymore," he replied.

And I could not take that. I announced that I would not seek re-election for a third consecutive term. But when my legislative seat opened up again two years later in 1986, I could not deny how much I missed public service. With the support of Nancy and the children, who were older now, I left a much more lucrative private-sector job to run for the legislature again. It was a big risk. Thankfully, I won, and served two more terms.

The leap from representing a local constituency to statewide office in Ohio is always an Olympic long jump. In 1989, I was ready to run statewide in pursuit of my long-held dream of becoming Ohio attorney general. Nancy, John, Cory, and I traveled all over the state that summer and were gaining support until a better-known candidate running for governor was muscled out of that race and dropped back into the race for attorney general. The party leaders asked me to run for auditor of state instead, even though no one expected a relatively unknown legislator to have a shot at defeating the incumbent, Tom Ferguson.

The Ferguson name was an institution in the Ohio Auditor of State office. Tom had served sixteen years in the office, succeeding his father, Joe Ferguson, who had been in the post for twenty years. When my race against Tom Ferguson began, ten months from the 1990 election, polls showed Ferguson tracking at 68 percent versus Petro at 18 percent, with 14 percent of the voters undecided. However, our scrappy, underfinanced campaign managed to gain some traction, spurred on by Tom Van Meter, a legendary Republican state Senate leader who became a political strategist and his smart, young associate, Bob Klaffky. The surprise of that election year was not that we lost but that we came closer—with nearly 48 percent of the vote—to toppling a Ferguson auditor than anyone had in twenty years. As a result of this strong finish, my spot on the statewide ticket in four years was secure.

I thought that I was out of public service for a while. But shortly thereafter, Governor George Voinovich tapped our Cuyahoga County commissioner, Virgil Brown, to become director of the Ohio State Lottery. I was nominated by the county Republican organization to fill Brown's vacancy and had the great opportunity to manage, with Democrats Mary Boyle and Tim Hagan, Ohio's largest county. It was a productive time in Cleveland and the county, as we worked with city and corporate leaders to build what are now Progressive Field, home of the Cleveland Indians baseball team; Quicken Loans Arena, where you can see the Cleveland Cavaliers basketball team, as well as hockey and arena football; and the Rock and Roll Hall of Fame.

Those years flew by, and soon I was joining the Republican ticket for my second attempt at statewide office. Although I could have run for attorney general, after our strong campaign for auditor of state, I chose to pursue the opportunity to reorganize that office, knowing that, if successful, I could have a future shot at attorney general.

CHAPTER 6

Rising to Opportunity

I N OHIO, THE AUDITOR WIELDS more clout than in any other state, with financial oversight, audit responsibility, and investigative authority over more than five thousand units of government. Permitting one family to be in control of a public office for the better part of forty years—and uninterrupted for twenty-four years—requires public diligence, as abuses can accompany protracted authority in an elected office. By 1994, the Ohio Auditor of State office was a strong argument for term limitations, which voters had instituted two years earlier.

The office had sunk to become an ineffective political hiring hall with untrained and mismanaged employees. Audit reports were too late to be useful as the financial tools they were intended to be. Even worse, some audits certainly appeared to be politically motivated.

The timing was right for me in 1994. Tom Ferguson's close call four years earlier was, no doubt, a factor in his decision to retire. The office became an open seat, and I easily beat Ferguson's handpicked successor.

Besides building a reputation for management, I also revealed through this job a personality trait that is required in any financial auditing office, although not always rewarded in politics: independence. It was independence that enabled our office to conduct audits that led to the criminal conviction of more than 110 public officials. Of those who held partisan office, about half were Democrats and about half were Republicans.

Most voters and public opinion leaders appreciated my approach. My independence went beyond the auditing work; it drove much of my decision-making. It was not an affectation or strategy. It is core to my personality, and its impact was not without cost: For the first time in my career, I was making political enemies, many of whom were in my own party. I knew that this would make future elections all the more difficult, but, as they say, "Politics ain't beanbag."[1]

Ohio's two-term limitation for state officeholders required that I move on from the auditor's office in 2003. I was ready. An excellent management team and committed workforce had accomplished what we'd set out to do. We had established a new professionalism, credibility, independence, and relevance in the office; tripled productivity; employed technology for paperless efficiency; and instituted performance audits of Ohio's school districts that saved hundreds of millions of dollars. During my first term, by mandated national peer review, our office went from worst in the nation to best.

The attorney general's office was an open seat that year, also due to term limitations, and, by the grace of God, it had my name on it. I won the election with 65 percent of the vote, the largest margin for that office in a century, and was sworn into office in January 2003. Many of our senior managers in the auditor's office moved with me to the attorney general's office to undertake the same approach toward new methods and new technology. This time, however, the office had been ably managed by my predecessor, Betty Montgomery. Still, exciting opportunities awaited.

THE ATTORNEY GENERAL is the state's lawyer representing every entity of state government, from state universities to state boards, commissions, and pension funds with assets of $130 billion. I oversaw a staff of 1,250, of whom 350 were lawyers. While most of our work was civil in nature, and only about one thousand of these cases were criminal, our office engaged with the criminal justice system in many ways. The Bureau of Criminal Identification and Investigation (BCI), Ohio's state-of-the-art forensic laboratories, was under the auspices of the attorney general. Our office worked with county prosecutors to assist in criminal prosecutions, particularly in capital cases. We worked with county sheriffs, police departments, and the state highway patrol by providing crime scene investigations and countless investigative support services.

One of my goals was to fully utilize emerging technology to enable more effective communication among law enforcement agencies, an effort to address one of the nation's painful lessons of 9/11. Over the ensuing four years, an enhanced department of forty-five technology professionals in our office built a leading-edge communications system that linked every law enforcement officer and virtually every crime report and piece of crime data in the state, in real time.

I also wanted to make the most of DNA technology. My vision was to add a DNA profile of every felon and every high-level misdemeanant to the national CODIS database. I felt certain that this would instantly solve dozens of cold cases and that it would step up the utilization of the best crime deterrent since the discovery of the fingerprint. During the campaign, I had said that with a criminal's DNA profile on file, he or she might as well leave a business card at the scene of the next crime.

The first step was to get the authority to proceed on this ambitious project. I personally advocated the proposal to the state legislature. Both houses voted to dramatically expand the attorney general's authority, enabling the office to require a mouth swab from every incarcerated felon and high-level misdemeanant in Ohio prisons as well as those on probation or under supervision. Ohio's corrections, probation, and parole agencies were trained to collect each person's saliva on a cotton swab and secure it in a plastic envelope. Our office provided the kits, transported them to laboratories, and entered the test results into the state and CODIS databases.

Because we were beginning a program that would collect tens of thousands of DNA samples, we were able to negotiate very favorable rates on the DNA analysis. We then contracted the samples out to the four labs nationally that did this work, at the lowest bid price: about $29 per DNA sample. In my four-year term, we would add 210,000 criminal DNA samples to our state's and the national databases.

Even at the reduced lab rates, this came at a large cost: more than $6 million. I learned at national meetings of state attorneys general that most states had not considered an effort like this because of the expense. My most frequent question was, "Where do you get that kind of 'extra' money?"

In the first six months of my term, we were working on the answer to that question when I got a rude surprise. I learned that thousands of untested DNA samples had been accumulating in the BCI labs in Ohio, just as they had in states nationwide. Robert N. Patton Jr., a serial rapist who had terrorized central Ohio, was arrested based on DNA taken more than two years earlier. It had finally been entered into the state database, which immediately identified Patton as the "Linden Area Rapist." He was indicted in the rapes of thirty-seven women over a period of fourteen years. Tragically, thirteen had been raped while his DNA was waiting to be processed. Patton's DNA and that of thousands of other offenders had piled up in the state's forensic vault after a federal grant had expired. The federal government had promised additional resources to address the backlog, but the resources had been delayed by weeks and then months.

The Patton case was tragic proof of the importance of DNA and the need to process it quickly. Finding a way to clean up the DNA backlog became an urgent priority, and we found at least a short-term answer to the cost issue by tapping the state's Crime Victims Compensation Fund for $571,000 to pay for the analysis of more than nineteen thousand DNA samples.

A tight-fisted fiscal conservative to the core, I knew that with some ingenuity and planning, we could pull together the resources to carry out the larger mandate of taking DNA samples from every Ohio convict. In addition to drawing on the Crime Victims fund, we made cuts from other areas of our budget. Through attrition, we reduced the office head count over the four years, varying from 5 percent to 10 percent.

However, we also found a way to generate revenues. A statute in the Ohio Revised Code provided for a percentage of the state's collections revenues to be taken as a collection fee by the attorney general's office. It was our responsibility to collect debts owed to the state, such as delinquent taxes and legal judgments. These numbered in the hundreds of millions, and the legislature had provided a 9 percent incentive for us to go get them.

We made collections a high priority, instituting the most aggressive collections operation in state history. Through focused management, support, and technology, we nearly tripled collection receipts from about $135 million to $335 million per year. It was good news for Ohio, as the bulk of these monies were applied to funding state operations, and it was good for our office because it generated revenues to employ an enhanced in-house technology department for the development of new communications systems for law enforcement. It also paid for a massive, nation-leading collection of criminal DNA.

CHAPTER 7

The Calling Card

D NA, THE ABBREVIATION for deoxyribonucleic acid, is the genetic material in the cells of all living organisms.[1] DNA carries the cell's genetic information and hereditary characteristics:[2] everything from eye color to a predisposition to certain diseases. At least a century of scientific study and experimentation directed at understanding genes, cells, and the genetic building blocks of life preceded the first application of DNA analysis in criminal forensics. I learned a lot about DNA. It was truly coming of age during my term as attorney general, and I was committed to fully utilizing it.

DNA profiling was first described as "DNA fingerprinting" in 1985 by Alec Jeffreys, an English geneticist. Jeffreys discovered that certain DNA regions contained repeating DNA sequences and that the number of these differed from one person to another. He developed a way to perform human identity tests by measuring the unique variations in length of these repeated sequences.[3]

In law enforcement, DNA typing was first utilized in an English immigration case and, soon thereafter, in a double homicide.[4] Early use of DNA in criminal forensics in the United States began in the late 1980s.

When most people speak of DNA, they are usually referencing STR DNA, also called "nuclear DNA." This is generally what prosecutors and defense attorneys use, because it is unique to every human with the exception of identical twins. A match between two full samples of STR DNA gives a statistical frequency of one in several quadrillion.[5] STR, however, cannot be used for hair (unless the hair includes the fleshy root), and it often cannot provide a conclusive reading in samples with mixed DNA.

Two other kinds of DNA came into use as the technology developed: Y-chromosome DNA (Y-STR DNA) and mitochondrial DNA (mtDNA). Y-STR reads the DNA profile in the Y chromosome, which is present only in men. The advantage of Y-STR is that it is distinguishable from female DNA when the two are mixed, as is often the case in a sexual assault. In cases in which a mixture of DNA has considerably more female than male DNA, STR (nuclear) DNA of the male can be totally masked. However, Y-STR is recognizable even when present in small traces. Because Y-STR DNA is a genetic marker, sons have the same Y-STR as their father. While it does not have the unique match advantage of STR, it is a highly sensitive DNA that is particularly useful for confirming a strong consistency—meaning a DNA similarity that would exclude most of a population—or, conversely, excluding someone from crime scene evidence.

Mitochondrial DNA (mtDNA) is a genetic marker for the maternal line. A son and daughter have the same mtDNA as their mother. An advantage of both Y-STR and mtDNA is that, if prosecutors do not have the DNA of a suspect to match to crime scene evidence, they can use the DNA of the father, a brother, or a son to confirm whether the genetic line is consistent or excluded from the evidence.

The amount of detectable variation is much less in Y-STR and mtDNA compared to STR DNA analysis, and thus the frequency numbers (how often one might find this particular configuration in the population) are lower. However, Elizabeth Benzinger, Ph.D., a BCI forensic scientist, pointed out to our office an important insight on these oft-quoted frequency figures:

> The individualizing (or discrimination) power of a method should not be confused with the reliability of the method: an exclusion using any method is 100%; a matching profile is a matching profile. Frequency estimates address only the relative possibility of a coincidental match.[6]

In 1994 Congress established the Combined DNA Index System (CODIS). Funded and operated by the Federal Bureau of Investigation, it became the core of the national DNA database established to enable laboratories throughout the United States to compare DNA data. Only STR DNA is entered into

CODIS, which contains two indices of data: the convicted offender database, containing the STR DNA of convicts, ranging from misdemeanants to felons, depending on individual state practices; and the forensic index, containing STR DNA from crime scene evidence, such as saliva, blood, skin, and semen.[7]

CODIS provided the opportunity for a quick scan of the DNA from crime scenes throughout the country. Law enforcement could now enter crime scene evidence and get a "cold hit": a match to a convicted person's DNA. A convicted felon's DNA could also be entered to ascertain whether he or she was involved in other unsolved crimes.

Many shared my view that DNA and the CODIS system offered the greatest potential for deterring crime and providing a safer world than any other tool in my lifetime. It is what motivated our aggressive effort to collect criminal DNA. While we felt certain that the outcomes would justify the expense, we planned to test this theory when we had a significant quantity of DNA samples completed.

I will never forget the day in early 2004 that we entered the first batch of more than 19,000 DNA samples from Ohio convicts into CODIS. Match, match, match, match, match—more than 130 matches provided strong leads or solved cold cases instantly!

Within a few days of that first batch of DNA in CODIS, our Bureau of Criminal Investigations got a call from the sheriff's office in Orange County, California. One of the profiles we had just added matched the DNA evidence from an unsolved murder that had occurred there thirty-two years earlier.

On October 29, 1972, Marla Jean Hires, a twenty-three-year-old married mother of a two-year-old was somehow abducted in the early morning hours from her car before she reached her work. She was brutally raped and murdered, and her body was rolled up in carpet and dropped near the Yorba Linda Country Club golf course. We were told that law enforcement suspected her husband was the perpetrator, but they were never able to make the case. The husband consistently proclaimed his innocence, but it was said that he never remarried and lived under the cloud of his wife's unsolved murder. It was one of the oldest unsolved kidnap-rape-murder cases in Orange County.

When DNA first surfaced as a tool, the forensic division at the Orange County Sheriff's Department performed DNA analysis on the evidence from this crime and entered it into the CODIS database in the early 1990s. There was no match. The long-awaited DNA match came when we entered our first large batch of DNA, and it fingered Edwin Dean Richardson, an imprisoned Ohio felon who had been convicted of the murder of another young woman. Not that any more evidence was needed, but we also learned that at the time of the Hires murder, Richardson had indeed been in Orange County, California.

On December 4, 2004, a press conference was conducted by Orange County sheriff Michael S. Carona, Orange County district attorney Tony Rackauckas, and Sheriff Thomas McCort from the Belmont County Sheriff's Office in Ohio. District Attorney Rackauckas summarized, "We are helping bring closure for all those who loved Marla Hires. We will never give up looking for those who commit these brutal rapes and murders. DNA has caught up with Mr. Richardson, and now he will never get out of prison."[8]

Those in law enforcement were euphoric over the remarkable tool of DNA, especially when paired with other technology. I did not attend the press conference in California but was quoted in the Orange County Sheriff's Department press release as saying, "This illustrates the remarkable power of DNA to overcome time, distance, and the absence of useful leads to solve a horrible crime. It also represents what can happen when law enforcement agencies share information without regard to jurisdictional boundaries and state lines."

Richardson pled guilty that month to the murder of Marla Hires. Redemption came after thirty-two years to Marla's unfortunate husband. The timing in his life could have been better: Today he would have been cleared as a suspect in a matter of days.

This scenario of solving cases was to occur hundreds, even thousands, of times in the ensuing months and years. I noted that an arrest based on a DNA match was made somewhere in Ohio on at least a weekly basis. Some of these were particularly satisfying and extraordinary.

Stephanie Hummer, an eighteen-year-old freshman at Ohio State, was abducted near campus in the early morning hours of March 6, 1994. She was raped and murdered, and her body was found in an abandoned field near campus. The murder was high-profile in central Ohio. It prompted fear throughout the Ohio State campus as well as an increase in security measures.[9] But the case was never solved and grew cold over the ensuing years.

Then, in 2003, Jonathan Gravely, a former Whetstone High School track star, was arrested for nonsupport of his two teenage children, a low-level felony. He pled guilty and was ordered to pay the accrued support. He also got five years' probation. While Gravely was on probation, the Ohio legislature passed the law authorizing the expanded capturing of criminal DNA. On a probation visit, Gravely's probation officer took a mouth swab, and Gravely's DNA profile was entered into the state and national CODIS databases. It was a stunning surprise when Jonathan Gravely's DNA matched that from the Hummer crime scene evidence. Although Gravely had not met his responsibilities as a father, he had never been convicted of a violent crime, and he was never a suspect in this case.

With this irrefutable evidence Jonathan Gravely admitted guilt, and in September 2007, he accepted a plea bargain to avoid the death penalty. Gravely pled guilty to counts of aggravated murder and kidnapping. He was sentenced to twenty-five years to life.[10]

My motivation for the aggressive use of DNA was obvious, and the results were gratifying. The effort more than lived up to our expectations. We were identifying suspects and solving cold cases that otherwise would have remained dormant indefinitely. I don't think that many in the judicial system or the public fully understood the impact of this new tool on criminal conviction. But I, too, had more to learn: DNA would also rearrange my thinking about wrongful conviction and innocence.

CHAPTER 8

Proving Innocence

M**Y FIRST REAL RECOGNITION** of the nightmare of wrongful criminal conviction began with a phone call in September 2005. After four statewide political campaigns and the government jobs I had held, I knew just about everyone in elected public office in Ohio, and in my view, Bill Seitz, a Republican state representative from Cincinnati, was one of the brightest. He also may have been the most conservative.

Seitz called my office because he respected two local men he had come to know: Cincinnati city councilman John Cranley, a Democrat, and Mark Godsey, professor of law at the University of Cincinnati Law School and director of the Ohio Innocence Project. I was not surprised that Republican Seitz would be working with Democrat Cranley. Seitz may have been a pure conservative, but he was also pragmatic when it came to getting things done.

Still, I would never have guessed the subject of the call.

Seitz explained that Cranley and Godsey had an issue they wanted to discuss, and, assuring me that they were honorable, asked that I hear them out. The two men then got on the call, and we were introduced. Cranley and Godsey explained that they believed a man named Clarence Elkins had been wrongfully convicted and imprisoned for murder and rape. Having had no success in this case's long history with prosecutors and judges in Summit County, they were trying an innovative strategy: involve the attorney general.

Never mind the fact that attorney generals, like prosecutors, are in the business of prosecuting criminals, not defending them. The *Dayton Daily News* later described the odds of getting an elected attorney general to intervene on behalf of a convicted felon: "It's a little like buying a lottery ticket. In hundreds of Innocence Project cases across the nation, a state attorney general has never publicly supported one."[1]

But again, Seitz was pragmatic, and perceptive. He knew that advancing the use of DNA was a priority in our office. He knew that I believed DNA was the most accurate form of criminal evidence. And he also knew that, like him, I was independent enough to do the unlikely.

Godsey summarized this case that had required an army of advocates: Elkins's wife, Melinda; private detective Martin Yant; Akron attorney Jana DeLoach; Cleveland attorney Elizabeth Kelly; the Innocence Project lawyers and law students; and pro bono attorneys from the Cleveland law firm of Squire, Sanders & Dempsey and the New York City firm of Weil, Gotshal & Manges. Then he got to the point of the phone call. Even though Clarence Elkins had managed to obtain a cigarette butt from the suspected real perpetrator, Earl Mann, and even though Mann's DNA on the butt matched the crime scene DNA evidence, the Innocence team had no confidence in gaining anything positive from the Summit County officials. Fearing that the prosecutor would claim that the cigarette butt was not from Mann, Godsey asked whether the Ohio Attorney General's Office would obtain a DNA sample from the imprisoned Mann to provide absolute proof that his DNA matched the crime scene evidence.

I presumed that this would be an easy one for me. I explained that it would not be necessary to get a sample. Under Ohio law, because Mann had been convicted of a felony, his DNA would already have been added to both Ohio's and the national CODIS databases. In the nearly eight years since Elkins's conviction, the advance of DNA promised more definitive results. As in most "completed" cases, the crime scene evidence from the Elkins case had never been tested or retested with the improved DNA testing options. Godsey explained that they would be utilizing testing that had not existed at the time of Elkins's trial. We sent off the evidence for that purpose.

I also asked for and received volumes of information from Godsey on the Elkins case. I went over it carefully and had to face a remarkable probability: Elkins was an innocent man. This was very troubling on many levels. I was now personally compelled to get involved. Before making this risky decision, I wanted another independent appraisal. I asked Chief Deputy for Criminal

Justice Jim Canepa, an accomplished prosecutor, to review the materials and let me know his thoughts.

The potential political liabilities of an attorney general getting involved in a post-conviction case on behalf of a convicted felon did not escape Canepa. For the sake of justice (and also for the sake of his boss), he took my request very seriously. He interviewed Mark Godsey to examine and fully discuss the evidence of Elkins's innocence, and, like me, found it compelling. Canepa thoroughly vetted the evidence with BCI lab scientists. He asked the scientists to review all of the analysis that had been completed. The analysts had no stake in this case and therefore were totally objective. They assured him that this new skin-cell DNA match with Earl Mann was very definitive and significant. In fact, it left Canepa with no doubt about what he had to do.

"This guy's innocent," he said as he returned the case files to me.

Now there was no turning back. I knew that we would have to do whatever we could to correct a terrible error.

None of us was surprised when the DNA analysis results came back: We had a very convincing match. In a letter to Sherri Bevan Walsh, dated September 21, 2005, Godsey and Elkins's attorneys, Jana DeLoach and Pierre Bergeron, informed the Summit County prosecutor that newly conducted DNA testing "conclusively exonerates Elkins and implicates Earl Mann in the murder and rapes in which Elkins was convicted." The letter explained that the full profile of the DNA from the girl's panties and Mrs. Judy Johnson's vaginal swab were "consistent with Earl Mann's DNA for full 12-point match."[2]

As in all Y-STR DNA analysis, the odds of finding a match are calculated on how many times that specific configuration of markers has been seen in a particular database. In this case, only Earl Mann's DNA, in a database of 4,000 samples, matched the crime scene DNA. The letter explained, "Thus far, it [Earl Mann's profile] is a unique Y-STR profile, and there is less than a 1 in 4,000 chance that it is not Earl Mann who left his DNA at the crime scene in the most highly probative areas."[3]

The next day, the Ohio Innocence Project went public with the new DNA results. "As a result of the efforts of the defense team, the true perpetrator of these crimes has now been identified beyond a reasonable doubt through DNA testing and other evidence," said Mark Godsey. "This individual is Earl Mann."

On September 23, the *Akron Beacon Journal* published an editorial calling for action in response to "DNA tests credible enough to remove him [Elkins] even from suspicion." The editorial went on unequivocally, "Summit County prosecutors should respond by doing the right thing: moving quickly to free Elkins from prison."[4]

But the immediate result for Elkins was just the opposite. With the release of the DNA results, prison officials transferred him to solitary confinement. Clarence may have thought that this was the result of his breaking the rules in collecting and mailing Mann's cigarette butt, but it was probably for his own protection that he was locked up separately, away from Earl Mann and his friends. Nonetheless, Elkins got no special treatment. Shackled, he was confined to a small solitary cell for all but a few moments each day.[5]

Meanwhile, we were disappointed with Prosecutor Walsh's apparent response to the latest DNA lab report, which seemed to cast doubt on the significance of the evidence. Astounded by this, I asked Jim Canepa to contact the prosecutor. I wanted him to work with her office privately and urge her to reconsider this evidence. I was happy to meet with Walsh as well if that could be helpful. Unfortunately, Canepa's phone calls to the prosecutor's office to try to set up a meeting with either Walsh or her chief prosecutor, Mary Ann Kovach, were not returned.

Thinking that perhaps a face-to-face meeting could be arranged if he demonstrated his willingness to go more than halfway, Canepa took a good part of a day to drive to Summit County with the thought of stopping by the prosecutor's office, but he returned without success: Neither Walsh nor Kovach could see him.

Fearing that the Ohio Attorney General's Office would be accused of failing to speak to the prosecutor's office about the case, now that it was destined by the evidence to move forward, Canepa found a way to obtain Chief Prosecutor Kovach's cell phone number and called her cold. She picked up, but when she found out who was on the other end, she was not pleased. Canepa described her tone as "hostile and antagonistic." Even with the history of resistance in this case, Canepa was surprised at Kovach's response. "I just wanted to talk to her about the evidence," he later reflected, noting, "We're all supposed to be on the same team."

When Canepa referenced the latest DNA match, Kovach "became defensive," he said. Her position was that, even if Mann's DNA was found at the crime scene, DNA from skin cells could have been transferred.[6] However, at the March 23, 2005, hearing before Judge Judy Hunter, Assistant Prosecutor Michael Carroll had questioned a Cellmark forensic analyst about whether or not skin cell DNA could be transferred, for example, if pieces of clothing belong to different relatives were comingled. She responded, "It's possible, but I don't know if it's likely."[7]

Expert Elizabeth Benzinger, who'd reviewed the DNA test results, confirmed in a memorandum to Godsey and me the unlikelihood of transferring this DNA: "The potential of secondary transfer of DNA from Earl Mann to a child to the evidence has been considered and deemed unlikely," she wrote. "With respect to the vaginal sample from Judith Johnson, a third transfer step would presumably be needed."[8]

The possibility of transfer of the skin-cell DNA in the Elkins case is almost beyond imagination. Forensic scientists are trained to choose their words carefully, but finding a DNA match between skin cells in the rape kit evidence of two victims in a home and the skin cells of a person who did not live in or frequent that home, is very strong criminal evidence.

I would hope that most prosecutors, if presented the evidence in this case, would have agreed with our conclusion that this was no longer a matter of just excluding a wrongfully convicted man but of identifying the real perpetrator. At a minimum, this possibility warranted a different reaction than what we were getting from the prosecutor. A rigid, uncooperative position seemed at odds with a more commonsense approach of working with the attorney general's office and the Bureau of Criminal Identification and Investigation to try to evaluate the new findings.

Whether it is arrogance, political posturing, tunnel vision, or loss of perspective, prosecutors who are closed to the possibility of error in the face of strong new evidence need to reconsider their stance in light of the goal to which all prosecutors are supposed to aspire: finding the truth, not just obtaining convictions.

Totally frustrated by the lack of cooperation from the Summit County prosecutor, I decided to use the tool of last resort—the bully pulpit of my office—to expand public awareness and put pressure on the Summit County officials.

On October 28, 2005, I held the first press conference on the case and publicly stated my confidence in the DNA evidence that proved Elkins's innocence.

During the time that we were attempting to meet with Prosecutor Walsh, we decided to go one step further: We sent the pubic hair found in the underwear for testing.

Meanwhile, on October 31, the Innocence Project team filed a motion for an evidentiary hearing based on the latest DNA evidence. The prosecutor appeared to be uncertain about whether or not to oppose the motion and was public in her criticism. In the November 2005 issue of her newsletter, the *Rap Sheet*, Walsh reported that the DNA evidence in the Elkins case was "inconclusive"[9] and "incomplete."[10] She wrote, "Numerous judges have reviewed this case and have concluded that the conviction was a just result."[11] She criticized me for saying that Clarence Elkins was innocent and for advocating his release, and claimed that I had not fully examined the case.[12] She indicated that her office and the Barberton Police Department were investigating the newest allegations and that additional DNA testing was being done "to obtain more complete and accurate DNA test results."[13] She added, "...[A]t the present time, DNA evidence has not cleared Mr. Elkins and has not established that another man is the killer."[14]

After all we had done to work with the prosecutor, I found these statements to be totally unfair. "I object so much to that charge," I fired back to reporters. "Where does she get off? We have been engaged for quite some time. Almost a year ago, we said we had real concerns in this matter because Elkins was totally excluded as a DNA match."[15]

A week later, a Cleveland *Plain Dealer* editorial criticized Walsh's resistance to act upon the overwhelming evidence of conviction error, saying, "...justice also calls for something that won't show up in the county conviction rate: humility and the wisdom to respect science, the evidence, and the law."

Walsh claimed that Ohio law, which allowed just one year for an inmate to apply for DNA testing, made this new evidence inadmissible. However, she agreed to schedule an evidentiary hearing for February 22, 2006. While that was welcome news, the wheels of justice continued to grind excruciatingly slowly.

Everyone on the Elkins team knew that it would be an added travesty for Clarence to spend another Christmas in prison. Fortunately, we received powerful information to help us apply more public pressure.

The DNA analysis of the crime scene hair came back: another match. This test had utilized mitochondrial DNA, which links genes in the maternal line. With DNA showing a match in both the paternal and maternal lines, the odds that any other person could have left this DNA evidence were bumped up to 1 in 19 *million*.[16]

We immediately submitted this evidence to the Summit County Prosecutor's Office. On December 9, I also directed a letter to Prosecutor Walsh, stating, "As the Christmas season approaches, I believe that Mr. Elkins, who most likely is an innocent man, should be free to spend the holiday with his family."[17] I used the conciliatory term "most likely" in the interest of opening up a working dialogue with Walsh, even though I had long been completely convinced that Elkins was innocent.

We waited for Walsh's response.

But this time, Chief Criminal Prosecutor Mary Ann Kovach responded to the media, asking, "If they feel they have clear and convincing evidence this time, why did they agree to put off the hearing date till February?" Kovach went on to charge that we had not made our charts and our DNA analyst available to the prosecutors, and that they would not consider Elkins's release until they had seen this material.[18]

Mark Godsey quickly came back, saying that he had, in fact, given prosecutors copies of the evidence and offered to set up interviews with the analyst. Regarding the hearing, Godsey returned a challenge to the Summit County officials: "We'll have it [the hearing] next week. They're the ones who asked for all that time."[19]

I scheduled another press conference for Thursday, December 15, and gave advance notice to Prosecutor Walsh that I would be releasing the latest DNA test results implicating Mann to an irrefutable level of certainty. That morning, Melinda Elkins made another trip to Columbus to stand with me yet again before the media.

In spite of all past dashed hopes, a cautious optimism over the promise of the new DNA test results and the February hearing filled those who had worked on this case for years—first and foremost Melinda, as well as

Mark Godsey and the Innocence Project lawyers, Clarence and his attorneys, Detective Martin Yant, and others. At this point, turning up the heat with public awareness was part of our strategy.

Fifteen minutes before the ten o'clock press conference, members of the media were gathering outside my office when a nondescript fax came in. It was from Judge Hunter of Summit County. Prosecutor Walsh had reversed her position and filed a motion to dismiss all charges against Clarence Elkins. The judge granted the motion and ordered his immediate release.

One of the most joyful moments of my life came with the great privilege of turning to Melinda Elkins and saying, "It's over, Melinda. All charges against Clarence have been dropped. He is being released. You can go get him now."

Melinda was ecstatic and overwhelmed with emotion. But she pulled herself together and called Clarence.

"Are you ready to come home?" she asked.

"I have always been ready," he replied.

"Well, pack your bags, you're coming home, baby."[20]

The scheduled press conference had an unexpected, unscripted message: An error in the execution of criminal justice had finally been acknowledged.

But even at this long-awaited moment, Melinda was moving on mentally to the second part of the promise she had made to both her mother and herself. She looked into the cameras and vowed with her never-wavering conviction, "And I'd like to say to Earl Mann: We got you."[21]

Clarence was stunned and also emotional. After so many disappointments, he had expected the process to drag on. His release after nearly eight years of wrongful imprisonment, ironically, seemed sudden. His one concern was that Melinda and his sons drive carefully on that wintry day.[22]

At four o'clock that afternoon, Clarence Elkins walked out of the Mansfield Correctional Institution.

CHAPTER 9

Life After Exoneration

WHEN INTERVIEWED BY CBS News after his release, Clarence Elkins said, "Words, I don't believe, can express the gratitude I have for my wife and the love I have for her."[1]

Melinda recalled, "When he walked out of there, and he put his hands up like in triumph, it was the most amazing moment. It just absolutely felt like a relief. He's out of there. He's out of there."[2]

It seemed like a Hollywood ending, but this marriage of nearly twenty-five years did not survive. In fact, Melinda and Clarence were under the same roof less than two weeks before Melinda suggested that it would be best for her husband to move in with his parents. Clarence filed for divorce nine months later.

MELINDA AND CLARENCE

Melinda and Clarence married when they were both eighteen years old. Their two sons were the strong glue in their marriage, keeping the couple together through the occasional rough patch. The two sometimes separated for a short time to clear the air. They were struggling through the aftermath of one of these times when the nightmare of the crime began. The prosecution had tried to base the case on a rocky marriage, but Melinda said that their troubles were overblown.

"Yeah, we had marital problems," she acknowledged. "Who doesn't? But it was nothing like they portrayed."[3]

Melinda had no assurance that Clarence would ever get out of prison, but she was committed to finding justice not only for him but also for her mother and niece. Judy Johnson had adopted Melinda when she was just an infant, and the two were as close as any biological mother and daughter. Melinda was not about to let her mother's killer off the hook.

In fact, she was so focused on the case, her job, and raising her sons that her personal life took a distant backseat for the eight years that followed her mother's murder. She walled off her emotions and focused relentlessly on finding justice and real closure to this long ordeal.

Although she did not have the benefit of a college education, by 2005, Melinda had a good job as a regional sales representative at the Timken Company, a bearing manufacturer headquartered in Canton, Ohio. She interacted with customers, suppliers, and distributors on the phone every day. One day, the conversation was different. The voice on the other end of the line struck a chord. Melinda said later, "I immediately felt this connection."[4]

Melinda's phone conversations with Patrick Dawson, a Timken supplier, became a kind of courtship that she had never consciously sought. After four months of conversation—and, ironically, just a few months before Clarence was released from prison—Melinda met Dawson in person for the first time. The instant connection she had felt on the phone was reinforced, and they became friends.

Clarence had been home only days when Melinda hit a wall. She was filled with anxiety. She kept thinking that the authorities were going to try to put her husband back in prison. There was a lot of media attention. She told the media that getting Clarence out of prison was a godsend, but she knew that people would not understand, as she did, that her delayed grief over her mother's death was now crashing down on her. All of a sudden, the murder felt as if it had happened yesterday. "All those years, I was pushing it back and pushing it back," she said. "That's what hit me."

The awkwardness she felt with Clarence didn't help. "It was like a ton of bricks. I didn't know how to help Clarence. I didn't know how to deal with it."[5]

When Patrick Dawson said that he could help her, it was as if Melinda responded from her very depths, "Okay."

"I had to do this," she said reflecting on this period in her life and on her divorce. "Otherwise, I don't think that I could have come out of what I was in. It was such a deep depression."[6]

Whether Melinda had met Dawson or not, no one knows if the Elkinses' marriage could have survived the changes that occur when two people are separated for years in circumstances that change each of them in different ways.

Bob Gilmartin, producer of *Dateline NBC*, observed in interviewing Clarence an incredible lack of anger: "How he kept his composure and gentility amazes me, considering the fact that he was in the Ohio state prison system for so long surrounded by violent inmates. How he could survive that environment without becoming bitter and angry is a mystery to me. I think his answer would be a profound belief in his wife, his innocence, and in religion. His constant companion, he says, was his Bible.[7]

"In the end, however, there is something quite sad about this man who lost his freedom for so long, and then once he gets out of jail, his marriage. While the rest of us turned our clocks forward one hour last night, all Clarence wants to do is rewind the clock nine years as if all of this never happened."[8]

Clarence's transition to life outside prison was difficult, as it is for most exonerees. Some have fared far worse. So much has been missed in the lives of their loved ones, but also in the advances of the culture. In today's environment, rich with personal options—even in the many varieties of coffee drinks offered at the java stop on the way to work—just choosing what to do, what to wear, and what to eat can be overwhelming for someone who has had no choice for years.

Financially, Clarence was more fortunate than many. By Ohio law, exonerated persons are eligible to be compensated $40,330 (or a greater amount established by the state auditor) per year incarcerated and for lost wages, attorneys' fees, and costs. As of 2010, nearly half the states in the country have no compensation statutes for the exonerated. Among those that do is a broad range of requirements and compensation levels. In Ohio, for example, the exoneree must not have pled guilty, must apply for compensation within two years of exoneration, and must be declared "actually innocent"—meaning the state must determine that the person had absolutely nothing to do with the crime.

If any exonerated person has not met the requirements, the Ohio attorney general has no choice but to oppose compensation. Elkins qualified and was awarded roughly $1 million by the state. He reimbursed expenses from the case and helped his family out financially. The money dwindled.

Clarence also filed a civil rights suit in U.S. District Court against the Summit County Prosecutor's Office, the county, and the Barberton police.[9] The court held that the prosecutor was immune from liability.[10] Other parts of the suit are still pending.[11]

I chafe at the thought of the state incurring this kind of expense. However, I also wondered if any compensation could address what this family had endured. After reimbursing expenses and meeting some family needs, the payment enabled Clarence to have time to sort things out.

The first year was tough as he adjusted to the fact that his marriage would not survive. Nevertheless Clarence has made the difficult transition after imprisonment and has gradually gotten his life together. He shared in the joy of his son's marriage and, a year later, the birth of his first grandchild. Four years after his release from prison, Clarence has established a new relationship and found happiness in his personal life. And Clarence has become a frequent public speaker on criminal justice.[12]

The Elkinses also had the pleasure of seeing justice finally delivered to Earl Mann. Nevertheless, it seemed a very long time coming. Clarence couldn't understand why it took prosecutors nearly two years to indict Mann, when, he noted drily, "It didn't take them maybe a couple of hours to come after me."[13]

I often reflect on an event that occurred just weeks after the exoneration, in February 2006. Mark Godsey invited Clarence, Melinda, and others involved in the case, including me, to participate in a forum at the law school. Melinda and Clarence, still a couple, at least publicly, were there to tell their story and answer questions. This was the first time I had actually met Clarence. I was struck by his gentle, even timid nature. He seemed to be a very private man who was not particularly comfortable in the limelight that had come after his exoneration. Clarence shunned interviews and media attention. It was as if he just wanted to reclaim some normalcy.

As for Melinda, she is one of the most remarkable people I have ever met. I said that day at the forum, as I have said many times, "I'm not sure I've met someone with the courage and determination I've seen in Melinda Elkins."

Still, Melinda's work on the case was not done. The promise she had made at her mother's grave would not be fulfilled until Earl Mann got his due. Justice moved slowly once Clarence was in prison, and it would move slowly in completing its work with Earl Mann.

I had once quipped at a press conference that, considering Melinda's detective skills, "perhaps we should hire her." As a matter of fact, she eventually did work for a time at the Innocence Project offices at the University of Cincinnati Law School. But she has also been able, at long last, to focus on her personal life. Melinda married Patrick Dawson and moved to the Dayton area. When justice was restored, she turned the page on this long chapter in her life.

THE ELKINS CHILDREN

The lives of the Elkins children changed dramatically that early Sunday morning when their father was handcuffed and taken away for the murder of their grandmother. "I became an adult that week. I had to. I lost my childhood," said the older son.[14]

The fifteen-year-old and the twelve-year-old experienced fear, pain, and lost innocence not only on that nightmarish morning but also in the months and years that followed. They instantly lost their grandmother and day-to-day life with a father who had been quite active in their lives. No more fishing trips and working on the family's four-acre plot of land with Dad. Instead they could only see and talk with their father—who, although absent, still tried to be their father—in a prison visitors' facility.

Melinda was nearly superhuman in her efforts to be both mother and father to the boys. She worked two jobs as she assumed the role of sole financial provider. Both boys showed signs of post-traumatic stress syndrome early on. They were not comfortable being in a crowd of people. They were depressed. That is why Melinda opted to homeschool them using educational resources from her church. Even with all of this on her plate, she spent at least some time every day—seven days a week—working on solving the case. Her sons gave Melinda no trouble; they knew she was doing her best with the problems she already had.

I thought that a very poignant comment revealed the boys' uncommon burdens. As with most young guys their age, the boys had baseball bats in their rooms. But for them, the bats were weapons. They feared that their grandmother's murderer would come someday to silence their mother, and the teens were prepared to protect her.[15] The deep sleep of their youth was another casualty of justice gone awry.

The brothers lived for the day their father would come home. When that day finally came, they went with their mother to walk their father out of prison. They looked forward to their first Christmas together in eight years. They would be a family again.

But this was not to be. Their father and mother would go their separate ways. "I always thought, once he came home, it'd be normal," the younger son said. "It was a big slap in the face. It ain't normal, and it ain't gonna be normal."[16]

When Melinda married Patrick Dawson and moved to Montgomery County, about two hours away, her sons stayed near their father. Both brothers have taken most of the training required to be police officers. Their struggle with post-traumatic stress syndrome has delayed the completion of their training, but they are confident that they will reach their goal. They want to try to prevent what happened to them from happening to other families.

THE CHILD VICTIM

The young victim's childhood was ripped from her by the brutality of Earl Mann. Her victimization continued for years as she lived with troubling uncertainty about her identification of her Uncle Clarence. This case illustrates what scientists know about memory—how easily it can be influenced by suggestion—and how a tentative identification can become more confident with reinforcement by persons of authority. Once Melinda and her sister restored their relationship, the girl began living with her aunt on and off over the years, because her mother's marriage was fragile. Her move to Montgomery County with Melinda and Patrick Dawson provided a new home—one that was removed from the bad memories of her early childhood. She has done well in high school and plans to go to college. She wants to become a forensic scientist.[17]

CHAPTER 10

Proving Guilt

EARL MANN

O N JUNE 29, 2007, more than a year and a half after DNA analysis linked Earl Mann's DNA to that of the crime scene DNA evidence, Prosecutor Sherri Bevan Walsh announced that a Summit County grand jury had indicted Earl Mann on "two counts of aggravated murder, a special felony, with four specifications for imposing the death penalty, for allegedly causing the death of Judith Johnson; one count of attempted murder, a felony of the first degree, for allegedly engaging in conduct that if successful, would have resulted in the death of a child...; one count of rape, a felony of the first degree, for allegedly raping Judith Johnson; two counts of rape, a felony of the first degree, for allegedly raping a child anally and vaginally; and one count of aggravated burglary, a felony of the first degree, for allegedly unlawfully entering the home of Judith Johnson and harming her and a child."[1]

On July 11, 2007, Mann pled not guilty.

And he decided to play lawyer. On January 10, 2008, Mann's motion to represent himself was granted by Common Pleas Judge Marvin A. Shapiro. The judge appointed standby counsel in the event that Mann might need it.[2]

However, Mann's career as a defense attorney was short-lived. He decided not to go to trial; instead he made a deal with Prosecutor Walsh.

TONIA BRASIEL

The neighbor who had acted so strangely when the young rape victim came to the door and whose testimony helped convict Clarence Elkins, was a codefendant with Earl Mann in the rape of the couple's three daughters. She was convicted of child endangerment and failure to protect her children, and received probation.

At about the time that Clarence Elkins's attempt to be exonerated became front-page news, Tonia Brasiel disappeared. Mann may have been in Brasiel's home when the little girl came for help the morning of the murder and the rapes. It would certainly explain her bizarre behavior in not calling an ambulance and the police. Most people would have immediately called the police out of fear that this predator might still be in the neighborhood. Most would have called an ambulance for the little girl and to make certain that Mrs. Johnson might not still be alive and need emergency care. If it is true that Brasiel was giving Mann cover, she knew that Clarence Elkins was the wrong person in prison those many years. Attempts to question her about the case by the Innocence Project team were unsuccessful.

PROSECUTOR SHERRI BEVAN WALSH

Prosecutor Walsh was not convinced of Clarence Elkins's innocence by DNA test results presented to her by the Elkins team. By mid- to late-2003, national television programs had brought attention to the case and, with it, pressure to pursue DNA testing and the truth. When Walsh agreed to release the crime scene evidence to the Elkinses for testing, the results excluded the younger suspect who had been identified by the Elkins team—but also excluded Clarence. It matched an unknown male.

Walsh needed to evaluate these DNA results. There was the question of the reliability of skin-cell DNA. Highly sensitive and very dependable in identifying gender-based genealogical markings that can include or exclude a person, skin-cell DNA is often definitive when other DNA may be unavailable or poorly preserved. Skin-cell DNA can be present in sweat, semen, saliva, and blood,[3] and can also be left by even a mere touch. At the March 23, 2005, hearing in front of Judge Judy Hunter, prosecutors sought in their questioning to present the possibility that the skin-cell evidence may have undergone "alteration"[4] in its transfers from police department to trial and from evidence room to laboratory, even though testimony indicated that professionals had handled the evidence within prescribed protocols of care. As it turned out, Judge Hunter based her denial of the motion on another argument of the prosecution: namely, that the new Y-STR DNA results would not have changed the outcome of the trial.

Professionals in the justice system bring their own unique histories and experiences to their work, to their assumptions, and to their decisions. Prosecutor Walsh's experience included a personal brush with a violent criminal. In 1986, a serial rapist known as the "Daylight Rapist" abducted and raped young women in the Akron area with a modus operandi that included duct-taping their eyes, leading them to a car at knifepoint, and raping them. Women in Akron were on edge as they read about the assaults of this rapist so bold as to strike in broad daylight.[5]

During this period, nineteen years before the 2005 hearing before Judge Hunter, Sherri Walsh, then a new lawyer in Akron, had just gotten into her car one snowy morning when a man armed with a knife suddenly yanked open the driver's-side door. He tried to push Walsh over into the passenger seat. The young woman screamed, kicked, and struggled with him as he tried to choke her. Her screams attracted the attention of people in the neighborhood, and her attacker fled.[6]

Gordon McRoy, the alleged Daylight Rapist, was apprehended, indicted, and convicted of twelve counts of rape, ten counts of kidnapping, one count of aggravated burglary, three counts of aggravated robbery, and five counts of felonious assault, but before he was sentenced, McRoy committed suicide in jail.[7]

This frightening experience had a lasting impact on the young lawyer. Walsh worked in her father's law firm, which specialized in worker's compensation, but she eventually ran for Summit County prosecutor and won a narrow victory in 2000. She inherited the Elkins case after Clarence's conviction.

Regina Brett, a reporter with the *Plain Dealer*, followed the Elkins case for ten years. After Elkins's exoneration, Brett wrote an article that told the case story from Walsh's perspective. While I respect Brett's writing,

I was not the only one baffled by the article's headline: "Summit County Prosecutor Sherri Bevan Walsh Fought to Convict Clarence Elkins, Then to Free Him."

The skin-cell DNA had not convinced Prosecutor Walsh of Elkins's claims of innocence. Later, when she was provided with matches of mtDNA and Y-STR DNA from both Mann's maternal and paternal lines, she still did not acknowledge to our office this very strong evidence of Elkins's innocence. However, after reviewing Earl Mann's record of rape and other assaults, Walsh wanted him to take a polygraph test. He was convinced to do so to prove his innocence. The testing occurred in the fall of 2005. First Mann insisted that he had not been in the neighborhood in months prior to the murder. When challenged to be truthful, he then admitted that he had been in the Johnson house briefly the day of the crime. Finally, he said that he had sex with Mrs. Johnson. The polygraph needle bounced wildly, confirming the lies that he was stumbling over.[8]

Walsh indicated to Regina Brett that Mann's record of violence and his failed polygraph finally convinced her of the terrible error in this case. She moved to discharge Clarence on December 15, 2005, and we were notified by fax fifteen minutes before the press conference at which we had indicated we would make public the maternal and paternal DNA match.

The unannounced fax handed to me that day—the state's motion to dismiss, signed by Prosecutor Walsh—read:

> The State hereby moves the Court for an Order dismissing the indictment in this case with prejudice, vacating all convictions obtained pursuant to said indictment and discharging the Defendant.
>
> For cause the State says that there is evidence that clearly and convincingly demonstrates that the Defendant is actually innocent of the offenses for which he stands convicted.[9]

Clarence and Melinda wasted no time after Clarence's release to make an unexpected call on Walsh at her office. Melinda recalled that Walsh seemed to be trying to win her over with small talk, but the Elkinses wanted answers, and they wanted Earl Mann's conviction. Walsh explained that the polygraph tests would be inadmissible in trial, and she still felt that the

DNA evidence was weak. She said that she intended to build a strong case against Mann.

With Earl Mann in prison, Walsh could take her time. She directed the testing of thirty pieces of DNA evidence. Eight months later, in May 2007, a bodily fluid DNA sample from the victim's panties revealed the most undeniable match to date: with odds of 1 in 96,990,000[10] that the DNA could have belonged to anyone else.

Ultimately, Walsh reached an agreement with Mann that included a particularly satisfying element: a confession of guilt. In return, he was sentenced on August 19, 2008, by Judge Robert M. Gippin to fifty-five years to life in prison, but no death penalty. Although Mann would be eligible for release at age ninety, the judge recommended that, "based upon the facts and circumstances of the case," he "not be granted parole at any time."[11] The Elkinses approved of this plea agreement.

Apparently the voters also approved. In 2008, Sherri Bevan Walsh easily beat her Republican challenger.

Prosecutor Walsh began her end-of-year 2008 newsletter with a commendation of her prosecutors for achieving a 96 percent conviction rate.[12] She also commented on the "full circle" that justice delivered when Earl Mann pled guilty to aggravated murder and rape in the case involving the murder of Judith Johnson and the rape of her granddaughter: "For him to take responsibility for these horrific crimes after allowing Clarence Elkins to take his rap and spend seven and a half years in prison was nothing short of shocking. We never expected it and were pleased to see it."[13]

THE ELKINS CASE finally may have been closed, but the impact it had on me was far from over. The seriously misguided and narrow investigation and the tragic lack of attention to the significant exculpatory evidence that should have eliminated Elkins as a suspect were troubling and begged difficult questions. How does this happen? How often does it happen? How many innocent people are in America's prisons? Who is to blame? Is there anything we can do about it?

The thought of innocent Americans in this nearly hopeless situation motivated my wife, Nancy, and me to learn as much as we could about wrongful conviction. The Elkinses' experience taught us that, once convicted, a prisoner's opportunity to prove his or her innocence is extremely remote and requires an army of pro bono lawyers and tenacious family members willing to work for years at great expense without any guarantee of restoring justice.

DNA analysis of crime scene evidence has led to the exoneration of more than 250 persons who had been convicted and imprisoned for serious felony crimes, primarily murder and rape. Of these, seventeen had spent time on death row. Each case is compelling, extraordinary, and tragic.

Nancy and I learned that there are six major contributors to wrongful conviction. We began to realize that these contributors are enabled and fueled by common misunderstandings about the justice system. These myths—we identified eight of them—set the stage for conviction tragedies.

A lifetime in politics has taught us that until we, as a nation, confront our misconceptions, fixing the system will be an uphill struggle. With knowledge, however, we can significantly reduce wrongful conviction, and, in the process, create a much safer nation.

These understandings, however, did not come instantly. In fact, our journey had just begun.

CHAPTER 11

How Many?

Q. How many convicts in American prisons today
   are totally innocent of the crime?

A. Only God knows.

A S RECENTLY AS 1989, this would have been the end of the discussion. However, on August 14, 1989, Gary Dotson was exonerated by an emerging forensic tool: DNA analysis of crime scene evidence.[1] The luckless Dotson, a high-school dropout from Chicago, had served eight years over a twelve-year period in and out of prison for a rape that was totally fabricated by the victim, Cathleen Crowell. In 1977, the sixteen-year-old Crowell, after having consensual sex with her boyfriend, invented the rape as a backup story in case she became pregnant. She fooled detectives, prosecutors, judges, and even a governor by basing her detailed story on a rape described in a novel by Rosemary Rogers, *Sweet Savage Love*.[2] Two years later, Dotson, then twenty-two, was sentenced to a minimum of twenty-five years in prison.

When Crowell discovered religion and recanted her testimony against Dotson in 1985, the prosecutors and judge chose to believe her first story.[3] However, the case had become high-profile, and the governor commuted Dotson's sentence to the six years served, with a parole-like stipulation of required good behavior. As if cursed, the alcoholic Dotson violated this by allegedly assaulting his wife and being disruptive in a bar. Only his attorney's decision to test the crime scene evidence saved Dotson from a return to prison.[4] Without DNA, it is unlikely that Dotson—doomed by a wrongful conviction and his own demons—ever would have found justice.

Dotson was not a terrific poster child for the exonerated. Nor was his case a particularly auspicious beginning for a new forensic test that would change crime and justice.

Until the advent of DNA, most Americans trusted that the nightmare of wrongful criminal conviction is a rare event in a criminal justice system thought to be the best in the world. However, confidence was shaken with the disturbing frequency of court-ordered exonerations, vacations of convictions (removing a conviction from a person's record), and prisoners being released after DNA analysis of crime scene evidence proved their innocence. Even with this truth-revealing tool, however, most of the exonerated had to fight for years with dedicated pro bono lawyers and tenacious loved ones to pry the tight grip of American justice from their lives.

Public response to the Clarence Elkins case was similar to that of other exonerations in the United States over the past nearly two hundred years. By and large, people view a wrongful conviction as a one-in-a-million unfortunate mistake. They pity the poor person who has such bad luck and believe that it could never happen to them. These cases arouse our curiosity and sympathy. Only occasionally does temporary criticism fall on the authorities responsible in a particular case. Until recently, rarely has this expanded to the notion of holding the criminal justice system accountable.

However, the mistaken convictions revealed through DNA technology have been like stubborn weeds difficult to ignore in the landscape of criminal justice. And some people have not ignored them. Researchers and legal pioneers have attempted to quantify the extent of error. Pro bono lawyers have worked to reverse error in specific cases. Academics have analyzed the DNA-triggered exonerations to identify the factors that contribute to error. This research has led to the creation of reforms designed to improve outcomes. Legislators have introduced bills and passed laws to enact new procedural requirements. An innocence movement has emerged, and it is growing.

Numerous individuals and organizations have estimated the number of innocent men and women in U.S. prisons today, and none of the estimates is comforting. Many believe that the 253 Americans exonerated through DNA represent the tip of the iceberg and that the wrongfully convicted remaining in prison number in the thousands, possibly tens of thousands. Some have said this ill-fated population is more than one hundred thousand.

Nancy and I wanted to come to some understanding of how extensive wrongful conviction might be. Even an intuitive analysis suggested significant numbers. The theory that the exonerated represent a small percentage of innocent people in prison is supported by what we know are significant barriers to exoneration, including:

- the hurdles, costs, and extraordinary effort required to achieve a reversal after conviction;
- the destruction of key biological evidence after trial;
- the lack of DNA evidence in most criminal acts;
- the concentration of corrective efforts on the relatively small percentage of the prison population convicted of murder and rape;
- the overwhelming number of imprisoned Americans, which would require countless pro bono lawyers and detectives to identify and pursue worthy post-conviction cases;
- the confidence that most Americans have in the justice system, making exoneration a low priority in the political environment that influences those who deliver justice.

The late Robert Dawson, a thirty-seven-year professor and cofounder of the Texas Center for Actual Innocence at the University of Texas School of Law, speculated on the Center's website, "If the Texas system is 99 percent accurate, there are 1,500 innocent people in prison. And if the system is 99.9 percent accurate, that's still 150 innocent people in prison. That is both reassuring and a depressing thought."[5]

CHAPTER 12

A Compelling Witness

"**Y**OU'VE GOTTEN ABOUT** three hundred fifty angry emails so far today."

Kim Norris, my director of communications, didn't sugarcoat bad news. A veteran from my Ohio Auditor of State years, she knew that I wanted information straight up and as soon as possible, even if it was unsettling. "They want you to pay Michael Green five hundred thousand dollars," she said.

I was into my fifth month as attorney general of Ohio. Eight years as auditor of state had been good preparation, but this job was very different. The work was incredibly diverse, spanning a wide swath of legal responsibilities from civil to criminal. Fraud. Identity theft. Consumer protection. Collections. Child and elder protection. Environmental enforcement. Criminal forensics. And these were just for starters. Some of our 35,000 active civil and criminal cases were of political interest. Decisions were often controversial. The media was always looking for a story, and critics were eager to pounce. Nevertheless, I felt good about our start. We had rewritten the organizational chart, a new management team was in place, every division had challenging objectives, and we were making good progress on a number of fronts.

Still, the morning of Friday, May 23, 2003, was not starting off well.

Only a few days earlier, I hadn't known who Anthony Michael Green was, but I had quickly learned. In 1988, Green was wrongfully convicted in Cleveland and had spent thirteen years in prison for a rape that he did not commit. The *Plain Dealer* had run a series of articles on his case. Green, by then thirty-seven, had been exonerated by DNA about a year and a half earlier. As the newspaper series concluded, a Rodney Rhines stepped forward to confess to the crime. DNA proved his confession was genuine: Rhines was guilty. Anthony Michael Green wanted the money that the state is required by law to provide to victims of wrongful conviction.

Connie Schultz, the writer of the Pulitzer Prize–nominated series on the Green case in the *Plain Dealer*, had railed against me in her column a day earlier. "Former Attorney General Betty Montgomery and her successor, Jim Petro, have ignored Ohio law, which stipulates that Green is owed at least $40,330 for every year he was in prison," she wrote.[1]

She then challenged her readers to demand justice for Michael Green by calling, writing, or emailing me.

This was nearly two and a half years before I got involved in the Clarence Elkins case, and, like most Americans, I thought that wrongful criminal conviction was extremely rare. But that wasn't the reason that our office had resisted authorizing payment for Green. The reason had to do with our job. The Ohio Attorney General represents the state and, by extension, the citizens of Ohio in virtually every civil and criminal legal case involving the state and the offices of state government. The attorney general's responsibility in the Green case was to protect the state's resources in the process of finding equitable compensation for the state's error in wrongfully convicting and imprisoning this man for thirteen years.

There would be no issue as to whether or not Green would get the stipulated $40,330 for each year he spent in prison. He had met Ohio's standards for compensation. Not only had he been exonerated and released from prison, but he had also been determined to be "actually innocent" by the exclusion of his DNA from the crime scene DNA. The unresolved issue was how much the state should pay for Green's missed wages. If he had been employed at the time of his arrest, we would have had a good basis for calculating a fair settlement. However, Green was unemployed then and did not have a consistent history of employment.

Green's case met the expected initial response from the assistant attorney general representing the state: a boilerplate denial of the claim. While the state would soon agree to pay the compensation for the lost time, our lawyer was seeking to delay any payment until the question of lost wages had been resolved through negotiation with Green's lawyers.

If it were not for Connie Schultz's article urging her readers to email me, I probably would not have known about the case. While I skimmed all of Ohio's major newspapers, and may have read some of the articles on Green, our office had nothing to do with the case until this question of state compensation for Green's wrongful conviction.

I took a phone call from Schultz, who gave little credence to my explanation that delaying payment until we had resolution on the lost wages question provided leverage to the state in this negotiation. I explained that this is the way legal cases are carried out.

To illustrate that the lost-wages question could cost Ohio taxpayers hundreds of thousands, even in excess of a million dollars, I asked her, "What if Green claimed, 'I was going to be a concert musician'?"

She asked me whether I honestly thought Green would make such a claim. "Well…no," I admitted.

I was not sensing any success in my efforts to explain to Connie Shultz how the legal system works. However, she was doing a great job of getting this case onto my radar screen. After hanging up the phone, I asked for a briefing on the Green case. I went through the file of our staff attorney, and I read Shultz's articles.

I made a decision by the next day. Anthony Michael Green was innocent. He had lost thirteen years of his life in prison for a crime he didn't commit. Now out of prison, he was just scraping by financially. His ambition to work with troubled youth had been thwarted by several potential employers who inexplicably would not hire an ex-con, regardless of guilt or innocence. I authorized payment of the uncontested portion of his claim, an unusual—perhaps unprecedented—step.

Even so, there is a process. It includes getting the approval of the Ohio Court of Claims, and it takes time. Two months later, after the court approved the payment, it was announced that the state would pay Michael Green $523,186, the amount stipulated for his wrongful incarceration.

"It's the right thing to do," I said at the time. "We're going to look for early resolution in all of these cases."[2]

The payment also had to be approved by the Office of Budget and Management controlling board. After that occurred on August 18, Green received a payment of $375,000. He chose to receive the remainder of the payment in 240 monthly payments of $2,200 beginning when he planned to retire, in 2020.[3]

Schultz congratulated her readers for their activism, and most of them no doubt believed that a few hundred emails, and the political pressure they sought to apply, had changed my mind on this case. Actually, the publicity and the emails brought the case to my attention. Looking into it personally resulted not only in partial payment for Michael Green but also in a new policy that made settlement in wrongful criminal conviction cases a priority in our office. When the state makes the horrific mistake of convicting and imprisoning an innocent person, it should move with all possible speed to acknowledge the error and to provide the stipulated compensation for it. Of course, this can occur only in those states that have such a provision.

I never enjoyed the rare occasions when I was painted as the bad guy in the press, but I consider Connie Shultz's series and follow-up articles on Anthony Michael Green—and the resulting flow of emails and letters to me from her readers—to be journalism and citizenship at their best. Justice requires the diligence of everyone. The series brought a number of positive, even remarkable, results, not the least of which was my introduction to the travesty of wrongful criminal conviction. I didn't realize it then, but for me, Michael Green had broken the seal on a Pandora's box.

OVER THE NEXT SIX YEARS, I would be drawn into the challenge of understanding wrongful conviction by encounters such as this one. I was one of countless Americans who had watched the February 1997 broadcast of the PBS *Frontline* report "What Jennifer Saw." I learned this story's lesson: A victim who provides eyewitness testimony can be very intelligent, very confident, very honest, very well intentioned—and very mistaken.

The Cotton case involved a rape, in Burlington, North Carolina; the well-considered, but incorrect, eyewitness testimony of a Caucasian victim, twenty-two-year-old Jennifer Thompson; and the conviction of Ronald Cotton, an innocent African American who was imprisoned for eleven years before eventually being exonerated by DNA analysis of rape kit evidence. Oddly enough, in 2009 the two collaborated on a memoir, *Picking Cotton: Our Memoir of Injustice and Redemption.*

The national exposure of the Cotton case raised awareness of the fallibility of memory, as well as common misunderstandings regarding how memory works. This story and others like it were opening slammed doors that would permit scientists to share explanations, some of which they had known for a hundred years.

FOR NEARLY TWO DECADES, legal and academic pioneers had been analyzing the growing number of wrongful convictions. With its many similarities to the Ronald Cotton case, the Anthony Michael Green case brought Nancy and me back years after Green's exoneration to take a close look. By thoroughly reading the trial transcripts and pursuing other relevant information, we hoped to identify the procedures, assumptions, arguments, and subtle persuasions that contributed to this imperfect human journey from crime to flawed conviction.

The process and outcome of the justice system in this case was as frightening and victimizing as any crime that steals reputation, dignity, and freedom. A host of people assumed to be professional, capable, and well motivated delivered a tragic error that, like a steamroller, became virtually unstoppable.

Unlike Ronald Cotton, Green would never reconcile with his alleged victim, who wrongly identified him as her rapist. The West Virginia nurse, a Caucasian single mother, died of cancer about a year after testifying under oath that Green was the black man who had raped her.[4]

The crime occurred at the Clinic Center, a hotel attached to the renowned Cleveland Clinic medical center, where the woman was undergoing treatment for her advanced cancer. She checked herself into a special floor at the hotel for patients who needed further testing but not constant care. It was Sunday, May 29, 1988, and she would not have to go back to the clinic until the next morning.[5]

The woman was resting in room 524 when, just after ten o'clock p.m., she heard a loud knock on the door. She was hoping it was her boyfriend, who had accompanied her to Cleveland. She had not heard from him all day, and, expecting him, she opened the door. She would later testify that "a man reached in...with his right arm and grabbed me around the throat and put a knife in my face and pushed me into the room."[6]

As the man pushed her into the room, the door slammed and automatically locked behind him. He kept the knife in front of her face while continuing to grip her throat as he moved in a circle around her. He had a "horrible, threatening, murderous look on his face," she told the jury.[7]

The man asked whether she had any money. She indicated that she did, and he let go of her so she could get it. She went to her wallet, took out the money—about $42—and handed it to him.[8]

The woman would testify at trial of her unrelenting focus on her assailant. "The whole time that he was in my room, I made eye contact with him. I never took my eyes from his face," she said.[9] "I told him that I was fighting for my life."[10]

It almost worked.

Standing there, staring at her, he revealed his own fears. "You're going to call somebody, you're going to do something," he said.[11]

He hesitated, but then he pushed her back onto the bed. He took his trousers off and he raped her.[12] Afterward he walked to the bathroom, wiped himself with a washcloth, and dropped it onto the floor.[13]

He rifled through her things and asked her how she pronounced her name. She told him, and he said, "My name is Tony."[14]

Before leaving, he revealed regret that would haunt him for years.

"This is going to hurt me more than it does you," he said.[15]

When the woman finished telling her story to the jury, thirty-eight-year-old Cuyahoga County assistant prosecuting attorney Timothy J. McGinty, a seven-year veteran of the prosecutor's office,[16] concluded the dramatic line of questioning with the anticipated question: "Looking about the courtroom, do you see the man in this room that forced his way into your room on May 29, 1988, who at knifepoint took your money and raped you?" he asked.

"Yes, I do," the victim replied confidently.

"Can you point him out and describe him?" McGinty asked.

"Yes, I can. Right there he is," she said, pointing to Anthony Michael Green.[17]

MICHAEL GREEN WAS in an uphill battle to overcome the impact of the state's first witness. In fact, even if there were no other witnesses, the confident testimony of the frail, terminally ill rape victim would prevail in a "she said, he said" contest with Green, the unemployed former dishwasher at the Clinic Center coffee shop.

But the state had other impressive witnesses, including four officers of the law from the Cleveland Clinic Police Department. The jury learned that the Cleveland Clinic, a large, internationally recognized medical center, has its own police department. Thomas Hinkle, a twenty-nine-year-old security officer, was working in the dispatch room when the call came in from his colleague, Officer Robert Beck, the first officer to respond to the call. Beck relayed the description of the perpetrator to Hinkle so that it could be broadcast by radio to the other officers on the force.[18]

The woman described her attacker as a "black male, mid-twenties, approximately five foot seven, short hair." He was wearing "a do-rag—a tight cloth on the head—and then a ski or stocking cap over top of the do-rag." He had a thin mustache. The male had "broad shoulders, a muscular build. He had a black or dark-colored T-shirt on with some rip or tear mark on the shirt." The victim thought that the sleeves had been removed from the shirt. His pants were tight at the waist and baggy in the legs.[19]

Bingo! Security Officer Hinkle had a suspect: Anthony Michael Green.[20]

Beck couldn't place him at first, but, with Hinkle's help, he remembered Green as the dishwasher who had worked at the Clinic Center coffee shop.[21] Green fit the woman's description, and Green had once shown Hinkle his small pocketknife. The security officer had often chatted with Green in the slow, early morning hours when both would take a coffee break. Hinkle later testified that Green had sometimes bragged about being an ex-con[22] and liked to talk about weapons and women. "He really liked women," Hinkle reported.[23]

Officer Beck testified at Green's trial that within fifteen minutes of his arrival on the crime scene, he had communicated the description, and Hinkle had identified Green as a suspect.[24] Fast work!

Security Officer Hinkle could not recall whether he was told immediately or later that the perpetrator had told his victim that his name was Tony. As I reviewed this case, it struck me that a criminal like this burglar-rapist who supposedly revealed his name to the crime victim was either very honest, very stupid, or a liar. The clinic officers must have dismissed the third possibility. For them, the fact that Tony is short for Anthony supported the hunch that Anthony Michael Green was the rapist.

Although no one knew how the assailant had gained access to guest rooms without being noticed by security, it would make sense that the perpetrator might be a former employee who would know the employee back entrance and pathways to get to the guest floors of the Clinic Center without having to enter the more heavily trafficked and staffed front entrance of the hotel.

The officers wasted no time in pursuing the theory of Green as perpetrator. The very night of the incident, Officer Beck picked up and brought the Cleveland Clinic foundation's album of identification photos of employees to security officer Hinkle to confirm Green's identity in the small photo that had been used for his employee identification badge.[25]

THE NEXT DAY, detectives showed the rape victim an array of photos.[26] Referencing Green's photo she said she saw one person who resembled her attacker, "but just not enough."[27]

The following day, Clinic Police Staff Investigator Lou DeGross and his colleague Herb Fortune came with larger photos, including the same photo of Green, enlarged. DeGross later testified at the trial, "We told her we had some photographs; that we had possibly the suspect in this situation."[28] This time the woman spotted her attacker, saying, "This is the one."[29]

Officer DeGross replied, "This guy's name is Anthony. Tony."[30]

CHAPTER 13

Flaws and Faulty Forensics

ANALYSIS OF EXONERATIONS proven by DNA analysis confirmed common-sense assumptions about criminal justice process and revealed new understandings about how conviction error occurs. In retrospect, I recognized a multitude of subtle contributors that played havoc with justice in the Green case.

1. Based on a limited description by the victim, detectives identified Green as a suspect and were building their case around him within a couple of hours of the crime. I got the impression that, as was also true in the Elkins case, detectives jumped to an early conclusion rather than permitting the evidence to lead to the suspect.

2. The detectives did not heed the victim's most important *first* response to the photos of suspects: She said that the man in one photo resembled her attacker *"but just not enough."* A victim's earliest response after a crime is the most reliable, since memory can easily be corrupted. Her response was *not* identification but only an indication of a similarity.

3. The detectives who showed the victim the second batch of photos told her that they "had possibly the suspect in this situation." It's recommended that law enforcement personnel conducting a photo identification explain that a suspect may or *may not* be in the array of photos, and that the investigation will continue whether or not she makes an identification. This protocol was not followed.

4. When the detectives showed the victim a second batch of photos, the only person whose photo was included in both displays was that of Michael Green. Experts indicate that she may have selected Green because she recalled him from the first batch!

5. By presenting the photos all at once, the officers gave the victim the opportunity to compare photos and select "the closest one." The victim assumes that the suspect is included in the batch and therefore begins a comparison process that can lead to an inaccurate identification. The preferred procedure is to present the photos sequentially, one at a time, so that the witness must make a decision on each independent of comparisons.

6. The detectives who presented the photos knew who the suspect was and may inadvertently have communicated some indication of him either expressly or through their body language. It is preferable to have "blind administration": an administrator who is unaware of the suspect's identity.

7. When the woman selected Green in the second photo array, the detectives reinforced her selection by saying, "This guy's name is Anthony. Tony." These kinds of statements contribute to growing confidence on the part of the victim, so that by the time of the trial, even those who made a tentative selection often have become totally confident in court testimony.

Sadly, focus on the evidence, instead of early tunnel vision on one suspect, and simple procedural improvements may well have prevented this tragic conviction error.

NEWSPAPER AND MEDIA accounts of criminal cases typically do not mention the early procedures in an investigation. The media accounts after Green's exoneration would focus instead on a particular witness for the prosecution. In fact, his role in this trial would eventually become a great liability for the City of Cleveland. Many thought that he was instrumental in the outcome of the trial. Nancy and I wanted to know whether this was a fair conclusion and whether it provided any insights into wrongful conviction, which was another reason to examine the exact questions and answers recorded in the trial transcript.

This witness was Joseph Serowick, a scientific examiner in the forensic laboratory of the Cleveland Police Department. Serowick said that he spent "approximately twenty-five to thirty hours analyzing"[1] the hair found on the washcloth used by the rapist.

He "found that the diameter of the hair on the towel was...smaller than that of the pubic hair sample" [from Michael Green], and, therefore, he "determined that it did not come from the pubic region."[2]

The scientist also determined that the hair was "dark brown...in respect to color," it was "a match to the head hair of the defendant."[3]

Serowick compared hair characteristics in the evidence sample to hairs from Green.[4] The scientist provided ample disclaimers. In fact, he testified that unless he actually saw two hairs plucked from the same individual, he could find that they were similar but "couldn't say they matched" or "that they came from the same individual."[5]

Nevertheless, he concluded, "the hair found on this particular towel is consistent with the head hair standard sample taken from the defendant."[6]

The prosecuting attorney inquired about the likelihood of two hairs matching when they originated from two different people. Serowick said that there had been several studies on that particular question without consensus. He did "recall a study that said one in forty thousand would be a pretty good estimate" for this.[7]

In similar fashion, Serowick testified about the testing of the washcloth dropped by the rapist. He described the tests that confirmed seminal fluid on the washcloth. The jury was told that 80 percent of humans secrete ABO antigens in body secretions such as semen. The rapist was included in this majority. Serowick said that his blood was type B, present in about 20 percent of the black population.[8]

The scientist estimated that only 16 percent of the population are type B secretors.[9]

Coincidentally, the victim was also a type B secretor.[10]

Neither the prosecution nor the defense questioned whether or not this fact was an issue in interpreting this evidence.

Nor did either side seek DNA testing, which was emerging at the time, presumably because, in Serowick's words, it was "extremely expensive."

To be precise, $585 per tested item.[11]

In all of the long testimony of the forensic scientist, no physical evidence conclusively tied Michael Green to the crimes. The scientist provided adequate disclaimers to what the science could determine: probabilities, not certainties. Nevertheless, to Nancy and me, McGinty's concluding questioning—and the answers he elicited—seemed to imply stronger probabilities than the earlier testimony had offered.

"Your analysis strictly is here on probabilities?" he asked Serowick.

"Right. It's a probability on physical evidence."

"You can never be absolutely certain, can you, sir?" he asked.

"Not at this point, no."[12]

"As to the possibility, sir," McGinty concluded, "there is also a possibility, is there not, that this building will be struck by a meteor—right?—overnight?"

To this, the forensic scientist replied, "I would hope not, but there is a possibility, yes."[13]

JAMES DRAPER, a forty-six-year-old former policeman and experienced attorney, offered two witnesses on behalf of his client: Green's cousin Johnnie Lee Whitney and Michael Green himself.

Johnnie Lee, who'd worked at the Clinic Center for ten years, said that he and Green really did not get along very well.[14] Nonetheless, he'd helped his cousin get a job in maintenance with him. Green had fathered a daughter, now two years old, and he was trying to support the little girl and his girlfriend, who also had a five-year-old daughter. Unfortunately, the job at the Clinic Center didn't last; Green was fired due to a dispute with another employee, and he went back to working odd jobs and as a mechanic.[15]

Although Whitney did not seem to be a particularly sympathetic witness, he did clear up the matter of his cousin's name. Despite the fact that even Draper, Green's own defense attorney, referred to him throughout the trial as Anthony, Whitney said that he had always known his cousin as Michael, not Tony. He testified that everyone called him by that name: "His mother does and neighbors do. Everybody in the neighborhood calls him Michael," he said.[16] When Johnnie Lee found out that his cousin's name was not actually Michael, he asked his mother why he had gone by that name. She said that his birth certificate was flawed; it was supposed to have read "Michael Anthony Green."[17] Because Green had to show his birth certificate to become an employee at the Clinic Center, his birth certificate dictated the name on his ID badge and on his paycheck—the name that others called him at work: Anthony Michael Green.

From what I could detect from the trial transcripts, after questioning by the defense and cross-examination by the state, Whitney's testimony boiled down to a few undisputed facts for the jury to ponder: (1) Green had once shown Whitney a pocketknife.[18] (2) Green sometimes drank beer. (3) He sometimes bragged about a criminal record and a stretch in prison, which, in fact, had never happened. (4) Johnnie Lee did not know what his cousin was doing between the hours of ten and eleven on the evening of the rape.[19]

Michael Green took the stand in his own defense. He said that he learned indirectly that he was the subject of a rape charge. "Everybody on the street was going around calling me Jack the Ripper and rapist," he said.[20] Green was never arrested for the crime because he voluntarily walked the more than thirty blocks from his home to straighten things out with the Cleveland Clinic Police Department. He was ushered in to speak to Herb Fortune, a consultant to the department, who was assigned to the case.[21]

Green wanted to know where he fit into the rape investigation. According to his testimony, Fortune told him the police had learned that he had been terminated from his job at the hotel, "so we figured you needed some money." They believed that the ex-employee had snuck into the hospital-hotel "to rob the woman, and raped her."[22]

Fortune also told Green that the victim had picked him out twice in photo arrays.[23] Green insisted that he had not committed the crime and even volunteered to give blood and saliva samples to prove his innocence. Later, on the witness stand, Green said, "I told him I'm willing to take any type of test you want to put me through to prove I'm innocent. I'm not turning no test down."[24]

After providing the blood sample, the police took Green home and said that they would get back in touch with him.

But the only "getting back" he got was a letter in the mail informing him that he had been indicted, with an arraignment date of July 14. On that date, he showed up alone, without an attorney. A not-guilty plea was entered for him. The judge set bond at $25,000. Because Green could not afford a lawyer, he was appointed one. Then he was locked up and stayed in the county jail until the trial began three months later.[25]

At trial, Green testified that on the night of the crime, he had been hanging out with friends near his home. They were challenging one another in foot races, and then he had gone to his girlfriend's house nearby. She wasn't home, so he waited for her, hanging out with a friend, for two hours.[26] The defense did not present anyone to corroborate his testimony and alibi.

Green denied under oath that he had ever bragged about prison or women or that he ever drank alcohol to the point of blacking out and not remembering what he had done while drunk. The only time that he had imbibed to such excess that he was taken to the hospital was the night his father died.[27] In all of these denials of various claims by other witnesses— even though not one was incriminating in and of itself—Green responded that they were simply not true: The other witnesses were either mistaken or lying.[28]

The most important testimony Michael Green provided was in his unequivocal answers to a string of questions posed by his attorney, Mr. Draper:

"Mr. Green, on May 29, 1988, at the Clinic Center, did you engage in sexual conduct with [a woman] by compelling her to submit to you by force?"

"No," answered Green.

"On May 29, 1988, up here at the Clinic Center, did you have a knife and use that to take something of value...?"

"No, I didn't."

"Did you on May 29 go up to [a woman's] room with a do-rag and a ski cap or some kind of hat or baseball cap?"

"No, I did not."

"And compel her to do anything?"

"No, I did not."

"Did you in fact go to the police yourself?"

"Yes, I did."[29]

The defense's hope for Michael Green rested on the possibility that at least one juror would believe that he was telling the truth and that everyone else—from the victim, to the Clinic Center police officers, to the forensic scientist—had it wrong. Just one juror would have to believe in the unemployed, illiterate Michael Green.

As it turned out, one did.

CHAPTER 14

Closing Arguments

IN REVIEWING THE WRITTEN trial transcripts—again, years later—I felt that the case against Michael Green was very weak. The strongest evidence was the victim's having identified him. Prosecutor McGinty was correct when he told the jury that twenty or fifty years ago, this was all the evidence needed to convict someone. Without DNA, things have not changed much.

The only real supporting evidence came from the forensic scientist, Joseph Serowick. But what did he really say? He claimed that the hair from the crime scene was "consistent" with a head hair sample from Michael Green. While he admitted that science could not confirm that a hair came from a specific individual, he referenced one study that suggested that the odds were 1 in 40,000 that hairs from two individuals would match.

Regarding the seminal fluid on the washcloth, Serowick said that only 16 percent of the male population could have left it there and that Green was in that 16 percent. He acknowledged at trial that the victim was *also* in this population, yet no one addressed how this might impact the test results. Finally, the prosecution offered the dubious argument that the perpetrator said his name was Tony, and Michael Green's formal name was Anthony Michael Green—even though he had always been known as Michael.

Unfortunately, the defense witnesses didn't provide much to support Green's claims of innocence. Green's cousin, Johnnie Lee Whitney, could offer only the not completely positive testimony that Green went by the name Michael, that he once had a pocketknife, and that he sometimes bragged about having a criminal record, which was not true.

I had an advantage over the jurors. I personally knew the prosecuting attorney, Timothy McGinty; the defense attorney, Jim Draper; and the long-time county prosecutor, John T. Corrigan. I had the benefit of knowing that both McGinty and Draper were competent lawyers with strong reputations. Notwithstanding the fact that Green could not afford a lawyer, he was more fortunate than most in drawing Draper, a former policeman and established defense attorney. As a county commissioner, I had recommended that Draper be appointed Cuyahoga County public defender.

Considering the lack of conclusive physical evidence, I wondered why Green was not given a lie detector test. Twenty years later, after DNA has proven that the system makes errors, I have developed a respect for county prosecutors who question or change the focus of an investigation if the suspect passes a lie detector test. While the question of the polygraph's reliability has not been fully resolved, I believe that when a suspect offers, even demands, to take a polygraph or to enthusiastically give blood, hair, or DNA samples, as Michael Green did, investigators and prosecutors should take pause and be particularly attentive to any exculpatory evidence.

Corrigan, Cuyahoga County prosecutor from 1957 to 1991, was tough on crime, and the voters loved him for it. He was a pre-DNA prosecutor, and I would not be surprised if his office did not generally stipulate the use of lie detectors for criminal suspects. Even today, many prosecutors will not permit the results of a polygraph test to be used as evidence in the trial.

WITH ALL WITNESSES having been heard, it was time for attorneys from both sides to present final arguments. Jurors are cautioned and may understand that final arguments have more relaxed rules of presentation than the testimony phase of the trial, but it may still be challenging for them to give proper weight to the final argument, which is just that: an argument, a point of view, an interpretation.

Jurors hear both sides. The prosecution and the defense each seeks to clarify and promote its case. They are often very different summations of what everyone has heard, which can be disconcerting to the jury. The final arguments are the last information, other than the judge's instructions, that the jury hears before retiring to make life-changing decisions. And, because the burden of proof is the prosecutor's, the prosecution has the opportunity to come back and rebut the defense attorney's points. The prosecutor always gets the last word.

"...How, you might say to yourself, could a man do an act such as the defendant, Anthony Green, did in this case. It defies imagination," declared Prosecutor McGinty, the first to present his final argument.[1]

"What does this woman, who is virtually leaning on the door to meet her maker...what motivation does she have to come in here?" McGinty asked the jury.[2]

"I'll answer that, ladies and gentlemen.... Her motivation is to see that justice is done. That the man who attacked her, Anthony Green, is suitably punished, and no other woman is put into the position that she was."[3]

McGinty stressed that "the way the system was designed, there was no need to put any evidence on beyond the victim herself. That is the evidence."

Council for the defense, Jim Draper, was not about to let the question of evidence slip by. He reminded the jury that the forensic expert could not identify a single pubic hair from the room, and that there was no evidence of the woman's underwear, no fingerprints, and no sperm from the hospital exam after the rape.[4]

"...Mr. McGinty says all you normally have is the victim. My goodness, he is the one that is going to bring that corroborative evidence and testimony in here, and he didn't do it. He didn't do it because it is nonexistent. If it existed, you better believe you would have it in front of you," declared Draper.[5]

McGinty then addressed the jury, speaking nearly three times longer than he had in his initial final argument. His tone, even in the printed transcript, appeared to change from philosophical to taking some offense at the defense's final argument: "You've heard some attempts to twist and connive what has been said, to cloud and to muddle some of the issues.... I ask you to reject each and every one of them, and act intelligently and with common sense."[6]

As expected of a good prosecutor, McGinty challenged virtually every point Draper had made, one by one. He was particularly persuasive on the matter of the physical evidence:

"Now the calling card. Think of the weight of the evidence, and the scientific evidence. If this were twenty years ago, or certainly fifty years ago, you wouldn't have the blood and hair; the serology and hair analysis and toxicology certainly were not sophisticated enough for testimony. This would be all you had in a jury trial twenty years ago. And think about it now. Think about you have blood work. The blood work eliminates eighty-four percent of the male population of possible suspects. This is probability, it eliminates eighty-six percent, there is only fourteen percent of the male population left that could have done this crime. Out of the fourteen percent, you will find that we have the hair analysis. And all the major and minor characteristics were the same."[7]

Still, as forensic scientist Serowick had done, Prosecutor McGinty provided disclaimers: "You can't have absolute certainty in this science at this stage."[8]

But then he went on to summarize the hair evidence in his own words: "Now, the root was one of the two, the onion or the bulbous. This was the onion type. Think of the process of elimination. We are already down to eighty-six percent of the males eliminated. Each one of these steps eliminates further...."[9] he went on.

Prosecutor McGinty concluded: "There has been a monumental effort to create smoke, but you can see through this. You can see the basic evidence here is very strong. And ladies and gentlemen, there can be no reasonable doubt that this individual, Tony Green, is a rapist and aggravated robber. That is the case, that is the evidence."[10]

"WE, THE JURY IN THIS CASE, being duly impaneled and sworn, do find the defendant, Anthony Green, guilty of rape in violation of 2907.20, by purposely compelling her to submit by the use of force or threat of force."[11]

"Not my son! He didn't do it! ... He wouldn't rape anyone! Michael! Michael!" Annie Green, Michael's mother, screamed in devastation as the jury foreman read the verdict.[12] Judge Frank Gorman ordered the sheriff to remove her from the courtroom; the woman's screams and sobbing were disrupting the reading of the verdict.

"Second count. We, the jury in this case, being duly impaneled and sworn, find the defendant, Anthony Green, guilty of aggravated robbery with a deadly weapon or dangerous ordnance, to wit: a knife, in violation of 2911.01, charged in the second count of the indictment.[13]

"Again, that is signed by all twelve jurors in ink," said the jury foreman.[14]

Defense attorney Draper exercised his right to have the jury polled.

Addressing the jury, the judge said, "The question the court asks is, are these your verdicts? Your answer is yes or no."

Judge Gorman began the polling. "Mrs. Poindexter?"

Juror number one had an unexpected answer: "No."

"Are these your verdicts? Yes or no?" the judge asked again.

A tearful Mrs. Poindexter replied again, "No."[15]

The jury had been deliberating three days. No doubt, Mrs. Poindexter, the lone holdout who believed in the innocence of Michael Green, had been pressured to conform to the opinion of the other eleven. It had been a long week. Everyone wanted to wrap it up, to get back to families and jobs.[16]

"Not your verdicts," Judge Gorman said, acknowledging the obvious— but unusual—lack of consensus. "The jury will retire and continue deliberating."[17]

Juror number one, Lucille Poindexter, a sixty-one-year-old black woman, mother of seven and retired seamstress, strongly believed that Michael Green was innocent. But when the jury was returned for further deliberation, the pressure mounted, and she could not convince any of the others. She was unschooled in the law. Like many, she probably felt that somehow this error would get corrected later. She would pray for justice for Michael Green. But on this Friday afternoon, seeing no options, she finally gave in.[18]

Who would have ever guessed that Mrs. Poindexter was the only juror who had it right?

CHAPTER 15

Surviving Injustice

ICHAEL GREEN WAS sentenced on the following Monday morning. For the count of rape, he received a term of ten to twenty-five years. On the second count, aggravated robbery, ten to twenty-five years. The terms were to be served consecutively.[1]

"Because of the viciousness of the crime and the severe psychological injury done to the victim," Judge Gorman said, "the court deems it necessary to protect the public from the defendant for as long a time as possible and has an obligation to sentence you to the maximum on each count."[2]

He assigned Green a public defender for his appeal.

"How can I be charged, though?" Green asked, still not fully comprehending.

"The jury found you guilty. That's the answer."

"But they didn't have any evidence against me," Green challenged.

"Council will take it up on appeal," the judge responded.

"But I still got to get sentenced to the penitentiary for no reason? I don't know. They didn't do me right. And they had not one thing of evidence on me. And they find me guilty. I don't think it was right. I'm not going for it. I don't think it was right. I don't think it was right. Don't try to charge me guilty. I don't think it was right."[3]

Thereupon the proceedings were concluded.

MICHAEL GREEN'S transition into prison life was not smooth. However, Connie Schultz's series for the *Plain Dealer* told the remarkable story of his eventual metamorphosis there. A twelve-year prison veteran who had been convicted of killing a man in a Cleveland bar became Michael Green's unlikely mentor and teacher. He encouraged Michael to manage his anger and become productive.[4]

While working to improve himself in prison, Green never stopped claiming innocence. In 1997, he heard about the Innocence Project and immediately inquired about getting assistance. As was true in the Elkins and other Innocence Project cases, someone has to be the inmate's eyes, ears, legs, and hands on the outside. Someone has to dedicate the time, endure the frustration, and assume significant expense to do the hard work that precedes exoneration. That someone for Michael became Bob Mandell. Michael's mother married Mandell while Michael was in prison.[5]

Green's hope for getting out of prison depended on finding the washcloth that the rapist had dropped after cleaning himself. For a year and a half, the sixty-one-year-old Mandell looked for it without any encouragement. When he finally found it in a storage box in the old Cuyahoga County Courthouse,[6] Mandell immediately called Vanessa Potkin at the Innocence Project in New York City. She took the steps necessary to secure the evidence. The Innocence Project hired a Cleveland lawyer to file motions and stay on the effort. But it would still take two years for the Innocence Project to be granted the washcloth for testing.[7]

The delays encountered did not surprise Potkin, a seasoned Innocence lawyer. Years later, she shared her recollections on this case and others like it. "This was before Ohio had a DNA statute, and there wasn't really a good provision for getting back into court to try to do DNA testing," she explained. "Having no legal entitlement to DNA testing put us in those early years at the mercy of the prosecutor. And from their perspective, this was a very low priority, because their office is dealing with prosecuting current cases."

When Assistant Prosecutor Carmen Marino finally released the washcloth, the evidence was sent to Forensic Science Associates in California.[8]

Potkin contacted Marino with the results, which excluded Michael Green. Marino's reaction was a common one from prosecutors. He countered that the victim had since passed away, but she had *identified* Green as the perpetrator.

"There's an initial reaction that there was an identification [by the victim]," Potkin recalled. "There must be something wrong with the testing.... And so then they wanted to do their own testing," she said, explaining how time is consumed on the way to exoneration.

CHAPTER 16

Truth and Redemption

I NTEGRITY, LIKE COURAGE, is difficult to prove until it is tested. That's why both can show up in the most unlikely places. Michael Green demonstrated his character every time he appeared before the parole board. He was asked repeatedly whether he was ready to show remorse for the rape at the Cleveland Clinic Center and to participate in the sex offender program. If he said yes to these two simple questions, he could be released before he became an old man.[1]

In releasing anyone earlier than the longest time called for in the judge's sentence, the parole board's significant responsibility is to return to society only those who are unlikely to repeat the offense and cause harm to others. Dozens of factors determine the parole board's decision for each convict. One that provides strong justification for denying parole in Ohio is found on page 51 of the *Ohio Parole Board Guidelines Manual*: "The inmate shows no genuine remorse for the offense."[2]

This requirement makes sense for most convicted criminals. It is another painful part of the nightmare—and a mighty test of integrity and character—for the wrongfully convicted. For the innocent, freedom is offered in exchange for a lie that the state wants to hear. Granted, the life potentially available for Michael Green was that of a labeled sex offender with restrictions that would go on for years, perhaps for the rest of his life. Still, for most, this beats spending life in prison.

The Ohio Parole Board does not ask these questions often. Once again Green resisted the temptation to shorten his sentence. He told the truth; he was innocent.[3]

Most cases don't make it to trial. Often the evidence is so strong that the defendant pleads guilty to a lesser crime. In light of the 253 exonerations established through DNA to date, I believe that a consistent claim of innocence should earn some consideration on the decisions that are made throughout the justice process. For example, this should be a strong argument in support of a request to release any DNA evidence that could prove guilt or innocence, whether the request is made while the convict is in prison or after completion of the sentence. When prosecutors rigidly oppose release of evidence for testing in cases in which a person has consistently claimed innocence—especially if at significant personal cost—I have to assume that the prosecutor is more interested in preserving a record than in pursuing truth.

Some inmates prefer to stay in prison because it's the only place from which they can prove their innocence. In Ohio, as an example, people who have been paroled from prison were, until recently, ineligible for DNA testing of evidence even though postprison life is hugely impacted by the existence of a criminal record.

As I began to look at issues such as these through the eyes of the wrongfully convicted, I joined many who were rethinking policy and procedures. On the way to that position, I have no doubt that many of my former colleagues in law enforcement and in the prosecutor ranks of Ohio wondered what had made me go over to "the dark side."

CUYAHOGA COUNTY PROSECUTOR Bill Mason refused to act immediately on the new DNA analysis before conducting the county's own analysis. The Innocence Project's cofounder Barry Scheck kept media attention on the case. "The faster they do replicate testing, the faster Mr. Green, in my judgment, will be released," Scheck said. "And they should move heaven and earth to get it done, because can you just imagine being in prison for a crime you didn't commit."[4]

The county's DNA analysis came to the same conclusion. On October 9, 2001, Michael Green was released. He was officially exonerated nine days later.[5]

Exonerations are big news in the communities where they occur. The impact of the Michael Green case was even larger than most, though, because Green's response to his injustice was larger than most.

As Green emerged from thirteen years of wrongful imprisonment, he expressed no anger toward the rape victim who had identified him, or those involved in convicting him. And his astonishing capacity for forgiveness would extend to yet another unlikely recipient: the actual rapist.

BESIDES RELYING ON the official trial transcripts and records in studying what went wrong in the Green case, Nancy and I reread the *Plain Dealer* series on the case by Connie Schultz. No doubt, thousands in the Cleveland area had read this series—and numerous follow-up articles—in October 2002, a year after Green's release. One of those readers was Rodney Rhines.

Rhines, forty-four, had been living for several weeks at the City Mission, a haven for the hurting, homeless, and hungry in Cleveland.[6] He had a criminal record dating back to the mid-1980s and had been released from prison more than a year earlier after serving years for drug trafficking, grand theft, and aggravated burglary. But, just as he had once predicted, he was hurting much more from the burden of a crime for which he had not yet paid a price.[7]

Reading the *Plain Dealer* series on the Clinic Center rape, Rhines realized that he would never be free until he admitted what he had done and paid for it.

Rhines was able to tell police details of the crime. They took him seriously. They also took swabs of his saliva for analysis. The DNA test results confirmed that Rhines was the Clinic Center rapist.[8]

None of the news accounts of this unusual outcome went so far as to make the former rapist, the man who allowed another man to be wrongfully convicted of his assault on a terminally ill woman, any kind of hero. Still, Rhines knew what it means to be in prison. He did not have naïvete to fuel his courage in coming forth to confess. He knew that he was a changed man and would never rape again. But he also recognized that he had an unpaid debt. Redemption made another appearance in this sad tale.

Connie Schultz wrote a follow-up story on Rhine's emotional account of the evening of the crime. Ironically, he had worked briefly in the kitchen at the Clinic Center Hotel. The detectives had it right that only a former employee would know the less-exposed employees' access to the guest floors. They just pursued the wrong former employee.

And as for the name Tony?

"It was just a name I threw out," he said.[9]

When Rhines went to court for his sentencing in late January 2003, Michael Green was in the courtroom. The judge granted Michael's request to speak. He turned toward Rodney Rhines. "I didn't come out of prison with a bitter heart, and I won't leave here with a bitter heart," he said. "I harbor no bitterness toward you, and I hope you can continue to walk the path you're on now."[10]

Judge Judith Kilbane Koch commended Green for his compassion, and then, looking at both men, acknowledged the challenge of eyewitness identification. "I'm sorry," she said. "You don't look alike."[11]

The judge then sentenced Rodney Rhines to five years in prison for the crime that had already cost Michael Green thirteen.[12]

CHAPTER 17

Dissecting Error

IN ADDITION TO THE STATUTORY damages that the state of Ohio paid Green—nearly $1 million in compensation for wrongful incarceration as well as lost wages—Green filed a lawsuit in May 2003 in the U.S. District Court. He sued the city of Cleveland, the Cleveland Clinic Foundation, and his former attorneys.

On June 8, 2004, the City of Cleveland entered into a settlement that would pay Green $1.6 million on a condition that the city would "conduct an audit of the files from the city's forensic laboratory involving serology and/ or hair analysis."[1]

"You understand that Michael Green gave up part of his own settlement to help fund this audit," Innocence Project cofounder Barry Scheck later told Nancy.

The agreement stipulated that the city would retain James Wooley, a former assistant U.S. attorney in the Department of Justice with significant experience in investigations of police and prosecutorial misconduct,[2] to review all of the cases in which Joseph Serowick testified as an expert at trial as well as all cases in which Serowick "performed serology and/or hair analysis and the defendant plead guilty before any testimony was offered."[3]

According to Mark Gillispie, writing for the *Plain Dealer*, attorneys for the city had reviewed damaging opinions from experts that indicated Joseph Serowick lacked proper training and supervision.[4]

Scientific expert Dr. Edward Blake of Forensic Science Associates indicated that Serowick should have concluded that "no man should have been excluded as a possible source of the semen on the washcloth."[5]

Another expert said that Serowick's reference to a 1 in 40,000 chance of similar hairs coming from two different sources was misleading because probabilities such as this were not substantiated by science.[6]

However, more than two and a half years later, based on the review of the lab's work by Robert Spalding, a retired FBI agent, the audit report indicated that, in spite of procedural shortcomings and an apparent lack of understanding of the scientific evidence, Joseph Serowick did not intentionally mislead juries.[7] "I haven't sent [prosecutors] a single thing that made me think they [should] act on this," said audit director Jim Wooley.[8]

This report was remarkable to me. While the results by no means redeemed forensic scientist Serowick, they did suggest to me that the neat explanation many had for the Green conviction error was not quite so neat, nor so simple.

SO, WHAT CAN WE LEARN from the wrongful conviction of Michael Green?

Having thoroughly delved into this case, I came to believe that Michael Green probably would have been convicted on the eyewitness testimony of the victim alone, even without scientific evidence. However, *any* corroborating testimony works to bolster eyewitness identification in such a way that it very often prevails against even strong conflicting or exculpatory evidence.

The scientific testimony provided in the trial was incorrect. The hair on the washcloth was not a head hair; it was a pubic hair. The seminal fluid and the blood type conclusions were equally flawed. The jury was nonetheless also provided many disclaimers in this testimony—many acknowledgments that the science could provide only probabilities (unsubstantiated as they were). Contrary to what I remembered as the prevailing public opinion, the trial transcripts indicate that Serowick never said that the odds were 1 in 40,000 that the hair on the washcloth and the sample from Michael Green came from different sources. This was a reference to just one case study of a hypothetical pair of hairs, but, especially following the prosecuting attorney's questioning and closing argument, the jurors easily could have applied this statistic to the hairs in the Clinic rape evidence.

Attempting to connect the dots of a witness's testimony is a common strategy in which attorneys walk a fine line between clarifying and confusing the jury's considerations. Jurors are not practiced in discerning where testimony stops and advocacy begins. Both defense and prosecuting attorneys need to consider this when framing questions and arguments if truth and justice are the goals.

I believe that Michael Green may not have been convicted if the detectives had captured the victim's eyewitness testimony using better procedures, if they had paid heed to the victim's failure to definitively select Green in the first photo display, or if they had pursued all leads and not focused solely on building a case around their first suspect. Green may not have gone to prison if Serowick had not given misleading testimony, if McGinty had not been as aggressive in his questioning and final argument, if Draper had demanded the DNA analysis or had been able to build a stronger case with alibi witnesses, or if the jury had been more discerning and listened to Mrs. Poindexter.

But the justice system is not carried out under perfect conditions or by perfect people. We humans are imperfect, and those in the justice system probably no less or no more so than in other professions. Therefore, the challenge is to identify where human imperfection consistently fails us in the justice process and change procedures wherever improvements can deliver more accurate outcomes. That is the goal of reforms that are being debated throughout the country, on back porches and all the way to the U.S. Supreme Court.

A final irony of this case is that everyone seemed to accept the notion that $526 was too costly for the DNA analysis of the crime scene evidence. The cost of DNA analysis was probably *more* than that at the time (a DNA analysis on one item of evidence today is usually between $1,000 and $1,500, and one crime may have several pieces of evidence to test), but DNA was just beginning to be used in criminal cases in the late 1980s. That is probably the real reason it was not utilized.

However, I couldn't help but think, *What if?* Had the DNA evidence been tested, Michael Green would have been excluded as a suspect. The state of Ohio and the city of Cleveland would have saved a combined $2.6 million in damages, plus the cost of Green's incarceration, nearly a quarter of a million dollars. I like to think that Rodney Rhines would have still come forward. If not, if he were under state supervision or ever arrested again after 2004, his DNA would have been taken as a matter of law—and this would have been one of Ohio's hundreds of DNA database matches, accurately resolving a long-unsolved cold case.

PART II

Pursuing Truth

It is one thing to show a man that he is in error,
and another to put him in possession of truth.

—John Locke,
Essay Concerning Human Understanding (1690)
dedicatory epistle

CHAPTER 18

Prisons and Executions

HOW MANY INNOCENT people are in American prisons today? Nancy and I discovered that an understanding of two factors is essential to any discussion of the scope of conviction error: the size of the prison population in the United States and the influence of the death penalty debate on this question.

The United States has the largest prison population in the world, more than any other nation, both in actual numbers and as a percentage of our population. Criminal justice legislation and policy in the 1980s and 1990s significantly changed American justice. In this period, conventional wisdom moved increasingly toward a tough-on-crime stance with measures such as "three strikes" and other mandated sentencing laws. The results were longer sentences and an explosion in the U.S. prison population.

From 1987 to 2007, America's prison population nearly tripled. In 2008, 2,319,258 adults were in American prisons or jails—1 in every 99.1 adults.[1] To put this number into context:

- China, with its much larger population, came in second in 2008 with 1.5 million prisoners.

- The United States has a larger prison population (by more than 400,000 inmates) than the thirty-six largest European inmate populations *combined,* even though these nations have a combined general population of more than two and a half times that of the United States.

- As a percentage of population, the United States imprisons more than nations such as Iran and South Africa; for example, we imprison at eight times the rate of Germany.[2]

The prison system is a major driver of both public employment and public expense in our country. In my work as a state legislator, county commissioner, state auditor, and attorney general, I experienced the various responses of Ohioans to issues relating to building, expanding, or closing a particular prison facility "in their backyard." Data from the Census Bureau indicates that in 2006, 11.8 percent of Ohio's state employee workforce was employed in the prison (corrections) system.[3] In 2007, Ohio spent more than $2.5 billion on corrections. For every dollar spent on higher education in Ohio in 2007, 69 cents were spent on corrections.[4]

The rapid growth of our prison population is an example of how public sentiment influences policy. The economic downturn following the housing correction and the subprime mortgage crisis of 2007–09 impacted state governments so adversely that all expenses were freshly examined in efforts to balance state budgets. This prompted public discussions on the costs of maintaining a large prison population. Whether public sentiment eventually dictates a change or not, the size of our prison population enables a small percentage of conviction errors to translate into a large number of innocent people incarcerated.

Applying the earlier-mentioned rationale of Professor Robert Dawson, if the system is 99 percent accurate, 23,192 innocent persons are in prison. If the system is 99.9 percent accurate, that is still 2,319 innocent people in prison.

C. Ronald Huff, Ph.D., who for ten years served as dean of the school of social ecology and professor of the school of criminology, law and society at the University of California, Irvine, and for six years as director of the John Glenn School of Public Affairs at The Ohio State University, performed an extensive survey of prosecutors, presiding judges of felony courts, public defenders, county sheriffs, and chiefs of police in Ohio. The survey, which also included attorneys general from all fifty states and four U.S. territories, asked the respondents to estimate, based on their experience, the frequency with which wrongful conviction occurs. Its definition of wrongful conviction included "only those convicted of a felony and later officially cleared." These official acknowledgments of conviction error sought to identify actual innocence, such as a new trial resulting in a not-guilty verdict, or an official pardon based on new evidence, overwhelming evidence of innocence, or innocence acknowledged in appellate court review.[5]

The survey response was 0.5 percent, indicating a 99.5 percent accuracy rate. Approximately 2.2 million arrests were made for index crimes (murder, non-negligent manslaughter, forcible rape, robbery, aggravated assault, burglary, larceny/theft, motor vehicle theft, and arson) in the United States in 2000. The Huff study used a conviction rate of 70 percent. Applying the survey estimate of .5 percent would indicate that about 7,500 wrongful convictions would have occurred in the U.S. annually at these levels.[6] (Arrest levels have gone up marginally with 2.28 million arrests in index crimes in 2008.)[7]

Unfortunately, the study's estimates of wrongful conviction, such as those from the well-intentioned judges, sheriffs, public defenders, chiefs of police, and attorneys general responding to Professor Huff, had scarce data to inform them. However, Professor Samuel R. Gross and a research team at the University of Michigan Law School led a comprehensive effort to quantify exonerations identified in media sources. His 2005 report, "Exonerations in the United States, 1989 Through 2003," summarized known exonerations in this period:

> Overall, we found 340 exonerations, 327 men and 13 women; 144 were cleared by DNA evidence, 196 by other means. With a handful of exceptions, they had been in prison for years. More than half had served terms of ten years or more; 80 percent had been imprisoned for at least five years. As a group, they had spent more than 3,400 years in prison for crimes for which they should never have been convicted—an average of more than ten years each.[8]

When the exonerations were analyzed, the details supported the "tip of the iceberg" theory. For example, 96 percent of the exonerations were for murder and rape or sexual assault—the crimes that usually have DNA-related evidence—even though these crimes represent only about 2 percent of felony convictions.[9]

Death sentences represent less than one-tenth of 1 percent of those sentenced, and yet 22 percent of known exonerations from 1989 through 2003 were from this sliver of the prison population.[10]

What could researchers reasonably deduce? One subset of the prison population examined in later research by Gross offered intriguing data.

Based on actual exonerations in all capital cases of those who had been on death row at least fifteen years in 2004, Gross and his colleagues determined that 2.3 percent is the rate of exonerations for those sentenced to death from 1973 through 2004.[11] (More recent death row convictions were excluded, as these would likely also result in a similar percentage of exonerations, which historically have occurred after more than nine years of incarceration on average.)

Gross points out that if this capital exoneration rate were applied to those sentenced for all other crimes, about 87,000 exonerations of prisoners not on death row would have occurred from 1989 through 2003. The report further suggests that "if the false conviction rate for prison sentences were 2.3 percent, about 185,000 innocent American defendants were sent to prison for one year or more from 1977 through 2004."[12]

However, does the death row population have enough similarity to the overall prison population to draw such comparative conclusions? Supreme Court justices do not agree on the answer. Justice David H. Souter (1990–2009) presumed that there was more error in capital cases than other felonies. He wrote in his dissenting opinion in *Kansas v. Marsh* that homicide cases yield "an unusually high incidence of false conviction,…probably owing to the combined difficulty of investigating without help from the victim, intense pressure to get convictions in homicide cases, and the corresponding incentive for the guilty to frame the innocent."[13]

Justice Antonin Scalia has argued the opposite: "Capital cases are given especially close scrutiny at every level, which is why in most cases many years elapse before the sentence is executed."[14]

Leaning toward Justice Souter's view, Professor Gross suggested that "there are strong theoretical reasons to believe that the rate of false convictions is higher for murders in general, and for capital murders in particular, than for other felony convictions." He explained that while more time is devoted to solving these cases, pressure to secure convictions in murders drives law enforcement and prosecutors to pursue investigations even when evidence is slim, resulting in an increased risk of error. There is a greater temptation to cut corners. The murder victim cannot assist investigators, obviously, and the heavy penalty for murder convictions motivates perpetrators to frame others.[15]

Another high-profile commentator on conviction error, Joshua Marquis, district attorney of Clatsop County, Oregon, challenged claims of significant conviction error and Professor Gross's study specifically with a much more positive view of the justice system in a January 26, 2006, Op-Ed article for the *New York Times*:

> So, let's give the professor the benefit of the doubt: let's assume that he underestimates the number of innocents by roughly a factor of 10, that instead of 340 there were 4,000 people in prison who weren't involved in the crime in any way. During that same 15 years, there were more than 15 million felony convictions across the country. That would make the error rate .027 percent—or, to put it another way, a success rate of 99.973 percent.[16]

Professor Gross, however, revealed a serious flaw in utilizing only rape and murder exonerations as a percentage of the total prisoner population in Prosecutor Marquis's calculation. Gross pointed out that most of the exonerations that he researched were from wrongful convictions involving murder (205 cases) or rape (121 cases). These exonerations occurred either because DNA proved innocence or because capital murder cases can attract the resources and attention required to prove innocence. Clearly, about 90 percent of prisoners convicted of crimes in which no DNA evidence exists will never prove innocence through this science, and the vast majority of cases, other than capital murder, will never attract the resources required to prove innocence.

"By this logic," Gross wrote in response to Marquis, "we could estimate the proportion of baseball players who've used steroids by dividing the number of major league players who've been caught by the total of all baseball players at all levels: major league, minor league, semipro, college, and Little League—and maybe throwing in football and basketball players as well."[17]

Questions on the frequency of conviction error have been raised before the likes of Supreme Court justices, professors, researchers, district attorneys, and other advocates, because the answers have great bearing on the death penalty debate. If the American justice system is error prone, executing an innocent person becomes too risky to be justifiable; conversely, if the system is highly accurate, the death penalty is a more viable option.

In fact, with the growing awareness of DNA-proven conviction error, the current national discourse on the death penalty has been reframed around conviction accuracy as opposed to the long-standing polarizing morality debate. The most widely known outcome of this was Illinois Governor George Ryan's unprecedented decision to commute the death sentences of 156 inmates on death row in January 2003. Prior to this, the Republican governor, a capital punishment supporter, had imposed a moratorium on executions in 2000 and established a commission charged with looking into capital punishment in Illinois. The commission's report had convinced Governor Ryan that the death penalty in Illinois could not continue as it was. Since Illinois had reinstated the death penalty in 1977, twelve inmates had been executed, and thirteen prisoners condemned to death had been released. The commission noted that of those released, "All thirteen cases were characterized by relatively little solid evidence connecting the charged defendants to the crimes."[18]

I made it clear in the prologue that a comprehensive analysis of the pros and cons of the death penalty is beyond the scope of this book. However, the premiere advocates for and against the death penalty are also quotable experts when attempting to quantify wrongful conviction. An unavoidable overlap must at least be acknowledged. And as a matter of disclosure, I have had more close encounters with the death penalty than most.

"YOU SEEM QUIET this morning. What's wrong?" Nancy asked.

"Oh, nothing."

"Come on, I can see it in your eyes."

Now into our fourth decade of marriage, we have a tough time hiding things from each other, and this particular morning, February 12, 2003, was no exception.

"Oh," she said, pausing as she figured it out. "Is today the execution?"

"Yeah," I answered. "Ten this morning."

"Who is it, again?"

"Richard Fox."

"That's right. He killed a young woman?"

"Yes. Leslie Keckler, an eighteen-year-old college freshman. Fox lured her into a fake job interview. She drove with him to review the supposed sales route for the job. He took her to a remote area, and when she refused his sexual advances, he stabbed her multiple times in the back. He later admitted that he then strangled her with a rope, 'just to make sure she was dead.'"[19]

"That's just so horrible."

"I know. It was a brutal, terrible crime. You can't feel the least bit sorry for him. Still, I have been dreading this day."

I couldn't avoid the irony of it: I was partly responsible for the existence of a death penalty in Ohio—and days like this.

CHAPTER 19

Capital Punishment Disclosures

A BOUT EIGHT YEARS BEFORE Richard Fox's heinous crime, in January 1981, I was in my first month as a freshman member of the Ohio House of Representatives and found myself thrown into deliberations that would determine whether the death penalty would be reinstated in Ohio. It was a quick and sobering baptism into the legislative process.

I had been appointed to the Ohio House Judiciary Committee, which was determining the future of Senate Bill 1. Ohio's death penalty had been declared unconstitutional by the U.S. Supreme Court in 1972. A new death penalty law in 1974 had also been struck down. This bill sought to restore Ohio's death penalty.

The bill before us had passed the Ohio Senate. Its journey to become law required passage out of the Judiciary Committee in order to proceed to a vote in the House. The committee members were deeply divided on the issue. With some still undecided, I knew my vote might determine whether the bill would go on to become law or would die in committee.

When I ran for state representative, the voters in my district supported the death penalty by a great majority. I supported the death penalty and said so. While I had thoughtfully determined my position, it is another matter to realize that your vote could determine whether or not there is a death penalty—that *your* vote could mean life or death for convicts.

It was a tougher decision than I would have predicted. Ultimately, I voted to move the bill out of committee. With some changes, it was narrowly approved by the Judiciary Committee and passed in the full House, 57 to 42. The new law took effect October 19, 1981.

As it turns out, the impact was not felt on death row for many years. I don't think that Ohio's governors at the time had much of a taste for executions. At the end of his term in January 1991, Governor Richard Celeste commuted the death sentences of eight persons on death row to life in prison. Eight years later, death row inmate Wilford Berry Jr. became "the Volunteer" by waiving all appeals. Prior to his execution on February 19, 1999, no one had been executed in Ohio since 1963, but after Berry, the pace picked up.

When I became attorney general, one of my responsibilities was to audibly monitor executions so that the state would be prepared to halt the proceedings in case of a last-minute stay of execution. I went to a specially equipped conference room in our offices to listen to the preparations and the execution. A dedicated open line to the execution chamber in Lucasville, Ohio, about one hundred miles away, put me in direct moment-to-moment voice contact with Terry Collins, deputy director of the Ohio Department of Rehabilitation and Correction.

I had been in office about five weeks when I experienced this for the first time with the execution of Richard E. Fox. Before the execution that day, I called members of Leslie Keckler's family. I said words to the effect that, on behalf of the state of Ohio, justice would be served today with the execution of Richard Fox; that I was sorry for their loss and the pain that Mr. Fox's actions had caused them. Today the justice system would complete its response to the crime that had changed their lives.

And then I listened for the first time to a man's execution. By then, Ohio used lethal injection. Those who implemented Fox's sentence verbalized each step of the procedure: the transfer of the convict, the strapping down on the gurney, the opportunity for last words (he had none), the activation of each vial of poison, the pronouncement of death.

When it was over, I walked back to my office, closed the door, sat down, and took a few minutes to pull myself together. I was shaken by this first one, and I never became callous to this ultimate execution of justice. In my four years as attorney general, Ohio had nineteen executions. I dreaded every one of them. Nevertheless, I still support the death penalty in cases where there is no question as to guilt in the most heinous of crimes.

As attorney general, I had no authority to halt an execution. I came to terms with my official responsibilities regarding the death penalty as "rendering unto Caesar what is Caesar's." The people of Ohio determined that this should be the state's response to one person's taking of another's life. Public sentiment shapes public policy through the election of legislators and judges who understand the peoples' mandate. Supreme Court Justice Scalia underscored this in his opinion on the death penalty in *Kansas v. Marsh* (2006): "The American people have determined that the good to be derived from capital punishment—in deterrence, and perhaps most of all in the meting out of condign [appropriate] justice for horrible crimes—outweighs the risk of error."[1]

I have given considerable thought to my personal views on capital punishment. Proponents of the death penalty are consistent in their justifications for it. First, they say that it is a deterrent. They also claim that it saves public money: that it is cheaper to kill someone than to house them for life. They contend that it brings closure for the victim's family. They view capital punishment as the reasonable, fair response for the state in its role of administering justice following acts that totally discount the value of human life—an eye for an eye in Old Testament terms.

None of these is among the reasons that I support the death penalty.

I don't believe that many of these justifications are, in fact, justifiable. In his book *Ultimate Punishment: A Lawyer's Reflections on Dealing with the Death Penalty,* best-selling author and lawyer Scott Turow—an on-again, off-again supporter of the death penalty—shares reflections, his experience, and research on the ultimate punishment. My takeaways from this book are consistent with my own experience and intuition. The deterrent theory is not much more than that. Some studies suggest that non–death row states have fewer murders per capita than death penalty states. Turow points out that Texas has a murder rate well above the national average even though more than a third of the nation's executions since 1976 have occurred there.[2] (Note that this observation was made in 2003.)

The economic theory is also questionable. An Indiana gubernatorial commission's research concluded in 2003 that it is about a third more expensive to pursue a capital case to its conclusion than to house a person sentenced to life without parole.

Similarly, the issues of closure for the victim's survivors and the state's moral and just response to heinous criminal acts are debatable.

My support for the death penalty is simple and pragmatic: It is all about public safety. My instructors in this lesson were Robert Daniels and John West, nicknamed the "Mad Dog Killers" by Ohio's newspapers.

From the early years of our marriage, I heard the story of horrific events that occurred in and around Tiffin, Ohio, the week of my wife's birth in July 1948. The Bero family, who lived in Tiffin, would remember this week for the early arrival of their first daughter, Nancy, but for many Ohioans the week would be marked by a murderous rampage.

Robert Daniels and John West, just released from the Ohio State Reformatory in Mansfield, apparently were determined to get revenge, although at least half of their victims would be random. The first person they murdered was a Columbus tavern owner. Daniels and West next drove to Mansfield, where they went to the home of John Niebel, the prison's farm superintendent. Daniels and West broke into his home, pistol whipped Niebel and his wife, raped their twenty-year-old daughter, forced all three to strip, and marched them outside into a field, where Daniels and West executed them.

The following day, they drove toward Tiffin, about fifty-five miles away. Nancy's parents, now in their eighties, still recall the terrible details. Daniels and West followed a newly married couple driving at night. Forcing their car to a stop, the two criminals approached the car and then shot the young man in the face. His bride miraculously managed to escape execution by running to a nearby farmhouse.

When Daniels and West needed to switch vehicles, they shot and killed a truck driver who was asleep in his truck near Old Fort, Ohio. Two days later, they were finally stopped in Van Wert, near the Ohio-Indiana border, when they came to a roadblock and engaged in a shootout with police. West was killed; Daniels was captured. He reportedly bragged about his potential date with the electric chair, which occurred six months later.

In those days, Nancy's grandparents had the forerunner of a bed-and-breakfast in Tiffin. In the 1940s, these were called "tourist homes." Nancy's grandmother loved to welcome traveling business people; most were regular customers. She recalled two strangers who came to the rear side door, rather than the front porch entrance, looking for a room the week that her grand-daughter was born. She had no vacancy, but she said that if they waited a moment, she would call the other area guesthouses to try to find them a room. They waited outside while she made the calls. She located a room for them two blocks away. Curiously, they used the room to clean up but left without staying overnight. Nancy's grandmother later realized that the tim-ing, appearance, and odd behavior of the men suggested that they might have been West and Daniels. She felt blessed to have been spared. That is why this story was told twenty-some years later when I started to visit Tiffin with Nancy.

I always had thought—and Nancy's parents thought—that West and Dan-iels were escapees. However, we learned that they had actually been released from prison early; ironically, for good behavior. That detail did not change my view that capital punishment is justifiable for reasons of public safety.

After hearing of the brutality of West and Daniels and others like them, I've determined that some people are the equivalent of wild animal predators. John Walsh, in addressing the National Association of Attorneys General at its February 2010 meeting, shared lessons learned in his years of seeking criminals through the television program he's hosted since 1988, *America's Most Wanted*. In 1981, his own son, six-year-old Adam, was abducted from a department store in Hollywood, Florida, and killed; the presumed killer, who died in prison before he could be charged, had committed several other murders.

Walsh, citing pedophiles as an example, said that these predators have an inexplicable sexual "compulsion" that is so strong that he has seen pedo-philes even in their eighties who are still compelled to seek despicable sexual acts with children. Like other sociopaths, they feel no remorse after commit-ting horrendous crimes.

We should no more release such a person than we would uncage a wild tiger from the zoo. The challenge is to identify those beyond a redemptive life in public society, but certain criminal acts warrant this indictment. If we were to find a 100 percent effective incarceration that enabled absolutely no chance of escape, I could oppose the death penalty.

The state appropriately has the responsibility to respond to unaccept-able crime, and in America, the citizens shape this response, whether they recognize their role or not. My view is that God will be the ultimate judge of the Robert Danielses and the John Wests—but also of us, if we should neglect to take every precaution against making a mistake when imposing the death penalty. When the state takes a life on behalf of justice, there is no room for error, and we can never become callous to the enormity of this responsibility.

Fortunately, I had a high degree of confidence in the guilt of the men who were sentenced to death during my watch. Except one.

John Spirko was convicted in 1983 of the murder of Mary Jane Mottinger, the postmistress in Elgin, Ohio. Spirko was the only execution scheduled during my term in which conviction was based solely on circumstantial evidence. He had served time for another murder and was not a good guy, but many were concerned about the weak evidence that convicted him of this crime. I ensured that no stone was unturned with regard to testing the crime evidence for DNA. The results were not definitive; I asked for another reprieve for testing. Then more testing, then another reprieve. Governor Bob Taft granted my multiple requests for reprieves until his successor, Governor Ted Strickland, inherited the case.

On January 9, 2008, after I had requested seven reprieves, Governor Strickland resolved the issue:

> Mr. Spirko's claims that his own lies led to his conviction for an offense that he did not commit are unpersuasive in the face of the judicial scrutiny this case has received. Nonetheless, I have concluded that the lack of physical evidence linking him to the murder, as well as the slim residual doubt about his responsibility for the murder that arises from careful scrutiny of the case record and revelations about the case over the past twenty years, makes the imposition of the death penalty inappropriate in this case.

Referencing the lengthy review of the case, he concluded, "I have decided to commute Mr. Spirko's sentence to life imprisonment without the possibility of parole."[3]

I was pleased with the governor's decision. When there is any legitimate doubt, commute.

WITH DUE ACKNOWLEDGMENT of my cautious support of the death penalty, I did not come to the question of the extent of wrongful conviction in America with a strong bias on either side of the debate.

Nancy and I considered the death penalty positions of those who sought to quantify conviction errors. District Attorney Joshua Marquis supports the death penalty in Oregon, a state that has executed two men since the death penalty was restored in 1984. His calculation of a .027 percent error rate was cited by Antonin Scalia in *Kansas v. Marsh.* In this same opinion, the conservative Supreme Court justice criticized Professor Samuel R. Gross's inclusion of some of the exonerated in Gross's study (the basis of his calculation of a significantly higher conviction error rate of 2.3 percent) as not fitting the definition of an innocent person.

Professor Gross responded by saying, "It is possible that a few of the hundreds of exonerated defendants we have studied were involved in the crimes for which they were convicted, despite our efforts to exclude such cases. On the other hand, it is certain—this is the clearest implication of our study—that many defendants who are not on this list, no doubt thousands, have been falsely convicted of serious crimes but have not been exonerated."[4] Gross opposes the death penalty, but his focus is wrongful conviction, his greater concern.

Justice Scalia referenced Marquis's error rate of .027 percent, less than three-hundredths of 1 percent, seeming to imply that this might be acceptable. "One cannot have a system of criminal punishment without accepting the possibility that someone will be punished mistakenly," he wrote.[5]

This raises the question of what is acceptable error in our justice system. A culture is defined in some ways by what it finds acceptable. When a commercial airplane crashes, the National Transportation Safety Board begins a painstaking investigation to determine the cause of the accident. Even the suspicion of a repeatable problem can ground an entire airline. Americans do not find errors in flight acceptable. The error rate in the justice system—whether the most conservative or most liberal calculation—would not be even remotely tolerated in the U.S. food industry or the U.S. pharmaceutical industry, for example. Why we have accepted it in the justice system is another question.

We believe that Marquis's conviction error estimate of .027 percent is flawed and a significant understatement. Nevertheless, if you apply that error percentage to our prison population in 2008, it would mean that 621 innocent persons were incarcerated in U.S. prisons that year. If these Americans were instead in a prison in a foreign land, it would constitute an international crisis.

If Professor Gross's death row 2.3 percent error rate were applied to the same prison population, it would suggest that more than 50,000 innocent Americans are imprisoned, but Gross believes that errors in the broader felony population are probably less frequent. The summary of his original study concluded, "Any plausible guess at the total number of miscarriages of justice in America in the last fifteen years must be in the thousands, perhaps tens of thousands."[6]

All things considered (including all that we had yet to learn), Nancy and I have concluded that Professor Gross's calculations are both credible and probable.

Another bit of information stunned us and supported the conclusion of significant conviction error. In 1996, the National Institute of Justice commissioned a landmark study, *Convicted by Juries, Exonerated by Science: Case Studies in the Use of DNA Evidence to Establish Innocence After Trial*, that sought to spark discussion by the justice and scientific communities on the challenges of incorporating DNA analysis in criminal justice. Included in the study, a commentary by Peter Neufeld and Barry Scheck revealed the surprising consistency of inaccurate identification of the perpetrator in rape cases where DNA testing could affirm or exclude the suspect:

Every year since 1989, in about 25 percent of the sexual assault cases referred to the FBI where results could be obtained (primarily by state and local law enforcement), the primary suspect has been excluded by forensic DNA testing. Specifically, FBI officials report that out of roughly 10,000 sexual assault cases since 1989, about 2,000 tests have been inconclusive (usually insufficient high molecular weight DNA to do testing), about 2,000 tests have excluded the primary suspect, and about 6,000 have "matched" or included the primary suspect.[7]

The evidence sent to the FBI in these cases was typically sperm from swabs taken from the victim (vaginally, anally, orally) or from the victim's clothing. Identification of the suspect was primarily from eyewitness testimony.[8] Generally, the prosecution not only confirmed these results with its own testing but also tested any males known to be in a recent relationship with the victim, to rule them out.[9]

In short, local authorities—law enforcement and prosecutors—thought they had their rapist, and over many years, rape kit DNA, tested either by the FBI or in private labs, consistently proved an error rate of about 25 percent.[10] Prior to DNA, there is no question that a percentage of these DNA-excluded suspects would have been tried and convicted. (State conviction rates for felony sexual assaults average about 62 percent.)[11]

What does this say about those in prison who were convicted of rape before 1989, before DNA? What does it say about people convicted of crimes today in which there is no DNA evidence to test?

This rate of incorrect arrest was shocking to us. It was irrefutable evidence of significant arrest and conviction error.

Scheck and Neufeld articulated the implications of these results: "The fact that these percentages have remained constant for seven years…strongly suggests that post-arrest and post-conviction DNA exonerations are tied to some strong, underlying systemic problems that generate erroneous accusations and convictions."[12]

Nancy and I came to the disturbing conclusion that the error rate in the criminal justice system—whether the most conservative or the most liberal view—is, nonetheless, unacceptable. It is unacceptable when compared to other industries and professions. It is unacceptable if we are capable of doing better.

What are the "systemic problems" Scheck and Neufeld referenced?

Fortunately, others had asked that question long before us.

CHAPTER 20

Classic Misconceptions

T HE FIRST WIDELY PUBLICIZED case of exoneration for murder in the United States involved the 1819 conviction and sentencing to death of two brothers, Jesse and Stephen Boorn, in Vermont for the murder of their brother-in-law, a fellow farmhand named Russell Colvin—even though Colvin's body had not been found at the time of the trial.[1]

This classic case of missteps has been inspiration for interpretation by both fiction and nonfiction writers—from Wilkie Collins, a Victorian novelist and nineteenth-century mystery writer (*The Dead Alive*); to Gerald McFarland, professor emeritus of history at the University of Massachusetts (*The Counterfeit Man*); to Rob Warden, executive director of the Center on Wrongful Convictions at Northwestern University School of Law (*Wilkie Collins's* The Dead Alive: *The Novel, The Case, and Wrongful Convictions*). The Boorn case is an instructive true account of how justice can awkwardly stumble.

The fact that there was no love lost between the Boorn brothers and their sister's husband, Russell Colvin, was well known in the town of Manchester, Vermont. Stephen and Jesse Boorn viewed Colvin as a lazy freeloader who not only didn't do his fair share on the family farm[2] but also thoughtlessly fathered a brood of children, further straining the family resources.[3] Colvin also had the inconsiderate habit of disappearing for days, weeks, and even months at a time, so no one thought much of it when, one day in May 1812,[4] he vanished again. As time went by, some folks in town wondered aloud whether Colvin had come to harm at the hands of the Boorn brothers. However, there was no evidence, and the mystery remained dormant for seven years.

The question of Colvin's disappearance was raised again, however, when Amos Boorn, uncle to the Boorn brothers, was visited in a dream by Colvin, who confirmed that he had indeed been murdered and that his remains were in a cellar hole. When a fire burned down an old barn on the Boorn property, the townsfolk speculated that the fire was set to hide evidence of the murder. Armed with the dream tip, the local authorities excavated the cellar hole remaining after the fire and discovered an odd collection of earthly possessions: a button, a large knife, and a penknife.[5]

The penknife and the button, as well as an old hat found nearby, were claimed to be Colvin's.[6]

With the entire town now engaged in the unfolding drama, incriminating evidence was discovered near the Boorn farm. A young boy, with the help of his barking dog, unearthed some bones, which were declared human[7] by four local physicians.[8]

Based on this growing body of evidence, Jesse Boorn was brought into custody. His subsequent interrogation by the local authorities put him in fear of a death sentence and most probably prompted him to name his brother Stephen as the murderer.

Stephen, who had previously moved to New York, was named in an arrest warrant.[9]

Meanwhile, after comparing the unearthed bones with human bones (requiring that they exhume a human leg that had been buried following a recent medically required amputation), the physicians changed their minds about the primary evidence in the case. The bones thought to possibly be Colvin's were determined to be of animal origin.[10]

While the lack of physical evidence was unsettling, Jesse's statement incriminating Stephen was bolstered by recollections, now years old, of an argument between Colvin and the Boorn brothers on the very day that Colvin disappeared. Indeed, some neighbors remembered statements in which the Boorns threatened to kill Colvin; others said that the Boorns' conversations implied that they knew that Colvin was dead.[11]

A posse went to New York, apprehended Stephen, and returned him to Manchester. Once Stephen had been thrown in jail, Jesse retracted his statement.

At about this tenuous time for the investigation, Jesse's jailhouse cell-mate, Silas Merrill (some accounts say he was a forger, some a perjurer), volunteered to state attorney Calvin Sheldon to testify about important evidence he claimed to have acquired in jail. Merrill said that Jesse had confided in him the facts of the case—namely, that Stephen had clubbed Colvin during an argument, and their father, Barney Boorn, finished the job by cutting Colvin's throat with Stephen's penknife.[12] While neither Merrill nor the state attorney would admit that Merrill was promised anything for his testimony, he was observed walking freely in Manchester after testifying.[13]

Both Boorn brothers denied Merrill's story. Nonetheless, based primarily on Merrill's testimony, Stephen and Jesse Boorn were indicted (their father was not charged). Stephen, faced with mounting incriminating evidence and having undergone a long and intense interrogation that convinced him that he would soon be at the end of a rope, eventually decided to confess to killing Colvin in self-defense,[14] a lesser crime, in the hope of avoiding death by hanging.

At trial, the jury gave credence to the testimony of eyewitnesses who discussed evidence, observations, and conversations, many resurrected from years past. Lewis Colvin, Russell's seventeen-year-old son, testified that he observed an argument between Stephen Boorn and Lewis's father. Jesse Boorn was there as well. When the argument between his father and Stephen came to physical blows with a riding stick and a club, Lewis, who was ten years old at the time, ran in fright without knowing the outcome. It was the last time that he saw his father. The day after the fight, Stephen told Lewis "not to tell of what had taken place the day before" and that he would kill him if he did.[15]

Silas Merrill provided a colorful account of Jesse Boorn's jailhouse confession, complete with Jessie's alleged claim that, a few days after Russell Colvin's murder, Stephen Boorn "had Colvin's shoes on."[16]

For whatever reason, the defense attorneys at the ensuing trial did not call upon the physicians to reveal the nonhuman nature of the bone evidence,[17] which had helped turn the tide of public opinion against the Boorns. In a risky move, the defense called for the reading of Stephen Boorn's confession,[18] which had been referenced by a witness, perhaps to show the inconsistencies in the testimonies of Silas Merrill and others.

In short order—about an hour—the jury returned a guilty verdict for both men. The same day, both brothers were sentenced to death.[19] The Vermont General Assembly later commuted Jesse's sentence to life in prison, but Stephen's execution was scheduled for January 22, 1820.[20]

According to Rob Warden, who has written extensively on the Boorn case, there are a couple of explanations as to how the "dead" Russell Colvin was resurrected, but the most likely account has come from the research of historian Gerald McFarland.[21] In *The Counterfeit Man*, McFarland details the fluke of events that delivered delayed justice to the Boorn brothers. The November 26, 1819, edition of the *New York Evening Post* included a reprint of an anonymous letter that noted the role of divine providence in solving the Colvin murder case. This account was read aloud in the lobby of a hotel in New York City and thus came to the attention of both James Whelpley, a former Manchester resident who had known the Boorn family, and Tabor Chadwick, a minister visiting in New York. He knew a Dover, New Jersey, farmhand named Russell Colvin who happened to work for his brother-in-law.

Chadwick wrote a letter to the *New York Evening Post*[22] regarding the possibility that the allegedly murdered Russell Colvin was living in New Jersey. Chadwick's letter sent Whelpley packing and off to New Jersey. He eventually found Russell Colvin, who had no intention of returning to Vermont. However, Whelpley utilized an attractive woman to lure Colvin to New York. From there he used other trickery to get Colvin by stagecoach to Manchester, where Colvin was greeted by those who had known him and could verify that he was not dead.[23] His return to life and Manchester came within only five weeks of the scheduled execution of Stephen Boorn.

As a legal means of freeing the convicted Boorn brothers, the authorities petitioned the Supreme Court of Vermont for a new trial based on the new evidence, and the prosecuting attorney refused the opportunity. Both Stephen and Jesse were released.[24]

The news of the returned farmhand and the subsequent release of the two brothers convicted of his alleged murder was a big story in newspapers on the East Coast. The conviction errors had been based on two confessions that turned out to be forced and false; bone evidence that turned out to be bad science; a jailhouse snitch's testimony that turned out to be lies; and eyewitness testimonies that turned out to be mistaken or irrelevant.

Curiously, these are the same factors that predominantly contribute to wrongful criminal conviction today, nearly two centuries later.

THE BOORN BROTHERS CASE was one of sixty-five errors of criminal justice included in *Convicting the Innocent: Errors of Criminal Justice* by Edwin M. Borchard, a Yale Law School professor. Published in 1932, this first landmark study of wrongful criminal conviction included Borchard's analysis of what went wrong in these malfunctions of justice. It is uncanny how consistent his observations were with the lessons from DNA exonerations today. We can no longer claim ignorance. The common contributors to wrongful conviction are: false confessions, use of unreliable informants and snitches, bad lawyering, unreliable science, government misconduct, and mistaken eyewitness testimony.

As Nancy and I pursued the reasons for wrongful conviction, we discovered that others had conducted painstaking research and analysis to identify and illuminate each major contributor. Much of this work, however, had never reached us and would not have without our focused interest and research. Academic treatises and comprehensive anthologies contribute mightily to the body of human knowledge; however, they often escape the awareness not only of those in the criminal justice system who would benefit most but also those who ultimately must be engaged to impact changes in policy: everyday Americans. And so, with all due credit to those who did the heavy lifting, we share, in a condensed summary, what we have learned from them.

CHAPTER 21

Lies and Other Disgraces

FALSE CONFESSION

LACKING ANY SUBSTANTIVE evidence, the Boorn case relied on the false confession of Stephen Boorn. But we do not have to go back to the early 1800s for cases of false confession. Fully 25 percent of DNA-proven wrongful convictions revealed since the late 1980s involved false confessions or admissions,[1] far more than we would have guessed. It is so counterintuitive that anyone would confess to a crime he or she did not commit that most in the justice system—including lawyers, judges, and jurors—often believe that this is the one true indicator of guilt. So convincing is a confession, that some states will not provide access to post-conviction DNA testing to anyone who confessed (a policy that should be changed now that we understand the frequency of false convictions).

Why would anyone admit to a crime he or she did not do?

Stephen Boorn confessed because his interrogators convinced him that he would be convicted and hung. In an effort to get a lighter sentence, he concocted a confession that he thought would reduce the crime. Stephen had been held with shackles on his hands and feet and chained to the floor in a dark cell without windows.[2] He was, no doubt, worn down physically, but it was the psychological ordeal that most likely drove Stephen to falsely admit guilt. Members of the court of inquiry relentlessly pressed him to confess. One told Stephen that he "had no doubt of his guilt." Another said that Stephen was "a gone goose."[3] If he confessed, his interrogators said they would support a reduced sentence.

DNA exonerations in cases that involved false confessions reveal that diminished reasoning ability—due to fatigue, substance use, stress, low mental capacity, or limited education—is often a factor. Dreams and offhand remarks have been interpreted by law enforcement as admissions, which have been utilized in courts of law in a manner very similar to a confession.

The landmark decision of *Miranda v. Arizona* (1966) sought to protect suspects from giving incriminating statements during interrogations without a fair understanding of the potential consequences by requiring that law enforcement inform all suspects in their custody of their rights to remain silent and to counsel. However, a well-documented study of actual interrogations indicated that 78 percent of custodial suspects in the study waived these rights altogether and that 64 percent of these suspects under interrogation provided incriminating statements or confessions.[4] Research has shown that young people, people with low mental capacity, and those inexperienced with the criminal justice system do not always understand their rights under *Miranda*. The innocent are more likely to waive Miranda rights,[5] possibly due to trust in the justice system and fairness in general to prevail. Officials who would use questionable means of eliciting a confession can use similar techniques—keeping the suspect in a prolonged, stressful process; discounting Miranda rights as a formality;[6] encouraging the suspect to "quickly clear up this matter so that you can go home"—to encourage the waiving of Miranda rights.

A review of cases in which false confession led to wrongful conviction would indicate that waiving Miranda rights is a perilous decision. Moreover, judging from the frequency with which Miranda rights are waived, we cannot count on Miranda rights alone to provide protection. To be effective, Miranda rights must be utilized by police detectives who respect this protection and recognize the value in a court of law of a statement that has been made without duress or manipulation. Fortunately, the great majority of police detectives who have embraced reform are of this mind.

Recommended Reform to Reduce False Confession

Videotaping of all custodial interrogations from the reading of Miranda rights on is the recommended reform for avoiding false confessions. Videotaping interrogations not only protects suspects but also law enforcement officers. A special report, *Police Experiences with Recording Custodial Interrogations,* by Thomas P. Sullivan of the Northwestern University School of Law Center on Wrongful Convictions, revealed the experience of 238 law enforcement agencies in thirty-eight states that recorded custodial police interrogations: "Virtually every officer with whom we spoke, having given custodial recordings a try, was enthusiastically in favor of the practice."[7]

The Sullivan report delineated many benefits in recording interrogations from the perspective of police detectives. These included enabling detectives to focus on the interview instead of note taking; fewer frivolous lawsuits and claims of interrogation abuse; less detective time spent on the witness stand in the courtroom; the opportunity to review the interrogation for important details that may have been overlooked; and improved training provided by the recordings.[8]

Wrongful convictions proven through DNA technology have spawned research into how and why false confessions occur. The goal of the interrogator is to break down the suspected perpetrator's resistance to confessing and to elicit incriminating statements. Many techniques to achieve these goals are considered acceptable until they are applied in an extreme manner.

Ohio Innocence Project Director Mark Godsey pointed out the importance of recent research that has enabled experts to "earmark" identifiable interrogation tactics prevalent in false confessions. As an example, studies show that the vast majority of interrogations last from thirty minutes to two hours. However, in proven wrongful convictions that included false confessions, the interrogations averaged 16.3 hours.[9]

Godsey indicated that an important benefit of recorded confessions is the emergence of experts who testify at trial to support claims of false confession by taking the jury through the videotaped recording and pointing out the earmarks of false confessions.

Taped confessions can be valuable investigative and learning resources for detectives. Jim Trainum, a detective with the Metropolitan Police Department in the District of Columbia, lectures on interrogation and false confessions after he had the experience of unknowingly taking a false confession in a homicide case. The interrogation was by the book, utilizing approved interrogation methods, with "no yelling, no cursing, and no physical abuse."[10]

In spite of the confession, the case was dismissed when the suspect's alibi proved beyond any doubt that she was innocent. Fortunately, the interrogation had been recorded, and Detective Trainum explained what his review of the recording taught him:

"We believed so much in our suspect's guilt that we ignored all evidence to the contrary," he reflected. "To demonstrate the strength of our case, we showed the suspect our evidence and unintentionally fed her details that she was able to parrot back to us at a later time. It was a classic confession case, and without video we would have never known [how the false confession occurred]."[11]

The advantages of videotaping were summarized by the Hennepin County, Minnesota, state attorney: "For police, a videotaped interrogation protects against unwarranted claims that a suspect's confession was coerced or his constitutional rights violated. For prosecutors, it provides irrefutable evidence that we can use with a jury in the courtroom. For suspects, it ensures that their rights are protected in the interrogation process."[12]

USE OF UNRELIABLE INFORMANTS OR SNITCHES

If the Boorn brothers' false confessions were not enough to indict them, Silas Merrill, the forger and cellmate of Jesse Boorn, was more than willing to share the details of the murder, which he claimed Jesse had revealed to him. Compensating a convicted forger for testifying in the Boorn case may seem questionable, but fast-forward nearly two centuries, and nothing much has changed. In more than 15 percent of exonerations resulting from DNA analysis of crime scene evidence, snitches and informants have testified for the prosecution.[13]

From the resumption of the death penalty in the 1970s until the release of *The Snitch System: How Snitch Testimony Sent Randy Steidl and Other Innocent Americans to Death Row*, a 2004 report from the Northwestern University School of Law Center on Wrongful Convictions, there were 111 death row exonerations, of which 51, or 45.9 percent, involved testimony from an informant or snitch. In this niche of wrongful convictions—capital punishment exonerations—the use of snitches is the most frequent contributor.[14]

The incentives for snitches to testify have been consistent over the decades. Jailhouse informants seek to reduce their sentence or accelerate their release from prison. Actual killers seek to incriminate others for their crime. The rewards for incriminating a fellow prisoner can also be more mundane. The late Robert Berke who served as the lawyer for California Attorneys for Criminal Justice, a group of defense lawyers, explained: "When you dangle extra rewards, furloughs, money, their own clothes, stereos, in front of people in overcrowded jails, then you have an unacceptable temptation to commit perjury."[15]

Leslie Vernon White, an articulate and savvy California convict, jarred justice system officials and everyday Americans when he demonstrated to a national TV audience how he could gain detailed information on a crime by calling various officials from prison and posing as a bail bondsman, a prosecutor, or a policeman.[16] From this information, he easily concocted a credible confession and claimed that a fellow convict had confided the crime details to him. White had testified or agreed to testify in a dozen or more cases in exchange for money, furloughs, and even a parole recommendation.[17]

The Snitch System references an interview on CBS's *60 Minutes*, where White quipped that the snitch system had spawned slogans such as "Don't go to the pen, send a friend."[18]

In 1999, the *Chicago Tribune* ran a series of articles on Illinois's convictions in capital cases and revealed that of more than three hundred such convictions, more than half had been reversed either for resentencing or for a new trial. Of these, forty-six had utilized snitches. This was some of the information that prompted Governor George H. Ryan to declare a moratorium on capital punishment in the state, to establish a commission in 2000 to study the Illinois criminal justice system, and to subsequently commute all death sentences in the state.[19]

Even though DNA exonerations have proven that many jailhouse snitches are about as truthful as Silas Merrill was, the practice of using them continues today.

Reform Regarding the Use of Snitches

A clear reform solution to protect trial proceedings from lying informants has not been implemented. Some believe that pretrial discovery, jury instructions, cross-examination, and the use of experts[20] would provide important caution and education to fact finders in evaluating this kind of testimony. Boston College of Law professor Robert Bloom, in a report for *Criminal*

Justice Magazine, expressed his view that "the only effective way to deal with this problem is to provide a pretrial exclusion process to ensure the reliability of an informant's testimony."[21]

The use of informants who are compensated for testimony is always risky, and, yet, perhaps because jailhouse informants can provide information that might not otherwise be discovered and because the use of informants has long been a tool of law enforcement, their testimony remains admissible. If the mind-set of police and prosecutors is to pursue truth rather than to just obtain a conviction, the use of likely unreliable informant testimony is at least reduced.

Bad Lawyering

The most significant piece of evidence in the Boorn case was the pile of bones that experts—four local physicians—contended were human and presumed to be those of the missing alleged victim, Russell Colvin. This discovery turned public opinion against the Boorn brothers. On closer examination, the doctors agreed that the bones were from an animal—but this critical fact was never raised in the trial. Legal affairs journalist and author Rob Warden, commenting on this inexplicable lapse, suggests that in view of the community's disposition toward the guilt of the Boorn brothers, perhaps the defense did not want to prevail upon the physicians to give such unpopular testimony. Now, *that's* bad lawyering![22]

Bad lawyering survives even today. Among the attorneys who represented those exonerated by DNA in the past twenty years were lawyers who slept during the trial, who were disbarred shortly after defending in a death penalty case, who failed to investigate alibis, who failed to consult or call forensic experts, and who failed to even appear at hearings.[23]

These inadequacies are almost comical until you consider the consequences.

Charles Chatman had a string of bad luck, including his draw of a court-appointed lawyer. In 1981, a white fifty-two-year-old rape victim identified Chatman as the black man who had broken into her home, raped, and robbed her. Chatman saw his lawyer only once before trial. After sitting in jail for seven months, he finally called him to see if he had any news. The attorney replied that, as a matter of fact, the trial would be the very next day.[24] Chatman's sister testified that he had been at work the night of the crime, but she had not been able to locate pay records to prove it, and his attorney didn't present all of the information to support this alibi either.

Contacted years later, Chatman's attorney revealed his lack of confidence in his ability to prevail in Chatman's defense. "Back in those days," he said, "a white lady takes the stand and points a finger and says, 'That's the guy,' he's dead meat."[25] Chatman was convicted and sentenced to ninety-nine years in prison. His luck finally turned when the Innocence Project proved through DNA analysis of the rape kit evidence that Chatman was innocent. He was released after serving *twenty-seven* years in prison for a crime he did not commit.[26]

When unable to afford an attorney, suspects must rely on a court-appointed one. Especially in times of shrinking budgets, funding for indigent criminal defense is sometimes cut back. Attorneys who do this work are often underpaid and overworked. Inadequate legal representation denies fairness in the criminal justice system, and many innocent people have paid for this inequity with their freedom and years of their lives.

Reforms Relating to Bad Lawyering

Evidence of wrongful conviction should weigh heavily on the public conscience and should raise in our public priorities the provision of fair legal representation for the poor. Inadequate legal representation results in conviction of the innocent and escape of the real perpetrator. If the human suffering of these cases does not move us to demand better, the high cost of trials, appeals, compensation to exonerees, and ongoing crimes by the real perpetrators should. Bad lawyering will exist as long as the American public does not demand proper funding for indigent defense—including the resources to perform forensic testing and call forensic experts—and overlooks unconscionable laziness and ineptitude from lawyers.

CHAPTER 22

Expert Mumbo Jumbo

BAD SCIENCE

THE FOUR PHYSICIANS identifying a pile of bones as human were wrong in the Boorn case, but they helped convince an entire town that the Boorn brothers had murdered and buried their brother-in-law. When Joseph Serowick said that Michael Green's blood type put him in a small minority of those who could have committed the Clinic Center rape, he was wrong. When Serowick said that the evidence hair in the washcloth was a head hair that was "consistent" with Michael Green's hair, he was wrong. It was a pubic hair, and it did not come from Michael Green.

Invalidated and improper scientific testimony has been a factor in more than 50 percent of DNA-proven wrongful convictions. While DNA has exposed this problem, it cannot solve it. Fully 90 percent to 95 percent of criminal cases have no biological evidence for DNA testing.[1]

Invalidated scientific testimony on bite marks, footprints, hair, soil, fiber, blood, semen, voice, fingernails, and even DNA was identified by Brandon Garrett and Peter J. Neufeld in a stunning study published in March 2009 in the *Virginia Law Review.* Titled "Invalid Forensic Science Testimony and Wrongful Convictions," its detailed examination of the trial transcripts of 137 cases where DNA proved innocence—that included testimony from a forensic scientist—revealed that in eighty-two cases, or 60 percent, witnesses for the prosecution provided invalid forensic testimony at trial. They presented either "testimony with conclusions misstating empirical data—that is, data based on quantifiable evidence, experiment, or observation—or [testimony] wholly unsupported by empirical data."[2]

Errors in forensic testimony offered by analysts from police laboratories were largely uncorrected in the trial process. Defense counsel was ineffective in revealing the inaccuracy of the testimonies either through cross-examination or by presenting contradictory forensic testimony from other experts. In fact, the defense utilized its own forensic experts in only 19 of the 137 cases.[3]

The courts have historically often provided prosecutors a broader range of "interpretation" of the evidence than many citizens might find acceptable or fundamentally fair, especially in light of the quasi-official role that the prosecutor, as the lawyer for the state, represents in the courtroom. When the defense did challenge the reliability of the prosecution's forensic experts in these cases, judges rarely provided relief.[4]

The study identified six kinds of errors in forensic science testimony:

1. The most frequent one, present in forty-eight of these cases, involves the "interpretation of nonprobative evidence as inculpatory evidence."[5] In other words, misleading testimony on non-determinative evidence falsely implied scientific support of the defendant's guilt. Joseph Serowick's stating that Michael Green was one of only 16 percent of the population that could have left the evidence on the rapist's washcloth is an example. Another expert years later said that Serowick's testimony should have been that this evidence excluded *no* male as the possible perpetrator.[6]

2. Ignoring scientific evidence that points to innocence was present in twenty-three cases in this study.[7] DNA analysis of the hair taken from the rape kit of Judy Johnson's granddaughter excluded Clarence Elkins and indicated an unknown male. This was known a month before the trial. Several factors contributed to the discounting of this important evidence so that it was not a significant consideration in the jury's decision. Some may have thought that this hair was random, but its location should have strongly suggested to the state, the defense, and the jury that Clarence Elkins was not the perpetrator.

3. In thirteen of the wrongful convictions in this study, the analysts misstated the frequency of an occurrence in the population. For example, all persons have an ABO blood type and can either be a secretor or a non-secretor. An analyst testified that type O secretors (the defendant was a

type O secretor) represent 17.5 percent of the population, suggesting that 82.5 percent of the population would be excluded as the perpetrator. In fact, type O secretors make up 35 percent of the population.[8]

4. Stating probabilities that are not supported by research nor widely accepted by the scientific community is another common misleading type of testimony. Serowick's reference to one study that indicated a 1 in 40,000[9] likelihood that two hairs with similar characteristics would come from two different persons was unjustifiable. Frequencies such as this have not been determined by science.

5. Subjective, non-numerical analyst testimony on probabilities in a forensic area that has no established probabilities based on empirical data also misleads a jury, and this type of testimony was present in nineteen of the cases in the Garrett and Neufeld study.[10] In several of the common areas of forensic study where there are little or no empirical data (for example hair analysis, bite marks, and shoe prints), forensic scientists are trained to select their words carefully so as not to imply a greater association than has been ascertained through quantified research. The Garrett and Neufeld study raises the question of whether or not even seemingly innocuous wording such as "consistent with" is "irrelevant and unduly prejudicial."[11]

If a defendant's hair in one metric is deemed "consistent with" a crime scene hair, what does this really tell us if in that particular metric the hair might be consistent with, let's say, 25 percent of the population? Or 55 percent? Or, more commonly, with an *unknown* percentage of the population? Some would argue that coming from a credentialed forensic scientist, the importance of this "consistency" is unjustifiably elevated. Until we know the frequency of such similarities, is science really ready to testify?

A 2009 national study, *Strengthening Forensic Science in the United States: A Path Forward,* in fact concluded, "No scientifically accepted standards exist about the frequency with which particular characteristics of hair are distributed in the population," and there "appear to be no uniform standards on the number of features on which hairs must agree before an examiner may declare a 'match.'"[12]

This same report referenced an FBI study of 80 hair comparisons that were "associated" through microscopic examination. When analyzed through mtDNA examination, 9 of these (12.5 percent) came from other sources. The report concluded, "This illustrates not only the imprecision of microscopic hair analyses, but also the problem with using imprecise reporting terminology such as 'associated with,' which is not clearly defined and which can be misunderstood to imply individualization."[13]

6. Stating that evidence conclusively identifies a defendant when science has not provided the empirical data to support such certainty is another form of invalid testimony. For example, in several cases a scientist testified that a defendant was absolutely the person who left a bite mark on the victim. Science has not developed the empirical data to support any such claim.[14]

Several forensic scientists are often cited as notorious purveyors of "junk science" or unjustifiable testimony, revealed through DNA exonerations. The allegedly misleading testimony of police chemists Fred Zain in West Virginia and Joyce Gilchrist in Oklahoma, and follow-up investigations, resulted in at least ten exonerations and millions in settlement costs[15] to the wrongly convicted.

Those responsible for faulty testimony range from the mistaken, undertrained, or inept; to those influenced by a too-cozy relationship with the prosecutor; to those motivated by any number of human failings. It is easy to view these as the exceptions in a much larger universe of competent scientists. However, Nancy and I began to fear that the advantages of the prosecution—for example, having the funds to hire forensic experts, enjoying the presumption of truthfulness generally afforded the state's attorney, and getting the last word in final argument—and the opportunity to push the limits of fair advocacy by the prosecution in forensic matters (with few judges affording relief when the defense objected, and the defense often without resources for opposing experts) may be much more common than just a few outrageous cases.

Garrett and Neufeld supported this frightening possibility. In the exoneration cases included in their study, invalid scientific testimony was offered from seventy-two forensic analysts from fifty-two laboratories, practices, or hospitals across the country.[16]

Nancy and I wondered: if these scientists and their work were audited, would this have revealed any violation of any standards? Or was this a case of many unrecognized failures in the system? With all of the apparent problems in the scientific testimony in the Michael Green case, the two-year audit of the Cleveland Police Department Forensic Laboratory and of forensic scientist Joseph Serowick's work did not produce evidence of wrongdoing warranting prosecution. James Wooley, the overseer of the audit, told us, "There was nothing that alarmed me." He indicated that nothing suggested an "obstruction of justice."

Wooley said, "What was remarkable about it, there was an absence of evidence...of intentional manipulation."

The Cleveland audit included a review of the trial transcripts in which Serowick testified. "In most cases, the testimony was presented in a way—based on what had been done in the lab—we didn't think was misleading," concluded Wooley.[17]

Nancy and I came to believe that, aside from some scientists who pursued illegal means to present invented testimony for the prosecution, the unreliable testimony that was contributing to wrongful conviction might not find its complete explanation in the laboratory. The testimony itself—the positioning of the analysis in the framing of the prosecutor's questions and in the closing argument and the forensic scientist's selection of words in weak scientific context—influenced the fact finders in ways that could contribute to wrongful conviction.

With due respect to the good intentions of most forensic scientists, we came to believe that new attention must be focused on this important investigative and evidentiary tool and enterprise, forensic science and testimony.

REFORMS RELATED TO FORENSIC SCIENCE TESTIMONY

The Supreme Court clarified the criteria for admissibility of expert testimony in modern times in *Daubert v. Merrell Dow Pharmaceuticals* (1993). The Court placed on the trial judge "the task of ensuring that an expert's testimony rests on a reliable foundation and is relevant to the task at hand."[18]

Unfortunately, in practice, *Daubert* has been used frequently to exclude questionable scientific evidence in civil cases, but it has almost never resulted in the exclusion of forensic evidence presented in criminal cases.[19] Once judges have determined that the scientific discipline meets the standards of *Daubert,* they do not, in the vast majority of cases, challenge the specific conclusions and the statistical claims and inferences of the expert in trial testimony. They leave this to defense counsels—who are usually ill equipped to challenge the expert or provide an opposing expert.[20]

IN FEBRUARY 2009, a congressionally mandated report based on a two-year study by the National Research Council (a private, nonprofit institution providing public policy advice under congressional charter) came to the following conclusion: "Badly Fragmented Forensic Science System Needs Overhaul; Evidence to Support Reliability of Many Techniques Is Lacking."[21] The report's conclusions noted "serious deficiencies in the nation's forensic science system" and the need for "major reforms and new research." Systemic problems, in summary, were:

> Rigorous and mandatory certification programs for forensic scientists are currently lacking...as are strong standards and protocols for analyzing and reporting on evidence. And there is a dearth of peer-reviewed, published studies establishing the scientific bases and reliability of many forensic methods. Moreover, many forensic science labs are underfunded, understaffed, and have no effective oversight.

Recommendations included:

- "[T]here is a tremendous need for the forensic science community to improve."
- Congress should "establish a new, independent National Institute of Forensic Science to lead research efforts, establish and enforce standards for forensic science professionals and laboratories, and oversee education standards."
- "[P]ublic forensic science laboratories should be made independent from or autonomous within police departments and prosecutors' offices."

- "Certification should be mandatory for forensic science professionals."
- "Accreditation for laboratories should be established."
- "Additional resources will be necessary to create a high-quality, self-correcting forensic science system."[22]

CHAPTER 23

When the Good Guys Aren't

GOVERNMENT MISCONDUCT

DNA-PROVEN EXONERATIONS revealed to Nancy and me that government misconduct is more prevalent than we had assumed. Police misconduct was present in 50 percent of the first seventy-four DNA exonerations, while prosecutorial misconduct was a factor in nearly 45 percent of the first seventy-four DNA exonerations.[1]

For me, this is a uniquely troubling contributor to wrongful conviction, because it reveals what happens when those in the criminal justice system lose their way. Most professionals in the system are properly motivated public servants. However, in focusing on what goes wrong in conviction errors, Nancy and I bumped into instances of corruption; unlawful tactics; misplaced motivations; arrogance; and abuses of power by district attorneys, police detectives, forensic scientists, and others. Our eyes were opened to troubling evidence that law enforcement and judicial process can be inconsistent with fairness, decency, and due process.

On November 4, 2009, the U.S. Supreme Court heard arguments on whether or not prosecutors are absolutely immune from prosecution not only for their work in the courtroom but also for illegalities in preparing their case. Absolute prosecutorial immunity is the legal doctrine that protects prosecutors from frivolous lawsuits and criminal charges.

This question arose from a case that involved a glaring example of alleged government misconduct. In 1977, Terry Harrington was a star high-school football player looking forward to college, with recruiting overtures from the likes of Yale University. Instead, Harrington and Curtis McGhee were convicted of using a shotgun to kill a retired police captain who was working the night shift as security for a car dealership in Council Bluffs, Iowa. Harrington and McGhee, both black, lived just over the state line in Nebraska and were convicted by an all-white jury[2] primarily on the testimony of Kevin Hughes, a sixteen-year-old with a criminal record. Police had stopped Hughes and his friends, who were driving a Cadillac stolen earlier from a Nebraska dealership.[3]

Probably feeling at risk of being charged with the murder, Hughes blamed the car theft on other people (lies that were apparent and quickly dismissed) before he eventually named Harrington and McGhee. Hughes's initial "testimony" about what he claimed to know about the crime was full of errors. Yet, detectives told him that if he would help them in solving the homicide, he would not be charged with murder, he would get some assistance with his other criminal charges, *and* he would have a shot at a $5,000 reward. Not surprisingly, Hughes took the deal.[4]

Both Harrington and McGhee were convicted, largely on the sixteen-year-old's testimony. Harrington, nineteen, was sentenced to life in prison despite having consistently maintained his innocence. After serving twenty-five years, Harrington finally won a reversal of his conviction in 2003 from the Iowa Supreme Court, which found that the prosecutor had failed to reveal another suspect investigated in the case. Withholding from the defense exculpatory evidence that is deemed material either to the conviction or the punishment was determined to be a violation of due process in *Brady v. Maryland* (1963). Such failure by the prosecution is a Brady violation, and it can reverse a conviction, as it did in this case.

In its decision, the court also indicated that the chief witness in the case was "a liar and a perjurer."[5]

This reversal never would have been achieved without the assistance of a prison employee, who got to know Harrington and his family. She obtained, through a public records request, police records relating to the case.[6] They revealed that Assistant County Attorney Joseph Hrvol, who was actively involved in the investigation, and County Attorney David Richter, who oversaw his office's work in the case, had engaged in activities that Harrington's attorney contended were tantamount to framing Harrington and McGhee for the murder. At the time of the investigation, Richter was running for re-election with the liability of an unsolved murder of a former police captain.[7]

Allegedly, prosecutors withheld information that pointed to another suspect, a white man. This man, who happened to be the brother-in-law of a city fire department captain, had been a suspect in an earlier homicide, and witnesses claimed to have seen him in the vicinity of the car dealership at the time of murder. He was said to have been walking his dog, and at least one witness observed him holding an object that looked like a shotgun. He failed a polygraph on the important question of shooting the victim. Furthermore, seven of eight crime reports written by the Council Bluffs police referenced the suspect as part of this investigation, but this was never disclosed to the defense. In fact, in post-conviction hearing discovery, Hrvol denied that the suspect had ever been identified as the man with the dog. Withholding this information was the basis of the Iowa Supreme Court's decision to overturn the convictions.[8]

The witnesses in the case eventually recanted their testimony against Harrington and McGhee. Pottawattamie County Attorney Matthew Wilber reluctantly dismissed all charges against Harrington. Curtis McGhee, who only a month before had pleaded no contest to second-degree murder in exchange for his testimony in an anticipated retrial of Harrington, was sentenced to time served and also released.

"As for the final justice for Terry Harrington," County Attorney Wilber proclaimed at a press conference, "I will defer that honor to a higher power."[9]

Harrington and McGhee sued the prosecutors in a civil law suit alleging that the prosecutors had helped put together false evidence to convict them. The prosecutors claimed that they had absolute immunity. The district court, ruling earlier on the question of absolute immunity in this case, found that immunity does not extend to "a County Attorney who violates a person's substantive due process rights by obtaining, manufacturing, coercing, and fabricating evidence before filing formal charges, because this is not 'a distinctly prosecutorial function.'"[10]

The Court of Appeals agreed with the District Court, and the case was appealed to the United States Supreme Court where oral arguments were heard. However, a $12 million settlement reached on January 4, 2010, concluded the high court's deliberation on the question of whether or not prosecutors' rights to immunity extend to their conduct prior to trial and, in particular, to the kinds of fraudulent misconduct alleged in this case. The settlement provided that Pottawattamie County pay $7.03 million to Terry Harrington and $4.97 million to Curtis McGhee Jr. in exchange for their dropping the lawsuit against the county.[11]

Matt Wilber said that the settlement did not imply an admission of guilt by the county, Dave Richter, Joe Hrvol, or him.

Rob Warden, executive director of the Center on Wrongful Conviction at Northwestern University School of Law, articulated the potential impact of this settlement. "This means prosecutors who step outside their traditional role and who act as investigators can still be subject to civil rights lawsuits just as police would be," he said.[12]

We have made two observations about government misconduct in the criminal justice system. First, despite the fact that most police detectives and prosecutors are honorable in their public service, a minority—and I want to believe it is a small minority—abuse their authority. Second, rarely have prosecutors been held accountable for irregularities and illegalities in the course of their work. "I couldn't give you five cases in the last forty years of criminal charges against prosecutors," said former prosecutor Bennett Gershman, now a law professor at Pace University.[13]

A notable recent exception was the Duke University lacrosse rape case in which District Attorney Mike Nifong was disbarred for two dozen ethics violations—including withholding exculpatory evidence from the defense, lying to the court, and making reckless derogatory public comments about the defendants. The three lacrosse players, accused of raping a hired dancer at a March 2006 team party, were suspended by Duke, and their families spent a fortune on their defense. North Carolina Attorney General Roy Cooper took over the case and the investigation. He not only dropped the case but also declared the defendants innocent. Nifong was disbarred, forced to resign as district attorney, and served one day in jail for contempt.

In May 2008, Dallas County district attorney Craig Watkins expressed an unusual view: Prosecutors should pay a price for intentionally withholding evidence from the defense. "If the harm is great, yes, it should be criminalized," he said. He was frustrated by the then forty-five wrongful convictions in Texas, which had cost the state $8.6 million. Brady violations were involved in twenty-two of the cases.[14]

The Innocence Project has identified government misconduct in many forms. These include deliberately flawed eyewitness identification procedures; withholding exculpatory evidence from the defense; delaying the defense's access to scientific evidence; deliberately destroying or mishandling evidence; encouraging suspects to waive their Miranda rights; utilizing unethical techniques to gain false confessions; and knowingly using unreliable snitches and informants.[15]

Reforms Related to Government Misconduct

Many reforms, such as video recording custodial interrogations and blind administration of line-ups, address important procedures that guard both suspects and law enforcement from unnecessary challenges when cases are presented in trial. The Innocence Project recommends the establishment of Criminal Justice Reform Commissions to study wrongful convictions and recommend reforms. These have been established in a handful of states to date.

However, beyond reform legislation, I place particular responsibility on prosecutors to seek justice, as does the law. In the courtroom, the prosecutor assumes a quasi-judicial role. The Supreme Court has recognized that the prosecutor is "cloaked with the authority of the United States Government,"[16] and that "it is fair to say that the average jury, in a greater or less degree, have confidence that these obligations [to serve justice], which so plainly rest upon the prosecutor, will be faithfully observed. Consequently, improper suggestions, insinuations and, especially, assertions of personal knowledge are apt to carry much weight against the accused when they should properly carry none."[17]

CHAPTER 24

Why We Can't Believe Our Eyes

MISTAKEN EYEWITNESS TESTIMONY

IN MOST INSTANCES OF KNOWN wrongful criminal conviction, one or more of the contributors that we have already examined worked in tandem with the most prevalent of all factors: eyewitness testimony, which historically has been the most valuable tool for solving crimes and convicting the guilty.

Extremely credible and convincing to jurors, eyewitness testimony often trumps alibis and strong conflicting evidence. Therefore, it is also the number-one reason that the innocent sometimes get convicted of crimes they didn't commit. DNA exonerations in the late 1980s and 1990s began to reveal that more than 75 percent of wrongful convictions were based in part or completely on mistaken eyewitness testimony.

The importance of eyewitness testimony to solving crimes and convicting criminals has made this a sensitive topic for law enforcement and prosecutors. In fact, until recently, the justice system has turned a deaf ear to what scientists have long known about how memory works. In light of the lessons of DNA exonerations, the standoff between law and science on the subject of eyewitness testimony is gradually softening, and reforms in eyewitness procedures are gaining acceptance. As an advocate for this reform, I stress that recommended reforms will not banish or limit eyewitness testimony; they seek only to ensure that a testifying eyewitness's memory is as untainted and as uncompromised as possible. This enhances accuracy, benefitting both the prosecution and the defense, and, more importantly, justice.

As Nancy and I considered the challenge of improving eyewitness testimony, we once again found ourselves mining the work of many who had been far ahead of us in this pursuit.

A brilliant Harvard scientist returned early from a family vacation after learning that his home had been burglarized. He anxiously went through his home to determine what had been stolen. He was called later in the summer to testify at the trial of a defendant who had been caught with the scientist's belongings. Under oath, the scientist reported that burglars had entered through a basement window. He knew the timing, he said, because he had found candle wax on the second floor. He testified that his large mantel clock had been wrapped in paper and left on the dining room table, an indication that the burglars had intended to return to the house. The burglars had taken some clothing, which he listed.[1]

This internationally known scientist had given some three thousand lectures without ever using notes or forgetting a name or losing his train of thought, but he discovered a few days after his courtroom testimony that most of his statements under oath were incorrect.[2]

The burglars had not broken the basement window but had broken the lock on the basement door to enter his house. The mantel clock was wrapped in a tablecloth, not paper. The candle wax droppings were in the attic, not the second floor. His short list of missing clothing was, in fact, too short.[3]

These lapses in memory might have been dismissed as the expected responses of an absentminded professor, but this scientist was no ordinary academician. He was Hugo Münsterberg (1863–1916), a pioneer in applying psychological research to the practical business of life, earning him the title of the "father of industrial psychology" as well as the "father of applied psychology."[4] The German-born psychologist was the esteemed director of Harvard's psychological research laboratory.

For Münsterberg, his own fallibility in remembering the details of his plundered home was just more proof that human memory applied to the mission of delivering justice in the courtroom is risky business. In his book *On the Witness Stand: Essays on Psychology and Crime*, Münsterberg explained the roles that imagination, police suggestion, substitution, forgetting, and faulty conclusions played in his flawed testimony. His errors were inconsequential, but we now know that these kinds of errors can send an innocent person to prison or to death row.

In this same volume of essays, Münsterberg boldly claimed what the Ronald Cotton case taught Nancy and me: The sincerity and the confidence of a witness have an imperfect relationship to accuracy in eyewitness testimony.[5]

Münsterberg noted another nonintuitive fact: "The public in the main suspects that the witness lies, while taking for granted that if he is normal and conscious of responsibility, he may forget a thing, but it would not believe that he could remember the wrong thing."[6]

The professor also claimed that confessions could not be trusted as true indicators of guilt.[7]

As current as these understandings seem, Hugo Münsterberg published this book more than a century ago! The emerging field of applied psychology and how it could benefit criminal justice was recognized then, and yet even today its potential to inform the criminal justice process is not fully realized. The 1908 *New York Times* book review of *On the Witness Stand* predicted, "Experimental psychology as Professor Münsterberg studies, teaches, and uses it at Harvard…promises—as soon as its already demonstrated potentialities reach the minds of judges, jurors, and lawyers, to revolutionize court procedure and to bring light and order in domains where all, or almost all, is now darkness and confusion."[8]

Instead Münsterberg's research findings were unwelcomed, even repudiated, by the very profession that should have embraced them. His seemingly mild-mannered book elicited a negative response that would be destructive to Münsterberg's reputation and devastating to his effort to inform eyewitness testimony with psychological insights.

Münsterberg compared the legal profession's hostility to psychological research with the more receptive response from other disciplines. He concluded, "Only Lawyers are obdurate."[9]

He wrote, "The lawyer and the judge and the juryman are sure that they do not need the experimental psychologist…They go on thinking that their legal instinct and their common sense supplies them with all that is needed and somewhat more; and if the time is ever to come when even the jurist is to show some concession to the spirit of modern psychology, public opinion will have to exert some pressure."[10]

This criticism of the legal profession drew the defense of a brilliant lawyer, equally gifted and accomplished. Ask any law school graduate to name the most influential legal scholar on the subject of the rules of evidence, and the answer will likely be "Wigmore!" Or, more precisely, "Dean John Henry Wigmore."

James M. Doyle, in his book *True Witness: Cops, Courts, Science, and the Battle Against Misidentification,* characterized the ensuing showdown over eyewitness testimony between Münsterberg and Wigmore as an historic battle between science and law.

John Henry Wigmore, author of the ten-volume *Treatise on the Anglo-American System of Evidence in Trials at Common Law (1904–05),* more commonly called *Wigmore on Evidence*—the foundational exposition on evidence in American law—was dean of Northwestern University Law School when these two titans represented their professions in a tongue-in-cheek confrontation that had unexpected outcomes. Both men were enormously productive scholars but pragmatists, and were probably much closer in agreement on the contribution that applied psychology could make to criminal justice than they would reveal in their unorthodox matchup.

Wigmore chose a method to his advantage for his response to Münsterberg: a mock trial written as an article for the February 1909 issue of the *University of Illinois Law Review.* In this fictitious trial, Wigmore's alter ego not only prevailed but also humiliated the hapless defendant, "Muensterberg." According to the testimony, "Muensterberg" had overstated the advances of psychology, which were not yet "exact" and "so incapable of forensic use that even their well-wishers confess that thousands of experiments and years of research will be required before they will be practicable, if ever."[11]

However, the fictitious judge's final statement in the mock trial revealed what may have been Wigmore's true belief, consistent with his future work in founding the nation's first forensic lab:[12]

No country in the civilized world was probably so far behind in the scientific study of the criminal law as affected by the contributory sciences of sociology, anthropology, psychology, and medicine. In no country had the legal profession taken so little interest in finding out or using what those other sciences were doing.... In the continent of

Europe there were not only a dozen monthly journals devoted exclusively to criminal law, but five or six of these were given exclusively to the modern science of Criminology.... In the United States there was not a single journal devoted to criminal law in any aspect.[13]

While we can theorize that Wigmore's objective was actually to shine a light on the importance of utilizing scientific findings in the courtroom, the result was the opposite. Münsterberg and applied psychology did not recover. Other factors certainly played a role. William Stern noted in his memoriam for Münsterberg that he suffered increasing unpopularity and estrangement from his friends and associates when, as World War I began, he identified with Germany and attempted "a spiritual war against the traditional English sentiment at Harvard."[14] It is difficult to imagine that after such an illustrious career, Münsterberg died in relative obscurity at age fifty-three in 1916.[15]

Without Münsterberg, and in light of what seemed to be an unresponsive legal profession, most psychologists remained in their ivory towers for the next many decades. James Doyle summarizes in *True Witness* the limited ensuing role of psychology in trial testimony: "'Law and Psychology' came to refer to clinical evaluations of insanity and competency to stand trial, to the study of the abnormal rather than the normal operations of the human mind."[16]

"ARE YOU AWARE OF THE FACT that what you are talking about isn't even science? You don't even have agreement in your own field about eyewitness testimony! Your experiments aren't like real life."

Fast-forward one hundred years, and the conversation has not changed much. Nancy and I were attending a presentation—"Strengthening Prosecutions: Improving Eyewitness Identification Procedures in Ohio"—sponsored by the University of Cincinnati College of Law in 2009. Attendees included lawyers picking up continuing legal education (CLE) credits, police detectives, sheriff deputies, prosecutors, and others in law enforcement.

We were about twenty minutes into a presentation by Nancy Steblay, professor of psychology at Augsburg College in Minneapolis. Steblay has spent the last sixteen years doing research, in the spirit of Hugo Münsterberg, on human behavior, law, and eyewitness testimony. Her focus is meta-analysis: the analysis of the accumulated research and analysis of colleagues—across different samples, labs, situations, stimuli, and various levels of realism—to identify reliable patterns, establish memory principles, and translate these to the field.

Steblay works with law enforcement organizations to implement better eyewitness identification procedures. Her presentation was intended to show the underlying research supporting these new methods. She led the audience through a photo identification in which even this group—experienced as they were in eyewitness evidence—stumbled badly on remembering what they had just seen.

But one seasoned assistant county prosecutor was not buying it.

"Your experiments aren't like real crimes. I have been dealing with real criminals and real witnesses my whole career," said the assistant prosecutor.

"You're not subjecting people to the stress of a real crime," added another. "Stress increases memory. Our victims remember what they saw because they were under great, *actual* stress."

I did not have the patience of the presenter, Professor Steblay, as I listened to this. "I am not sure who is teaching you that," I came back, standing up from the last row. "Stress does *not* increase accuracy. Ask Jennifer Thompson. She was under a lot of stress when she was being raped, but she forced herself to focus on the face of her attacker. She was totally confident when she identified Ronald Cotton as her rapist, and she was dead wrong. *That's* what we are talking about here today!"

Professor Steblay calmly followed with the assurance of what thousands of research experiments have revealed. In fact, researchers *do* agree on many findings. As examples, the belief that our "common-sense" view of memory is good enough, is a myth. Memory is *not* like a video recorder. Confidence in a memory does *not* indicate accuracy. People under stress do *not* have increased memory of faces and events. Yes, we remember a horrific event, but stress impairs our ability to remember the details of it. The stress-increasing presence of a weapon reduces our ability to identify a person's face. Furthermore, people are more able to identify someone of their own race than of another race.

The contrary prosecutors pulled back, but their body language was clear; they were not convinced. I suddenly thought of Münsterberg: Are *only* lawyers (and law enforcement) obdurate?

Defensiveness and resistance from many in the justice system were still alive and well, but things had quietly progressed since the days of Hugo Münsterberg, and I sensed that momentum was beginning to side with meaningful reforms in criminal justice.

While seventy years of opportunity for progress in psychological research in the area of memory and eyewitness testimony were all but lost after Münsterberg, occasional researchers made contributions until new leaders emerged, particularly in the 1970s. Psychologist Bob Buckhout articulated to a broader audience the fallibility of eyewitness testimony when he appeared as an expert witness for the defense in the high-profile trial of Angela Davis, a former instructor at the University of California and an admitted member of the Communist Party. Davis was indicted on multiple counts in a hostage/ murder case. She denied that she was involved in a horrific crime involving a group of Soledad prisoners. Their misguided effort to bring about an escape resulted in the death of the trial judge as well as three of the perpetrators. Eyewitness testimony that linked Davis to a perpetrator was critical to her prosecution.

The defense called Robert Buckhout as an expert. He gave a comprehensive and compelling presentation on the factors that can impact reliability in eyewitness testimony. There is little doubt that his testimony contributed to the outcome of the trial.[17] The jury found Davis not guilty of murder, kidnapping, and conspiracy charges on June 5, 1972.

Buckhout went on to testify approximately 150 times as an expert witness on memory and eyewitness identification and published "Eyewitness Identification" in *Scientific American*.[18] This oft-cited article was credited with a resurgence of interest and research in eyewitness reliability.[19]

MORE THAN TWO THOUSAND scientific studies on eyewitness identification had been published by 1995.[20] These studies, often experiments that exposed individuals to carefully designed situations with or without the subjects' awareness, tested their recall afterward and revealed new truths about memory.

In the experience of Professor Münsterberg, however, legal and criminal justice professionals ignored or resisted the research findings. As recently as the late 1990s, the U.S. Supreme Court revealed a lack of awareness of research findings on human memory. In *Manson v. Braithwaite* (1997), the high court established broad guidelines for police identification procedures. In the majority opinion, Justice Harry Blackmun stated that law enforcement could use any procedures it chose as long as these were not "so unnecessarily suggestive as to give rise to a substantial likelihood of an irreparable misidentification."[21]

In the event that an overly suggestive procedure was used in the capture of eyewitness testimony, *Manson v. Braithwaite* relied upon five components set forth earlier in the 1972 case of *Neil v. Biggers* for judges to consider to determine whether the testimony should nevertheless be admitted: "the opportunity of the witness to view the criminal at the time of the crime, the witness's degree of attention, the accuracy of the witness's prior description of the criminal, the level of certainty demonstrated by the witness at the confrontation, and the length of time between the crime and the confrontation."[22] In *True Witness*, James Doyle cites an example of how this opinion ignored science: By 1997, exonerations through DNA analysis had proved witness certainty (the fourth item on the list) to be a very poor indicator of eyewitness accuracy.

For decades, trial judges had routinely denied the testimony of eyewitness experts. Before *Manson v. Braithwaite*, one standard was that expert testimony had to "conform to generally accepted explanatory theory" (*Frye v. United States*, 1923) in the scientific community. The "generally accepted" rule and other guidelines in landmark cases such *United States v. Amaral* (1973) enabled prosecuting attorneys to argue successfully to exclude scientific expert testimony. Judges ran little risk of denying the testimony of eyewitness experts, because the state courts had not reversed any cases based on such denial until 1983. In that year, the Arizona Supreme Court ruled reversible error in *State v. Chapple*, opining that a trial judge had abused his discretion by refusing to allow Elizabeth Loftus to testify as an eyewitness expert.[23]

Loftus, a psychologist nationally recognized in eyewitness identification research, had published *Eyewitness Testimony* four years earlier. This book, which won the 1980 National Media Award for Distinguished Contribution from the American Psychological Foundation, examined the results of experiments regarding more commonly known contributing factors to flawed memory, such as exposure time (the length of time the witness viewed the perpetrator) and situational influencers (for example, the distance between the witness and the perpetrator). However, it also revealed subtle factors, such as the witness's biases and expectations.[24] The important finding that a memory can be significantly altered by all kinds of influences dispelled the "tape recorder" concept of memory, namely, that our minds accurately record and preserve memories without risk of alteration.

Just one example of the hundreds of experiments that confirmed the vulnerability of a memory was performed in 1974 by Loftus and J.C. Palmer. Designed to show the impact, if any, of the subtle suggestion implied in the phrasing of a question, subjects were shown a film of a traffic accident. They were divided into two groups of fifty persons each. Those in one group were asked, "About how fast were the cars going when they *smashed* into each other?" Those in the other group were asked, "About how fast were the cars going when they *hit* each other?" A week later, the groups were asked, "Did you see any broken glass?" There was no broken glass in the accident. Of the subjects who'd heard the impact described as "smashed," 32 percent, or nearly a third, responded that they had seen broken glass; whereas in the group that had been asked the more mildly phrased question, only 14 percent said that they'd seen broken glass.[25]

Loftus and other researchers proposed that two types of information go into one's memory: (1) the information gathered during the original perception of the event, and (2) external information that is introduced after the event. Many experiments revealed that these two could merge into a single memory.[26] As results were consistent over many experiments in different locations, with different subjects, researchers came closer to understanding how memory works, how it can be corrupted. This experiment and others like it revealed that memory is as fragile as a fingerprint.

CHAPTER 25

Observations on Eyewitnesses

I N THE COURSE of my work on the Clarence Elkins case, I learned a lot about memory and eyewitness testimony that surprised me even though as a prosecutor I had been cautious and aware of the fallibility of this form of evidence. At the time, DNA was proving again and again that even a victim's seemingly certain eyewitness testimony could be absolutely wrong. Tragically, victims were victimized again by the hard truth that their testimony had cost innocent persons years in prison.

DNA exonerations were revealing that law enforcement had often contributed to eyewitness error—usually unknowingly but occasionally through purposeful acts that skirted best practices in order to get eyewitness testimony to support their case. I have heard statements from many accomplished law enforcement officers, police detectives, prosecutors, attorneys, and judges that indicate even today a surprising lack of understanding about this critical evidentiary tool.

As if this weren't enough, most jurors remain woefully unprepared to evaluate eyewitness testimony. Even those who may be intellectually aware of its inherent problems dismiss these as not applying to "their" case when the crime victim confidently says, "That's him! I will never forget that face!"

The tragic conviction errors exposed by DNA were a force for new thinking on the use of scientific evidence in the courtroom. In the foreword to Attorney General Janet Reno's seminal 1996 U.S. Department of Justice report, *Convicted by Juries, Exonerated by Science: Case Studies in the Use of DNA Evidence to Establish Innocence After Trial*, Edward Imwinkelried, professor of law at the University of California, provided historic insights on the rules of admissibility of scientific evidence in the courtroom. The standard requiring that this evidence has "gained general acceptance" in its particular field, established in *Frye v. United States*, was "abandoned" by the high court in 1993 with the adoption of *Daubert v. Merrell Dow Pharmaceuticals*, "a more flexible validation standard." But because this was decided "on statutory, rather than constitutional grounds," the states could determine their own standards, and in 1995, nearly half of the states were clinging to the more conservative "general acceptance" standard.[1]

U.S. courts have a tradition of caution regarding the admissibility of scientific evidence due to the perceived "mystic infallibility"[2] that jurors give such evidence. We observed how Joseph Serowick's "scientific" testimony bolstered a mistaken eyewitness identification to convict Michael Green. However, I believe it was primarily the jury's belief in the mystic infallibility of eyewitness testimony that convicted Green.

In what may have been a fear that courts would rule the emerging science of DNA inadmissible, Professor Imwinkelried wrote that by restricting the use of scientific evidence, "we force the courts to rely on inferior types of evidence, such as eyewitness testimony."[3]

While DNA testimony became admissible in the courtroom, expert witnesses on eyewitness testimony are still denied in some jurisdictions. Still, perhaps in part because DNA-proven conviction errors were prompting questions that psychological research could answer, after more than one hundred years, the scientists were being heard, and in venues beyond the courtroom.

Translating the many new understandings from research on memory to practical application in the justice system was becoming a reality. Two insights were helpful to me in understanding where research could be applied to improve the criminal justice process:

1. First, commonly accepted among the psychologists we researched was the three-stages-of-memory analysis that Elizabeth Loftus delineated in *Eyewitness Testimony*:

    First, there is the *acquisition* stage—the perception of the original event—in which information is encoded and entered into a person's memory system. Second, there is the *retention* stage, the period of time that passes between the event and the eventual recollection of the event. Third, there is the *retrieval* stage, during which a person recalls stored information.[4]

2. Second, Gary Wells, Amina Memon, and Steven Penrod identified in their 2006 treatise, "Eyewitness Evidence: Improving Its Probative Value," two types of variables that impact eyewitness accuracy: system variables, which the justice system can control, and estimator variables, which are part of the event circumstances and not under control of the justice system.[5] Clearly, the opportunity for improvement is with the system variables. The authors suggested that system variables generally fell into two broad categories: "One category is interviewing eyewitnesses, a process that generally involves recall memory. The other category is the identification of suspects, a process that generally involves recognition memory. It is important to note that neither interviewing nor identification is considered by eyewitness scientists to be purely a memory process. Social influence can be a huge factor in both."[6]

While those in the justice system cannot control the estimator variables, understanding them can help ascertain the quality of the memory. For example, conditions such as lighting and length of time observed should be taken into account in evaluating an eyewitness identification. In the Elkins case, the six-year-old girl was attacked in the dark of night, was knocked unconscious, and was deprived of oxygen. As obvious as these impediments are to an accurate observation, detectives and prosecutors apparently ignored these problematic factors in accepting the victim's testimony.

In 1998, under Attorney General Janet Reno, the National Institute of Justice created the Technical Working Group for Eyewitness Evidence to develop recommended procedures in investigations involving this evidence. The working group included law enforcement, legal, and science research professionals, who worked for a year to create *Eyewitness Evidence: A Guide for Law Enforcement*, a practical handbook that incorporated research on memory and eyewitness evidence with the experience of law enforcement. Notably, Gary Wells, a leading eyewitness psychological researcher, and six other research professionals were at the table. In fact, they represented a third of the initial planning committee and a fifth of the thirty-four-person working group.[7] It was a historic collaboration of national leaders in law enforcement, law, and research, with due recognition of each group's unique experiences and mind-sets. The result was a new set of guidelines for law enforcement to improve processes and results in first-responder (initial investigator) response, mug books and composites, witness interviews, and eyewitness identification.[8]

In early 2000, under the auspices of this group, training teams were formed to create *Eyewitness Evidence: A Trainer's Manual for Law Enforcement,* published by the Department of Justice under Attorney General John Ashcroft in September 2003.

It is beyond the scope of this book to relate in detail the evolution of new understandings, as well as their acceptance, their application, and the emergence of reform recommendations that were occurring in this productive period and continues today. A confluence of forces was fostering new alliances and progress:

- A resurgence of psychological research in memory and eyewitness testimony beginning in the 1970s;

- The emergence of DNA as a crime-solving tool in the late 1980s;

- The Innocence Project's acceleration of DNA-proven exonerations, analysis of wrongful conviction, and identification of reforms in the 1990s;

- And leadership from the Department of Justice under Attorney General Janet Reno, involving law enforcement and justice system professionals, psychological researchers, legislators, public officials, journalists, and academics.

Reforms Relating to Eyewitness Testimony

Training of law enforcement regarding the critically important first interviews with witnesses and the use of recommended procedures in capturing eyewitness testimony are essential to preserving a memory that is vulnerable to contamination from a multitude of sources.

Reforms that have become standard procedure or have been legislated in progressive jurisdictions (New Jersey, North Carolina, and Wisconsin were the first states to legislate reform) seek to protect the witness's memory by addressing variables that law enforcement can control.[9]

Recommended reforms that have been either adopted operationally or legislated are constantly being refined and can be reviewed on the Innocence Project's website at www.innocenceproject.org. In photo and live lineups, blind administration (often called *double-blind administration*) requires that neither the administrator of the lineup nor the witness knows which person is the suspect. This eliminates the possibility of even subtle influences—verbal or nonverbal, intentional or not—communicated from the administrator, or accusation of this influence later in the courtroom. It also eliminates any bias in recording the witness's confidence level. Because the witness's degree of certainty can increase dramatically over time due to factors unrelated to accuracy, it is important to capture his or her earliest expression of certainty in the identification process.

The composition of a lineup should include people who resemble the witness's initial description of the perpetrator. The suspect should not stand out from the "fillers" in the lineup. The selection of fillers is important to the integrity of the lineup results. A witness should not be shown the same suspect in more than one lineup.

The witness should be given the instructions that the suspect may or may not be included in the lineup and that the investigation will continue regardless of the witness's response. Video recording of the lineup provides proof to the jury that the procedure was done according to recommended guidelines.

A more controversial reform is the use of the sequential lineup. Whether using a live lineup or a display of photos, research shows that the sequential lineup requires absolute judgment.[10] In other words, the witness must make a decision on each photo without comparing it to the others.

When all persons are shown to the witness at one time, the witness, perhaps believing that the suspect is included, may seek to determine the person who is "most like" the perpetrator. Professor and psychological researcher Nancy Steblay explained that this kind of "relative judgment"[11] might work if the perpetrator is present, but if the suspect is not there, the process can result in a false identification.

Selection is more cautious in sequential lineups. In fact, there is an 8 percent reduction in witnesses identifying someone by this method. However, in studies in which the perpetrator was not included in the lineup, there were 22 percent fewer *incorrect* selections. When a witness selects a person by this method, the odds are higher that the selection is accurate.[12]

ALL OF THESE RECOMMENDATIONS would inform a memorandum that Mark Godsey and I would take to a new Ohio governor and a new attorney general in 2008. A bill would be introduced into the Ohio Legislature that same year by legislative leaders who "got it." But in the meantime, this information about memory and eyewitness testimony was inadvertent preparation for a more practical challenge. I was about to be asked to assist in a case in which the conviction was based entirely on an eyewitness identification process that had violated virtually every one of these recommendations.

PART III

Doing Justice

And what does the Lord
require of you
but to do justice,
to love kindness,
and to walk humbly
with your God?

—Micah 6:8

CHAPTER 26

When the DNA Is Gone

MOTHERS TELL THEIR children that there is safety in numbers, but for twenty-two-year-old twin sisters from Sidney, Ohio, this timeworn guidance would be as false as the security it promised. The midsummer sun was still high in the sky at seven in the evening on Saturday, August 20, 1988, when the young women left the Best Products store near the Dayton Mall. Their shopping trip for a bridal shower gift[1] had been fruitless, and they decided to give up for the day and head home. They had just slid into their red Chevy Camaro when a tall, stocky man suddenly appeared. He said that he was a store security officer and that he needed to see their purses.[2]

The women were more annoyed than alarmed; they knew that they hadn't stolen anything. Not surprisingly, they both showed some attitude to the guy. "Here, look through my purse, I didn't take anything," one sister said, swinging her purse to him.

"Where are you from?" he asked.

"Sidney, Ohio."

"Why are you shopping at Dayton if you live in Sidney?"

"We'll shop in Dayton if we want to shop in Dayton," she shot back.

In an instant, the man slipped into the backseat of the car, pulled out a small handgun, and stuck the gun roughly into the ribs of the sister who was at the wheel.

"All I want is a ride out of town," he said. "I have to get out of this town. If you do everything I say, nobody will get hurt."[3]

He said that he had just gotten out of prison. He wanted to go to Columbus, and he didn't know his way around. The young women were suddenly shaken and scared.

The driver followed the man's instructions. He kept the gun in her ribs as she started the car and began to drive. He warned her not to try anything, not to draw any attention to the car. If they got pulled over by a cop, they would be dead.[4]

The man revealed his unpredictable nature throughout this ordeal. Chatty one minute, he would quickly change and become verbally abusive. He told one sister to light a cigarette for him, but she didn't do it quickly enough. "Give it here, bitch!" he demanded.[5]

He asked the women whether they were scared. They both were; one admitted that she was scared to death.[6] Yet, he still asked whether the women wanted to go to Columbus with him. They said no.[7]

He explained that his gun was a .32 automatic with nine rounds. It would kill only at close range. "I'll be at close range, though," he said.[8]

Within a half hour, the man instructed the driver to park the car in a secluded wooded area near Bear Creek bridge in Miami Township.[9] Fear had become silent terror as the young women were ordered to get out of the car. The man marched them into the woods. He must have been mistaken about the intended location, because he said that it was not right, and he forced the women back to the car. He told them to get into the backseat, and he drove them to the other side of the road. He made them get out again, told one of the women to bring two bandannas that were in the car, and then marched them about a half mile into the woods. With the commanding voice of a drill sergeant, he ordered them to stop at a fallen tree where he could sit down—and interrogate them.[10]

He asked them humiliating questions, ordered them to reveal their breasts, and then forced them at gunpoint to give him oral sex. When he ejaculated, semen spilled onto one victim's t-shirt[11] as he stroked her head with his gun.[12]

Curiously, the man, who wore sunglasses the entire time, waited until he had been fully satisfied to demand that the twins blindfold themselves with the bandannas. One sister was terrified, fearing that he was going to shoot them.[13] But he led them back to the car and ordered them to lie down in the backseat. While driving, he rifled through their purses, taking cigarettes and a lighter, asking about the photo of a boyfriend, and stealing their money, about $80.[14]

The man reeked of alcohol,[15] which may have prompted his nonchalant chatting as he drove the women back to the Dayton Mall. Before leaving the car there, he had revealed a lot about himself. He said his name was Roger.[16] He was from Columbus, and he also had spent time in Corpus Christi, Texas.[17] He bragged about working as a hired killer. He said that he got paid $1,000 per hit. He explained that he didn't care about his victims because he wouldn't see them again.[18] As if to justify what he had done to the women, he revealed that when he was twelve years old, his grandfather had raped him, and he had lived with that horror his whole life.[19]

Once back at the mall, he told the twins to stay down until two songs on the radio had finished. He would be watching. If they got up, he would shoot them. Then he left.[20]

In the nearly two terrifying hours from abduction to release, the twins had become victims of crimes legally defined as kidnapping, robbery, rape, and gross sexual imposition.

The case became high-profile in the region when, after the rapes were reported in the local newspaper, another young woman revealed that, two weeks before, she had been abducted and assaulted in similar fashion.

Based on the victims' descriptions, a black-and-white sketch of the perpetrator, with a mustache and sunglasses, was compiled by the Miami Township Police Department. The sketch prompted leads, but for months detectives followed them only to dead ends.

Many believe that another victim emerged from these crimes: Roger Dean Gillispie. Nearly two years after the abduction, the victims identified Gillispie, then twenty-five, from a six-photo array in a process that was seriously flawed in its execution. As of this writing, June 2010, Gillispie has served nearly twenty years in prison for these crimes. Many believe his unwavering claim of innocence.

No evidence tied Gillispie to the crimes, and his life provided no indication that he would have committed them. He came from a loving home in Fairborn, Ohio, had been popular in high school, had no prior problem with the law, and held a good union job working security at the local GM plant.

Dean Gillispie did make one mistake, however. He did not get along with his supervisor at work, who happened to be a former Miami Township police officer. Their growing animosity eventually resulted in Gillispie's termination. It was only then, after the composite sketch of the Dayton-area rapist had been on display in the GM plant lunchroom for nearly two years, that the supervisor presented Gillispie's employment photo to Steve Fritz, the Miami Township supervising police sergeant in the rape case. Fritz was attentive. He and Detective Gary Bailey had pursued many leads from the sketch. None turned out to be credible, however, and Fritz's hope for a meaningful lead quickly faded.

"Bailey and I eliminated Gillispie as a suspect because of the extreme differences in Gillispie's physical appearance compared to the description of the rapist, and because Gillispie, with a solid job and clean record, did not fit the profile of the brazen rapist in this case," Detective Fritz reflected. Noting the contentiousness between the supervisor and Gillispie, Fritz added, "As tips go, the one from [the supervisor] regarding Roger Dean Gillispie was a particularly unreliable one."[21]

Many people can resemble a black-and-white sketch of a man with sunglasses and a mustache, but the victims' first descriptions following the crimes provided full-color detail. The three victims said the perpetrator was a white man, between six foot and six foot three, 200 to 250 pounds, and twenty to twenty-five years old. He had short brown hair with a reddish tint, a mustache,[22] and acne along his jawline.[23] The sisters noted that, although he was white, the man had an unusually dark tan. He wore a short-sleeved unbuttoned shirt exposing his chest. One sister later testified in court that he did not have chest hair.[24] The third victim said that her abductor wore a chain and medallion around his neck and smoked.[25] One of the twins noted that the man had an authoritative voice.

Although Dean Gillispie's size was similar to the victims' description, nothing else matched. The most distinguishing feature of Gillispie's dark brown hair was his premature grey hair, which started coming in when he was in high school and earned him the nickname "Silver Fox."[26] Gillispie had fair skin that burned easily but did not tan. He wore his shirts buttoned in the summer to avoid burning.[27] Gillispie has an unassuming voice, and he has never smoked. In fact he disliked smoking so much that he had a "No Smoking" sign in his truck in those days.[28] Dean wasn't much of a drinker, either. A friend said that he would have a beer, but that was about it.[29] As an adult, he always had a thick mat of hair on his chest that prevented him from wearing chains or medallions.[30] Gillispie was never in the military and never went to Texas. He has no brother who committed suicide.

Had Steve Fritz remained in the police department, Dean Gillispie's life would have been entirely different. However, Fritz retired from the force in July 1990 with one regret: that he had not solved the Dayton rape case.

His replacement was Scott Moore, the twenty-two-year-old son of the chief of police. Fritz, having supervised Moore, said that the young detective "was often overaggressive and would try to cut corners." He and Detective Bailey had to "constantly rein him in and keep an eye on him" because Moore was "difficult to supervise." In law enforcement slang, he was a "cowboy."[31]

Gillispie's former supervisor had been told by Detective Fritz that Gillispie was not a viable suspect, but when Fritz retired, the supervisor presented Gillispie's photo again, along with photos of several others from the GM plant, this time to Detective Moore, who had inherited the case. The rookie detective may have recognized a chance to establish his credibility on the force with the unsolved case. From this point, Moore focused on Gillispie as the suspect.

Gillispie dismissed Moore's initial attempts to question him, but Moore did not give up. Eventually Dean decided to provide reason for Moore to dismiss the allegations. He asked for a polygraph, usually granted to suspects who volunteered, but Moore refused.

The Gillispie family hired J. D. Caudill, the preferred polygraph administrator of the local police departments. Dean was eager to prove his innocence. Sure enough, he passed the polygraph. Caudill's report indicated that Gillispie's numerous responses denying any involvement in the crimes were "truthful."[32] In fact, following the test, Caudill, a retired Dayton police officer, confided to Fritz, "They've got the wrong man."[33] Unfortunately, the test results could not be used in the eventual trial.

Without any evidence connecting Gillispie to the crimes, the case depended on the eyewitness testimony of the victims. Moore contacted the rape victims individually after nearly two years had passed without any progress on the case. He asked them to come in to view a photo lineup. As if it were not obvious enough, he told each of them that he had a suspect, setting the stage for the victims to select the closest person out of the six presented. This effectively canceled the intent of the recommended instruction to eyewitnesses that a suspect *may or may not* be present in the lineup.

Moore's lineup had numerous other flaws. Gillispie's photo ID jumped out from the five others. Gillispie's head was considerably larger in the photos than the men in the other five photos. His photo had a matte finish, while the other five had a glossy finish. The background in Gillispie's photo was yellow; in all the others, it was blue. Gillispie's headshot was so different in its presentation from the other five that the *Dayton Daily News* later reported that it was all but "circled and starred."[34] Research has shown that these kinds of conditions can make mistaken eyewitness identification almost predictable. In fact, in 38 percent of 175 DNA-exoneration cases studied, two or more witnesses made incorrect identifications, fingering the same innocent person![35]

In a case that involved important victim observations regarding the distinctive voice of the perpetrator and unusual hair and skin color, a live lineup would have provided a better opportunity for identification. Experts indicate, however, that even identification from a live lineup is very difficult, if not impossible, two years after the crime. Steve Clark, professor of psychology at the University of California, Riverside, who conducts graduate-level courses on the psychology of eyewitness identification, shared in a declaration attached to Gillispie's 2007 new trial motion a research study showing that after eleven months, the rate of an accurate identification decreased from 67 percent to 11 percent, no better than would occur by chance.[36]

Numerous factors conspired to result in Gillispie's conviction, but the verdict was based solely on the eyewitness testimony of the victims. While the first twin to view the photo lineup could identify Gillispie with only 90 percent certainty,[37] her sister, who went to view the photos the next day, did identify Gillispie. Afterward, Detective Moore told the twins that they had picked the same man and that he was their suspect.[38] The third victim also identified Gillispie from Moore's photo lineup.

Any hesitancy regarding the fact that Gillispie's hair was grey, and not reddish as described by the victims, was explained away by Detective Moore, who told the victims that Gillispie may have dyed his hair.[39] The witnesses did not hear testimony at trial from Gillispie's longtime barber and a forensic scientist. Both said that Gillispie had not dyed his hair.[40]

In spite of one of the twin victims' inability to identify Gillispie with full certainty from the photo array, by the time the victims were called to testify at trial, they were absolutely convinced that Gillispie was the man who had terrorized them. Eyewitness identification experts now know what the jurors did not: that many factors contribute to an increasing certainty by witnesses following a more tentative initial identification; that growing conviction is often the result of tainted memory; and that a witness's increased confidence does not make his or her testimony more reliable.

Gillispie reminds anyone who will listen that prior to the trial he was given the opportunity for a nominal sentence if he would plead guilty to a lesser charge. Dean was not about to live life labeled a sex offender. He refused any plea bargain, and he has steadfastly maintained innocence.

Gillispie was convicted in February 1991 but was granted a new trial months later, due to the discovery of hairs—including one pubic hair—found on the clothing of the victims. The jury, having learned that these hairs did not belong to Gillispie, at first hung, voting 8–4 for acquittal. However, the judge urged them to continue to deliberate and to try to reach a verdict (an instruction known as an Allen Howard charge). Within hours the same day, the jury delivered a guilty verdict. In later interviews with the jurors, Juana Gillispie learned that the eyewitness testimony of the victims, which seemed even more certain in the second trial, had prevailed. Gillispie was convicted and sentenced to 22 to 56 years in prison.

CHAPTER 27

Advocacy After Politics

I N 2006, I WAS A CANDIDATE in the Republican primary for governor of Ohio. Three Republican state officeholders were destined that year for the train wreck of a highly publicized mutual run for governor in a particularly bad year for Republicans.

Contested primary elections can run the risk of electing the most ideologically extreme candidate, who then often cannot survive the general election, and that is exactly what happened. The race eventually came down to two persons. Secretary of State Ken Blackwell campaigned primarily on social issues, while I promoted a plan for operational reform in state government.

As we approached the primary in May 2006, polls showed Blackwell running ahead, but I received every major newspaper endorsement in the state except for my opponent's hometown paper. This was encouraging. I could not remember an election in which a candidate so dominant in newspaper endorsements did not win.

On election night, our family gathered for dinner with the local campaign staff. A few hours later, it became clear that Blackwell had won. I called and congratulated him. Then Nancy, and Cory and John (now twenty-seven and twenty-nine years old, respectively), joined me on the ballroom stage to thank our wonderful campaign workers and supporters. Not prevailing in this enormous effort was very disappointing. Yet, the love I felt for my family at that moment was overpowering. I had lost an election that would deny me the opportunity to implement long-envisioned plans for Ohio. Still, at the end of my comments, as the four of us came together in a tight hug, I felt exceedingly blessed.

Once my successor, Democrat Marc Dann, was sworn in as attorney general on January 8, 2007, I began to look for work. I joined Waite Schneider Bayless & Chesley, a successful boutique law firm. However, within weeks, Republican State Chair Bob Bennett suggested that I think about a vacancy that would be coming up in three years. Tom Moyer, 70, who had served as Chief Justice of the Ohio Supreme Court since 1987, would be ineligible due to age and therefore would not be running in 2010.

FOLLOWING THE SUCCESS of the 2005 Clarence Elkins exoneration, Innocence Project Director Mark Godsey contacted me in the spring of 2007 to ask whether I would join the pro bono team working on the Gillispie case. Dean was coming up for a parole hearing, and Godsey had prepared a comprehensive argument for his release. He knew that Gillispie once again would refuse to acknowledge guilt, and that would work against him. If Gillispie were turned down again, Godsey, armed with new evidence, would prepare a motion for a new trial. In the event that came to pass, he asked, would I be Gillispie's attorney of record?

I reviewed the entire history of the Gillispie case, including Laura Bischoff's excellent series of articles in the *Dayton Daily News*. She reported that when the father of the twin victims read Godsey's presentation on the case to the parole board, even he said that Gillispie did not appear to be guilty of the crimes.[1]

I was leaning toward the same conclusion and told Godsey that I was willing to learn more and would consider getting involved.

Godsey was hoping that Gillispie's record during his sixteen years of incarceration might move the parole board even without an expression of remorse. A model prisoner, Dean had logged more than twelve thousand hours of community service. He had been named one of the Top 100 Individuals for Outstanding Contribution to Community Service by the Ohio Department of Rehabilitation and Correction.[2] Over the years, Gillispie, a talented landscape designer, had received recognition for his work on exhibits, including the "Best in Show" exhibit at the Cincinnati Flower Show. This time, he would have an unusual asset with him when he appeared before the Ohio Parole Board: eight offers of employment on the outside.

Godsey also would share with the parole board new exculpatory evidence that was not revealed during the trial. He would argue that if this evidence had been known by the jury, it would have reached a different verdict.

Dean Gillispie, by then forty-two, had served more time than many convicted murderers. Despite strong advocacy on his behalf by Mark Godsey, who became involved in the case in 2003, parole was again denied in July 2007. Gillispie's next parole hearing was scheduled for February 1, 2011.[3]

When Mark called me at my new law office to discuss the case, he knew that I was supportive of his work. Working with Godsey on the Elkins case had been a pivotal experience for me. The more I had gotten to know him over the past three years, the more impressed I became. Early on, I wondered what kind of guy commits to so many uphill battles. Had he no other options? Godsey's legal writing in the Elkins briefs would tip off anyone to the broad scope of his options: He has a brilliant legal mind and is an excellent writer.

Godsey was an editor of the *Law Review* and graduated Order of the Coif (an honors society for law school grads), summa cum laude, and second in his class from the Moritz College of Law at The Ohio State University. Then he landed a coveted law clerk position for Chief Judge Monroe G. McKay of the U.S. Court of Appeals for the Tenth Circuit in Salt Lake City, Utah. His are the kind of credentials that lead to a partner-track position with a major national law firm. Godsey practiced civil litigation and white-collar criminal defense at Jones, Day, Reavis and Pogue in Chicago and in New York City. He could have stayed on this prestigious and lucrative track.[4]

Instead, Mark chose to become an assistant U.S. attorney for the Department of Justice. Living in Manhattan, he prosecuted federal crimes such as political corruption, organized crime, and hijackings for the Southern District of New York. He supervised FBI investigations, prepared and presented cases to federal grand juries, prosecuted cases before juries and before the bench, and argued before the U.S. Court of Appeals. In the process, some of his work received national attention, and he racked up national awards from the Department of Justice and the FBI.[5]

After six years of this intense work, Godsey accepted a faculty position at the Northern Kentucky University Salmon P. Chase College of Law, where he was a faculty supervisor to the Kentucky Innocence Project. In 2004, he joined the University of Cincinnati Law School. There he has excelled as an award-winning teacher and in his life-changing work with the Ohio Innocence Project.

Godsey had been a pro bono lawyer for the Federal Public Defenders while with Jones, Day, Reavis and Pogue in New York, but it is not surprising that this former federal prosecutor was very skeptical about prisoners' claims of innocence. "When I first got to Northern Kentucky," he recounted, "the law students working with the Kentucky Innocence Project came back one day from a prison trip. They were convinced after speaking with a convict named Herman May that he was *so* innocent. I thought, 'What a load of crap! Can they tell he is innocent just by looking into his eyes?' But a year or so later, DNA proved that May was innocent of the rape and sodomy crimes for which he had been convicted and sentenced to forty years, and he was released from prison. I was stunned and realized that I had to reconsider my own intuition."

It's the same lesson I learned with the Elkins case. That experience prompted me to question my assumptions about those who claim innocence and about those who choose to listen to them. For these reasons, when Godsey called, I listened. Since cofounding the Ohio Innocence Project at the University of Cincinnati College of Law in 2003, his free legal clinic had reviewed more than 4,500 requests from convicts seeking legal assistance. The OIP needed pro bono lawyers like me, and plenty of them.[6]

The Gillispie case, however, was an even tougher challenge for me than the Elkins case. Just as there is no DNA evidence in the overwhelming majority of cases—more than 90 percent of criminal convictions—there is no surviving DNA evidence to rescue Dean Gillispie.

But there is a man we will call KC.

KC's life and lifestyle could best be described as menacing. A former girlfriend, who had a sexual relationship with him from 1999 to 2002, characterized her relationship with KC as "abusive." In an affidavit obtained by Godsey, she described KC. Even though he was "outgoing" and could be "the life of the party," he would become "violent when he drank." She was afraid of him. He had a noticeably loud, authoritative voice. KC had an exclusive fetish for oral sex. He stole from her and burglarized her home, which eventually led to a prison sentence. "I would not be at all surprised if [KC] has raped women and forced them to give him oral sex," she said in the written statement. "That would be right up his alley."[7]

She said that KC always talked about Columbus because of family there, and he also mentioned a connection to Texas. He had some African American ancestry, which may have accounted for his deep tan in summer. He liked to brag about having been a contract killer. He also told her that he had been sexually molested as a child by his father or grandfather, maybe both. He told her that his brother Roger had committed suicide.[8]

In truth, his brother's name was Lavaughn, but he had indeed committed suicide in 1988, about six weeks after the Dayton area rapes. The suicide threw KC into a deep depression. At that time, KC was a correctional officer at the Lebanon (Ohio) Correctional Institution. He often frequented bars around the Dayton Mall; he was picked up once in the afternoon by the Dayton police for driving under the influence of alcohol.[9]

An anonymous caller tipped off the Innocence Project team to look into KC. The ensuing investigation revealed a crime with modus operandi similar to the Dayton-area crimes. It occurred in Fairfield, Ohio—not far from both Lebanon and Dayton—on September 27, 1990, two and a half years after the Dayton-area rapes. An intoxicated young woman left a local tavern with friends and, once outside, exposed her breasts. KC, impersonating a police officer, approached and said that he was taking her in "to press charges."[10]

He quickly ushered the young woman into his car. Her friends alerted police and provided the license plate number. A Fairfield police officer went to KC's apartment and found KC and the abducted, frightened woman.[11] The officer described KC as having light brown hair with a reddish tint and a line of acne along his chin. He wore a chain and medallion. A small handgun was found in his apartment. The officer said that KC appeared to be a white man, but with a very dark tan.[12]

KC was arrested and charged with committing a felony while impersonating a police officer, kidnapping, and unlawful restraint.[13] The charges were later dropped when his victim refused to appear before the grand jury. She left the area without notice.[14]

Remarkably, when a photo taken of KC is placed alongside the composite sketch of the Dayton-area rapist, they are virtually identical.

CHAPTER 28

Discerning
Guilt and Innocence

E VEN THOUGH I WAS no longer in public office—and no longer subject to newspaper coverage that comes with elected positions—joining the Gillispie case felt riskier than my intervention in the Elkins case. I had to be certain that Gillispie was innocent, and without DNA evidence, I could not rely on science. The case for his innocence was compelling, though, plus I respected Mark Godsey's confidence in this determination.

Still, for me, the decision to work on behalf of a convicted felon to reverse a conviction carried a stronger requirement to be on the side of truth than is assumed by many prosecutors and defense attorneys who believe that their primary responsibility is to provide capable representation for their client, be it the state or the accused. Many defense attorneys defend people at trial even when they know or assume guilt. Everyone deserves legal representation in our system, and I am glad that there are those who provide it; however, as a young lawyer, I decided that, for me, it would be difficult, if not impossible, to defend someone I knew to be guilty. I *could*, in good conscience, advocate upon his or her behalf to reach a fair punishment. But this is not the mind-set of successful criminal defense attorneys, and so I did not pursue criminal defense work.

Early in my career, trusting the accuracy of the justice system, I assumed that most persons who were indicted were guilty. I believe that most jurors make a similar presumption. While I still believe that truth sides more often with the prosecution than with the defense, I have learned that the opposite is true in enough cases that the only just presumption that we as lawyers, jurors, and citizens can assume, is the foundational precept of our justice system: A person is presumed *innocent* until proven guilty.

As a young lawyer building a new law firm with my father and my brother, I took nearly every legitimate case that came in the door, including even some defense work. These early career experiences still inform my thinking and did so as I contemplated the Gillispie case.

I remembered the day a well-dressed young African American man came into my office. He needed a lawyer for a serious criminal matter. A high-school graduate and a tradesman, he had never been in trouble with the law. Yet, he had been indicted for felonious assault in the shooting of a parking lot attendant in a bungled burglary attempt. The bullet hit the attendant in the leg and caused him pain, loss of work, and a long period of rehabilitation.

The indictment was based on the eyewitness testimony of the victim, a white man. The young black man, who had been referred by a client of my father's, was scared and worried. He knew that a conviction could carry a sentence of five to ten years in prison. He said that the eyewitness was just plain wrong. He did not carry out this crime.

I was familiar with the fallibility of cross-racial eyewitness identification, and I decided to take the case. Knowing that the state's entire case was based on eyewitness testimony, I moved to suppress this evidence. However, the judge denied the motion. This case was going to come down to whether the jury believed the victim or my client.

As the trial date approached, the prosecutor contacted me to negotiate a plea bargain. He would accept a plea of guilty for aggravated assault, a step down from felonious assault. For this, my client would get up to two years in prison, as opposed to the five to ten years he risked if convicted under the current indictment.

I took the deal to my client. "Absolutely not," he said. "How can I plead guilty to something I didn't do?"

I reported back to the prosecutor, and we prepared for trial.

On the morning of the trial, as all parties and a handful of spectators gathered in the courtroom, my client and I noticed the crime victim, still dependent on a cane from the bullet injury, sitting in the courtroom. He was waiting to be called as a witness.

Just minutes before we were to begin, my client turned to me and asked, "Do you think the prosecutor would still take that deal?"

"I don't know," I answered. "I'll find out."

I approached the prosecutor's table and asked the eleventh-hour question. The prosecutor thought for a minute and said, "Sure, I'll still take the plea."

As I walked back to the defense table, my mind was racing. This unexpected turn of events presented only two explanations, and both were very troubling. Either my client was guilty, or he was innocent but unwilling to gamble ten years of his life on the decision of a jury. How many people—especially those of a racial minority—faced with this decision, have pled to lesser offenses rather than risk getting sentenced to prison for a decade or more? I could not guarantee that we would win this case. It was his life and his gamble. It had to be his decision.

He said that he would take the deal.

The judge was not one to take a guilty plea lightly. He quizzed my client repeatedly. Was he sure he wanted to do this? Did he understand his options and the consequences?

My client stuck with his decision.

The trial was over before it got started, and the outcome made me half sick. I couldn't imagine pleading guilty to something I didn't do. The likelihood that this probably often occurs dawned on me for the first time.

My client and I walked out of the courtroom. He was out on bond and would return in a few days for sentencing. We rushed to hit the elevator button to catch it as the door was closing. It reversed, opened, and we found ourselves staring into the eyes of the parking lot crime victim. We got on the elevator. An awkward silence filled the long moment as we waited for the door to close.

Then my client turned, stared directly at the man, and broke the silence.

"I'm sorry, man. I'm really sorry."

"That's okay," the man answered quietly.

His generous response was moving. He seemed to acknowledge that the tragedy of this event was not limited to his own suffering.

I was shocked. The elevator door opened, and we got off.

I pulled my thoughts together and said, "I am really glad that you told that man you were sorry. You did it, then, right?"

"Yeah," he said soberly. "I never intended to shoot him, I never intended to do that."

He paused and then said, "I was out with friends. It was a dare. One of my friends had a gun, and he pushed it into my hand. I was so nervous, the gun just went off. It was a nightmare."

"Okay," I said, collecting my thoughts. "You will do your time for this. And when it's over, you can put this behind you. Do that. And then get on with your life. You can still have a good, productive life."

He was sentenced to six months to two years. He served five months and got out a month early for good behavior. He called to tell me he was out and thanked me for representing him. I never heard from him again.

Experiences like this breed cynicism in law enforcement officers and prosecutors, and clearly some skepticism is justified. More than thirty years had passed, but this experience is what I thought about when Godsey asked me to get involved in the Dean Gillispie case. I was more worldly wise than I had been at twenty-eight years old, but I still needed to know in my heart that Gillispie was innocent. The fact that he had never wavered on his claim of innocence when he could have pled to a lesser crime and served a minimal sentence was a strong argument in his favor.

I decided to go to meet him.

CHAPTER 29

Seeking Assurance

E VEN IF YOU ARE JUST A VISITOR, a felony prison is a sobering place. Visiting a loved one there must be close to excruciating. I was preoccupied the day I drove to meet Dean Gillispie at the London Correctional Institution. I had been to London, Ohio, many times. As attorney general, I had overseen the operations of the Bureau of Criminal Identification and Investigation (BCI) located there. BCI is Ohio's headquarters for criminal forensic investigation, including the laboratories where fingerprints, DNA, and other criminal evidence are analyzed. Now I was returning, not as the state's attorney, but as a potential pro bono lawyer for a convicted rapist. I wanted to make the most of this visit. I wanted to know unequivocally whether or not I should commit myself to working on behalf of Dean Gillispie.

I asked Mark Godsey to join me. We met outside the prison and went in together. Godsey, of course, knew Gillispie and had met and spoken with him many times. Perhaps that's why he left most of the talking to Gillispie and me that day.

The London Correctional Institution is much like other prisons I have visited. Once we entered the brick building, which dates from the mid-1920s, I felt as if I had entered a world painted in shades of grey. Literally. Humans do not warm up to institutional environments. Think hospitals and grade schools of decades past, before attempts were made to humanize these important institutions. Nothing screams, "Institution!," though, more than a prison. As I walked toward the grey steel security stop, I began to empty my pockets.

"Oh, that's okay, sir," the guard said. "We know who you are."

In spite of the fact that I am more private than some politicians, I was pleased that this law enforcement officer remembered my public service.

"Oh, thank you. How are you?" I said, extending my hand. "I'm Jim Petro."

"Yes sir," the guard responded, shaking my hand. "We were expecting you. Please come this way. I will escort you."

We walked down a grey hallway to another entrance marked by grey bars. A guard was waiting. The barred gate was opened, and I entered. We continued to walk to another closed grey door, this one solid. The guard unlocked it with a key. Godsey and I entered a small room with a table, two chairs, and Dean Gillispie, dressed in a chambray work shirt and blue jeans.

Dean stood up. "Hi, Mark," he said, and turning to me, "Jim, it's nice to meet you."

"Hi, Dean. It's good to meet you as well."

We shook hands and sat down on opposite sides of the table.

Dean Gillispie was forty-two years old. He could have passed for fifty-two. He was fit and had the voice of a younger man, but the grey hair that had started to come in when he was in high school now had turned his head completely white. Only his eyebrows and mustache retained a hint of the darker tint of his youth.

We talked for an hour and a half. Dean Gillispie was not at peace with what had happened to him. Understandably, he would never fully acclimate to the unexpected life he was living. While calm, collected, and productive in prison, his exasperation and frustration surfaced a few times throughout our visit.

I reflected on his initial response to the detective who first contacted him about the rapes some twenty years ago. Detective Moore had also been a young man—a rookie detective described as "a cowboy." When Moore contacted Dean to talk about the rapes, Dean told him he knew nothing about them and had nothing to discuss with Moore. In short, he blew the detective off. I wondered whether the machismo of two young men fanned an escalation of events that had led to a terrible mistake.

Anyone could empathize with Gillispie's frustration. I would have wondered how he could have possibly been convicted if I didn't now understand the power of eyewitness identification. In this case, the identification was made from a sketch, two years after the crime had blurred the glaring dissimilarities between the initial description of the perpetrator by the victims and Dean Gillispie.

And, of course, there was the greatest frustration of all: The evidence that contained the DNA of the rapist was gone. It occurred to me that the victim's semen-stained T-shirt—returned to her by police detectives and apparently discarded long ago—could have prevented the conviction that cost Gillispie nearly two decades in prison.

Dean was likeable, genuine. He seemed honest and uncompromising. Perhaps that is what gave him the stuff to refuse all these years to admit guilt in exchange for his freedom. All the denials made it unnecessary for me to ask him again. He assumed that I believed in his innocence, and he was more right than wrong.

When I felt that I had spent enough time with Gillispie, we stood up and shook hands good-bye. I told him that I was leaning toward getting involved in his case and would decide shortly.

Before doing so, I wanted to talk to two other people: Dean Gillispie's parents.

WE MET FOR LUNCH at a Bob Evans restaurant. I would tell Nancy afterward that Gillispie's parents, Juana and Roger, were "the salt of the earth." They were Christians—not hiding the fact that they were people of faith—living in a small community, and proud parents. Dean, like his siblings, had been popular in school. The Gillispies did not appear to be in any way "dysfunctional." In fact, unlike many complicated family arrangements that can follow one or more divorces, Dean's parents had survived the kind of stressful event that can tear people apart. Everything about them seemed normal, except for the fact that their son had been in prison for nearly eighteen years for a crime they were certain he did not commit.

Dean's father was quiet; his mother was articulate and obviously bright. The Gillispies told me about Dean's once-promising life, his plans for marrying his fiancée, his progress on fixing up the home he had bought, the nightmare of his arrest and conviction, the frustration of all of the failed attempts to receive justice.

I recalled Steve Fritz, who had rejected Gillispie as a suspect in part due to the veteran detective's conclusion that the perpetrator who committed the bold act of abduction and sexual assault of two women in broad daylight was a "brazen, out-of-control criminal." This did not match Dean Gillispie—or his stable family, home, and life history.

Even though Mrs. Gillispie struck me as a strong woman, throughout the conversation, she became emotional, her eyes filling with tears. This had been going on for nearly twenty years, but it was still raw for her.

The Gillispies wanted me to get involved in the case. I didn't know whether that would even help, but I was past the point of walking away. I told them I would join the Innocence effort on behalf of their son.

MY INVOLVEMENT PRESENTED another opportunity for the press to revive its coverage of this case. The Gillispie conviction had been controversial from day one, and the Dayton media had followed the case for nearly two decades. The original detectives on the case and many friends and supporters believe that Gillispie is innocent. I like to think that the media had been partially motivated over the years not just to report this story but also to pursue truth, to prod the system for true justice.

Notwithstanding his outstanding record as an inmate, Gillispie had recently again been turned down by the parole board. Godsey had presented to the board a compelling argument for his release and new evidence of his innocence—work that represented hundreds of hours of investigation and preparation. This work would not be in vain. It was preparation for the next move.

CHAPTER 30

Arguing from the Other Side

ON FEBRUARY 13, 2008, the Innocence Project legal team, on behalf of Dean Gillispie, filed a motion for a new trial. The justice system does not easily grant new trials or hearings after conviction, and trying to achieve this is often a long, difficult process. Respecting verdicts is a cornerstone of our justice system, and for good reason. The system would be in chaos if verdicts were routinely overturned or cases were commonly retried. An appeal process that can go on for years seeks to ensure that the convicted have ample opportunity to challenge any unfairness or error, or to raise new evidence. My experience has been that judges at every level will use every credible reason to deny a new trial.

Our efforts on behalf of Gillispie would need to meet many tough legal requirements. We had to convince the judge that our new evidence was, indeed, new,[1] and that, if the jury had known about it, there was "a strong probability" that it would "change the result" if a new trial were to be granted.[2]

The law required that any new evidence must have been discovered since the trial and that it also could not have been discoverable with due diligence (expected thorough investigation) before the trial. The new evidence must be material to the case, must not just be cumulative to earlier evidence (that is, not just more of the evidence already presented), and it must do more than simply contradict former evidence.[3]

We were convinced that we could meet these standards. Mark Godsey and his legal team claimed new evidence in three areas:

1. "Police corruption, perjury, witness tampering, and other official misconduct of various types by Detective Scott Moore";

2. An alternative suspect, KC;

3. "New scientific understandings in the field of eyewitness identification."[4]

Our team had thirty-four witnesses—including the original police detectives in this case—ready to testify in a new trial to support these claims.

We detailed four areas of serious police misconduct: "(a) the photo identification process; (b) missing supplemental reports; (c) missing campground registration cards for the weekend of August 20, 1990; and (d) witness tampering by Detective Moore."[5]

I thought that our best opportunity for a new trial was our claim of a Brady violation, the withholding of exculpatory evidence from the defense Brady v. Maryland (1963). We argued that Gillispie's lawyers were never given the file that had been accumulated by the first detectives on the case. Not only that, but it subsequently disappeared! The Innocence team learned of its existence only long after the trial when Fritz, the original detective on the case and now a hired private detective working with Gillispie's legal team, mentioned the file. Fritz had always assumed that this record had been turned over to the defense as required by law, but it had not.

As a result of this breach, Gillispie's attorneys did not have the opportunity at trial to provide expert testimony from veteran detectives that would have contradicted Detective Moore. Defense attorneys could have attempted to challenge his tactics, professional demeanor, and conclusions. The records also contained factual information, favorable to Gillispie, which never saw the light of day.

Detective Moore's photo identification procedure was like a demonstration of how to ensure mistaken eyewitness identification and wrongful conviction. We argued that new understanding about how eyewitness testimony is tainted is based on the lessons of DNA and fifteen years of new scientific studies. It had the strong probability of resulting in a different verdict if it could have been presented, especially since the victims' eyewitness testimony was the only evidence that convicted Gillispie.

In our petition for a new trial, we described Detective Moore as "apparently hell-bent on jump-starting his career by cracking the big 'cold case' that the veteran detectives who preceded him could not solve."[6] To that end, we had evidence that Moore had obtained campground receipts that could have collaborated Gillispie's alibi—he was camping with friends the weekend of the crime—yet Moore never turned them over to the defense.

Our motion also presented the compelling evidence that KC was the likely perpetrator of this crime. KC matched the victims' original description in appearance, habits, voice, and revealed history. Furthermore, in addition to KC's being in the area at the time, he was subsequently arrested for abducting a young woman, a crime with a similar modus operandi.

In the hope of confronting KC, Godsey and a private detective drove to Kentucky and were fortunate enough to spot him outside the halfway house where he had been living since his release from prison. He had served time for the burglary of the home of his former girlfriend. Once they had identified themselves, Godsey told KC that they were investigating a rape that occurred in Dayton, Ohio, in 1988. KC claimed no knowledge of the crime. But then he became inexplicably chatty and had many questions about the case. Curiously, he asked what "the ladies" had said about the guy involved. To Godsey, this was very telling, because he hadn't revealed that the crime involved multiple victims!

While we could not prove unequivocally that KC was the perpetrator, given what was now known, he was a far more likely suspect than Dean Gillispie.

The state of Ohio answered our motion and requested summary judgment (outright dismissal) in writing, claiming that our motion offered nothing new. On May 28, 2008, our team replied, countering the state's position. We waited with some confidence for the judge's decision.

Five weeks later, on July 9, 2008, Judge A. J. Wagner ruled. It was almost as if we were reading the prosecution's brief again. The court overruled our motion for a new trial, overruled our motion for post-conviction relief, and sustained the prosecutor's motion for summary judgment. We lost across the board.

Every time I have a disappointment like this, I remind myself that I will still go home to have dinner with my wife. Dean Gillispie's hopes had hung for months on one judge's decision. As in previous failed efforts for reconsideration, he had no consolation, and his disappointment must have been unfathomable.

WE WERE NOT the only ones frustrated by Judge Wagner's ruling.

"Our View: Wagner Sided with Prosecutor Too Fast on Gillispie Case." On July 20, the *Dayton Daily News* ran an editorial that took the unusual position of criticizing a trial judge's decision on a criminal case. "Roger Dean Gillispie should have a new trial or at least a hearing about whether he should have a new trial," it said.[7]

The editorial said that Judge Wagner's decision "ignores too much" and is "dismissive of the possibility that an innocent man has been in jail for almost two decades."[8] The paper called the judge to task for not taking note of new statements from witnesses that contradicted the prosecutor's claims on the key question of the missing police case files.[9]

"The Innocence Project and Mr. Petro say they will appeal to the Second District Court of Appeals," the editorial concluded. "They should. Even if the decision is again not to have a hearing, that decision will have more legitimacy as the result of needed—and more thorough—scrutiny."[10]

Indeed, we made timely notice within thirty days to appeal Judge Wagner's opinion. We recognized, however, that we were running out of options, and all the while, Dean Gillispie was sitting in prison. The case haunted Nancy and me, and everyone working on it. Another year would pass before we would have fifteen minutes to argue on Dean's behalf in front of the Court of Appeals of the Second Appellate District of Ohio.

CHAPTER 31

A Higher Authority

WHY SHOULD IT TAKE a full year to appeal a judge's decision? The process of justice grinds slowly, and this was not an extraordinary amount of time to receive the court records of Judge Wagner's court; to obtain requested materials from the prosecutor's office (they were in no rush to respond), to prepare the appeals brief, to give required time for the state's response, and to get on the court of appeals docket.

Our forty-four-page brief submitted to the court on February 20, 2009, documented abundant legal precedence to demonstrate what we believed were the errors in the trial court's opinion. The failure to turn over evidence to the defense that could discredit the caliber of an investigation has been deemed a Brady violation in other cases. In 2006, an Ohio federal district court ruled in *D'Ambrosio v. Bagley* that "opinions and conclusions of original officers who investigate the case, which contradicted the theory of State presented at trial, would have been admissible at trial and State's failure to disclose them constituted reversible Brady violation."[1]

Could there be a more similar case?

The state's arguments suggesting that the missing files on the original investigation of Gillispie were known or could have been known by the defense at the time of the trial were discredited by the sworn affidavit of Detective Fritz. Defense attorney Dennis Lieberman could never have discovered these original records because, we argued, Detective Moore lied to him personally and again under oath at trial when he claimed that he, Detective Moore, not the original detectives on the case, had initiated the investigation of Gillispie.

In similar fashion, we said that the court erred in its finding that the missing campground receipts were not Brady material. These records could have substantiated Gillispie's alibi. We had submitted as evidence a taped interview with Wade Lawson, a retired homicide detective, who said that Detective Moore had admitted to him that he or a member of his staff had gone to the camp to obtain the records for the weekend of the crime.

We also contended that, consequently, Moore committed perjury at trial "when he said that he only telephoned the campground and asked them to mail some cards to him."[2] The detective left the jury with the impression that when he telephoned the camp and requested registration cards under the name of Gillispie or his friends, no cards related to the weekend in question had been sent. He submitted only three cards not related to the weekend as evidence. However, Lawson said that Moore told him in a casual, impromptu comment, that he, Detective Moore, had taken the registration cards for the weekend of the crime. Our brief reported, "Moore suggested to Lawson that it was not a big deal, because Gillispie's name was not on any of the registration cards for that weekend anyway."[3]

It *was* a big deal, however, because only Gillispie would recognize which of his friends happened to sign the registration card that weekend.

Lawson said that he was 100 percent certain[4] that he had heard Detective Moore correctly. He recognized the importance of this conversation and knew that Moore was contradicting his own testimony at trial. The defense team was disappointed when Lawson subsequently refused to provide an affidavit to this effect. He was concerned about the impact it would have on his relationships with friends in the local police forces. The Gillispie team had anticipated this possibility and had taped its interview with Lawson, without his knowledge.

The Lawson tape was important evidence to the defense. When Judge Wagner received the motion to include the tape as evidence, he requested a conference call with the prosecutor, Mark Godsey, and me. The judge expressed anger at Godsey and stated with some urgency that Godsey's taping the conversation with Lawson without Lawson's knowledge might be illegal and could be referred to the U.S. attorney.

There was a moment of silence on the line before I spoke up: "It would be my opinion, your Honor, that there was no violation in taping that interview."

"He's right, your Honor," the prosecuting attorney agreed.

A violation occurs only when *neither* party to the conversation knows that the conversation is being taped.

The conference call ended and while Judge Wagner took no action against Godsey, he still ruled the tape inadmissible as evidence.

The state's response to our appeal motion recited the long history of Gillispie's attempts to get a different outcome from the justice system. The implication was that this man had been given every opportunity to be heard and that nothing was new. To my way of thinking, Gillispie's long case history could just as easily support his innocence. I asked myself, if I were innocent, would I ever stop trying to prove it?

Gillispie's case history, outlined in the state's appellee's brief, documented the exhausting, expensive struggle that many of the nation's eventually exonerated have experienced:

- The first trial in 1991 resulted in Gillispie's conviction of three rapes that occurred more than two years earlier in two similar incidents with three female victims.

- Gillispie motioned for a new trial based on the discovery of hairs from the crime scene; the motion was granted. The second trial provided the opportunity for the defense to submit new evidence that the hair found on the victim's clothing was not from the victim or Gillispie. After considerable deliberation, the jury was deeply divided. The judge could have declared this a hung jury, a split decision, but instead chose to give an Allen Howard charge. When Lieberman spoke with jurors after the trial, some said that the Allen Howard charge made them believe that the judge thought it should not be so hard to come together in a verdict.

- Gillispie's lawyers filed an immediate second motion for a new trial, alleging prosecutorial misconduct and an abuse of discretion in the court's decision to give the jury an Allen Howard charge. Gillispie's appeal was denied, and he was given an indefinite sentence of twenty-two years to fifty years.

Gillispie was twenty-five years old.

- Gillispie appealed his second conviction, and the court affirmed his conviction. This one was a real heartbreaker. In denying the defense's motion for a new trial based on the argument that Detective Moore's failure to provide the campground records was a Brady violation, the court ruled that even if the jury had learned that Gillispie had spent the weekend at the campground, this would not have changed the verdict because Gillispie would have had time to return home and commit the crime on Sunday. But wait! The crimes occurred on *Saturday*. The court had relied in its decision on a critical factual error: the actual day of the crime![5]

- After hiring new counsel, Gillispie filed a third motion for a new trial, which was denied on July 29, 1993.

- Citing ineffective counsel on several counts, Gillispie filed a petition for post-conviction relief, but on May 18, 1994, the court denied the petition without a hearing.

- On February 1, 1995, the court of appeals affirmed the denial of post-conviction relief, requested in Gillispie's second appeal.

- In 1997 and 1999, Gillispie asked the court for an order to preserve the crime scene evidence for DNA testing and moved for the fourth time for a new trial. He also asked that hairs from the crime scene be tested in the national FBI database. He was denied a new trial but granted the release for DNA testing on September 17, 1999. However, when the packet of hairs was opened, at least one was missing. Gillispie asked the court to hold the state in contempt of its order to preserve the evidence. The court denied this request. At the hearing, the defense attorney "dropped the slide to the floor, shattering it and compromising the integrity of the remaining hairs within."[6]

- The court of appeals affirmed the lower court's refusal to hold the state in contempt over the hair evidence and denied Gillispie's third appeal.

- In March 2003, Gillispie filed a motion for mitochondrial DNA testing, and the court signed orders to allow it. However, the state objected, and the trial court denied another application for DNA testing in 2004, in part because the only surviving hairs had already been determined not to belong to Gillispie and therefore would not have changed the jury's decision.[7]

Dean Gillispie was thirty-nine years old.

CHAPTER 32

Waiting Eighteen Years for Fifteen Minutes

T HE GILLISPIE ARGUMENT before the court of appeals was scheduled for July 7, 2009. This was different from many of Godsey's other cases. With all due respect to the enormous effort required in his success-ful efforts, DNA eventually proved unequivocal innocence. But there was no surviving DNA in this case. Mark had taken it on because he believed in Gillispie, and he had made a commitment from his heart. I could identify.

I prepared as much as I ever had for any other case. This had to be the best argument of my life. Performance in a courtroom is very much like any other competition. I don't like the sports analogy, but it comes to mind. The American system of criminal justice is adversarial and competitive. I now believe that conviction errors are more likely when boundaries are pushed by participants on either side in the heat of the competition that occurs every day in hundreds of courtrooms. Like a professional athlete, I had the train-ing, the experience, and the technical skills to do the job, but there can be good days and bad days for any competitor.

I was also especially concerned that day over an increasing problem. For months, my voice had been raspy. I assumed it was from overuse. Years of advocating by day and giving political speeches at night can take a toll. As we had approached this argument, it had gotten worse. Still, Mark and I had decided that I should argue this one. My voice sounded horrible to me on this important day, but at least it might get the judges' attention. The fact that they might have to focus more than usual to hear might be an advantage.

Our goal was to convince the three-judge panel—Judges James Brogan, Mike Fain, and Jeffrey Froelich—to either grant Gillispie a new trial or order a hearing on the new evidence we were presenting. Our preference was a new trial, because we felt certain that the evidence now in hand would make it very tough for the prosecutor to make the case against Dean. A less favorable decision would be the hearing. The outcome that would be most consistent with Gillispie's past efforts would be a denial of both a new trial and a hearing.

I led off with our argument supporting the Brady violation. Within a few moments, the judges interrupted me, as expected. Having read the motions, judges typically jump in early with questions. They were most interested in the evidence about KC. We went back and forth on many details concerning our evidence implicating KC. I have always performed best in a question-and-answer format and, thank God, I began to feel on top of my game. The judges made an exception to the fifteen-minute rule. They acknowledged that this was an important case, that significant issues had been raised. Ultimately, both sides had closer to thirty minutes, and we had the final word. When it was over, I felt that I had made the points we had wanted to make, and I had done my best.

I returned to the defense table, and Mark Godsey, always generous, said, "You were spectacular."

I didn't need the flattery, but I did cherish the fact that he was satisfied with the effort.

I caught the eyes of Dean's parents and went into the gallery to hug Juana Gillispie. She was clearly pleased, although emotional. "I don't know what they will rule," I said, "but I think we gave Dean our best shot today."

CHAPTER 33

Tough Decisions

"**L**OU GRIECO SAID THAT you did a good job arguing the Gillispie case last week," volunteered one of the reporters at the *Dayton Daily News*. His colleague Grieco had been covering the most recent evolution of the Gillispie saga for the paper and had been in the court of appeals courtroom. "We were talking about how this might help your run for chief justice. What do you think?"

Twenty-eight years in elected public office, and a question like this still grated on me. "I haven't even decided whether or not I am running," I replied. "I doubt that my involvement in this case will have any impact."

I guess I could not blame the speculation. However, there is a cynicism that implies there has to be a political motive behind everything an elected public official—or a former one—does. This is one of the "cons" on my list every time I have considered running for office. Clearly, the "pros" usually prevailed in the past, but as I made the transition from my late fifties into my sixties, after a very stressful gubernatorial primary, the cons had become more competitive.

Honestly, I was not sure that chief justice was a good fit. My strength had been in executive positions. Still, as attorney general, I had been personally involved in overseeing the opinions of the attorney general, which were similar in authority and format to judicial opinions. My legal background was substantial at all levels of the justice system. The chief justice had a significant management role as the overseer of the entire court system in the state. Perhaps this could be an avenue for utilizing my experience.

Still, I was very torn. Sitting Justice Maureen O'Connor had come off of a strong re-election campaign in 2008. Not only had she announced that she planned to run for chief justice, but she was making appearances all over the state to boost her candidacy. Nevertheless, I was receiving considerable encouragement to run.

Down deep, however, I could not get fully excited about this race. Instead of asking myself the same question the reporter had asked, I found myself wondering just the opposite: How would a campaign for chief justice impact my work on the Gillispie case, as well as a half dozen other involvements that had the potential to change public policy? I would have to give up all of these efforts if I were fortunate enough to run and win.

And, of course, there was the raspy voice. I finally went to a voice specialist and had a laser scraping of my vocal chords. The doctor said my voice would be back in a few days. But that didn't happen. Weeks and then months later, I still sounded as if I had laryngitis. How could I campaign without a strong voice?

Uncertainty brings its own stress. At about this time, a burden I hadn't even acknowledged began to lift. I began to value my emerging role and envision new ways to be productive. My past experience had opened doors to meaningful challenges and gratifying work. And, for the first time in years, none of these depended on an election.

I made the decision. I might not be finished with public office, but I would not run for chief justice.

Not long after this, I changed law firms. I had discovered that I needed the broader legal backup of a full-service firm. I went with Roetzel & Andress, a firm with all of the support talent I could imagine.

Sadly, several months later, after presiding over cases on Wednesday of the first week of April 2010, Ohio Supreme Court Chief Justice Tom Moyer admitted himself into the hospital on Thursday morning. He unexpectedly died the next day. Moyer, the longest-serving chief justice in the country, left a sudden void on Ohio's high court. Governor Strickland appointed Franklin County Probate Judge Eric Brown to fill the position. But to keep it, Brown would have to prevail over Justice Maureen O'Connor in November 2010.

CHAPTER 34

A Partial Victory

O N JULY 24, 2009, just over two weeks after our arguments on behalf of Dean Gillispie before the court of appeals, the court released its decision. The three-judge panel's decision was consistent with prior decisions in ruling that no Brady violation had occurred in the state's handling of the campground records.

"Even if the campground registration cards could have confirmed that one of Gillispie's friends had registered a campsite," the judges wrote, "the jury would still have been required to accept testimony that Gillispie had been there. That testimony was presented to the jury."[1]

I was really surprised by this conclusion. Two of Gillispie's friends had testified at trial that they had been with Dean on the day of the rapes. However, the written camp registration records to support this testimony could have tipped the scales for Dean. Eyewitness testimony from victims is not easily discredited. Without the records, it was a classic case of "he said, she said." In the Clarence Elkins case, we had seen that the alibi testimony of someone close to the defendant—in this case, his wife—is often trumped by the victim's eyewitness testimony. In our view, supporting recorded documentation could definitely strengthen the testimony of alibi witnesses and make a difference in the trial's outcome.

The court said that even if Detective Scott Moore's alleged statements regarding how he obtained the camp records might contradict his courtroom testimony, Moore's comments "are not material to whether Gillispie was actually in Morehead, Kentucky, during the weekend of August 20, 1988." The decision contended, "We fail to see how Moore's 2003 statements would 'disclose a strong probability that it will change the result if a new trial is granted.'"[2]

The court added that any error by the trial court in its denial of Gillispie's motions to supplement the record (with the taped interview with Lawson) was "within the trial court's discretion."[3]

The court further ruled that there was no Brady violation regarding the original records of the first investigation of Gillispie by the veteran detectives. "If this evidence existed, the defense knew of its existence because its investigator, Fritz, put it into the file," the court opined.[4]

Once again, a court gave no credence to Detective Steven Fritz's sworn affidavit that he did not know that the file had not been turned over to the defense attorney, that he had no opportunity to discover this.

The court ruled that even if the detectives' opinion that Gillispie was not a viable suspect had been known, this information had "little, if any relevance" because the "affidavits do not assert that the detective's opinion was based on the discovery of evidence that would have exonerated Gillispie, such as evidence to support an alibi."[5]

The court distinguished Gillispie's claim of a Brady violation from that of the similar example in *D'Ambrosio v. Bagley*, in which the Brady violation was upheld, saying: "Unlike the reports in *D'Ambrosio*, Bailey and Fritz's affidavits do not indicate that their supplemental reports contained undisclosed information that contradicted the State's theory of how the rapes occurred or that tended to show that Gillispie was not the perpetrator. Simply stated, Bailey and Fritz's affidavits contain no facts that undermine the State's case against Gillispie, which was based substantially on the eyewitness identifications."[6]

But, indeed, there was factual evidence that could exonerate Gillispie in the original file. Detective Bailey remembered that one of the victims had made an important observation. When the rapist lowered his trousers, she observed his pants size. Dean Gillispie was a bigger man. He could not have fit into those trousers!

The court also overruled our second assignment of error: the lower court's decision to ignore evidence of witness tampering in Detective Moore's treatment of Gillispie's former girlfriend. She stated that Moore "harassed her and pressured her to testify against Gillispie 'the way he wanted me to.'"

She felt that she had been manipulated and lied to by Moore and that her resulting comments were, in essence, edited by the detective as he selectively recorded only parts of his interviews with her.[7]

She wanted to testify for the defense, but she felt that the transcript of her interview with Detective Moore was not an accurate reflection of the conversation. Gillispie's lawyer concluded, "Her testimony…was not worth the risk."[8]

Two strikes. But we weren't out.

The third error we argued was the trial court's decision to not grant Gillispie a new trial in light of our compelling new evidence of Dean's innocence with the emergence of the new, alternative suspect, KC. On this one, the court agreed with us:

"…Gillispie has presented new evidence regarding KC, consisting of statements that KC has used the name 'Roger' to refer to his brother, even though that was not his brother's name; that KC's voice was distinctively authoritative; that KC had bragged that he was a contract killer; and that he had asked how the 'ladies' had described their assailant even though he was not told that there were multiple rape victims."[9]

The court particularly noted the new evidence that KC liked to brag that he was a contract killer—an unusual bragging right and a significant fact, since both sisters had written in their statements to the police, "the assailant had said that he kills people for a living for $1,000."[10]

"In our view," the court continued, "the additional evidence regarding KC constituted 'new evidence' and was sufficient to require a hearing to flesh out the evidence and to determine whether a new trial…is warranted based on that evidence."[11]

Finally, the court ruled that the advance in eyewitness research we submitted was, at best, cumulative and did "not create a strong probability that it will change the result if a new trial is granted."[12] However, the court suggested that the trial court "may consider the effect that such testimony [regarding eyewitness identification] might have in conjunction with any new evidence regarding KC."[13]

The *Dayton Daily News* called the decision a "partial victory" for Dean Gillispie.[14] I was initially disappointed but, at the same time, relieved. Post-conviction relief—outright vacation of the conviction or a new trial—would have been a home run, but given the history of Gillispie's strikeouts, this decision was at least a double. Finally a door had been opened a crack for Dean Gillispie. We would have the opportunity to go back to the judge who had ruled against us and try to change his mind with evidence pointing to a much more likely perpetrator.

CHAPTER 35

Brady's Catch-22

BEFORE FOCUSING ON the hearing before Judge Wagner, I suggested to Mark Godsey that we submit to the court of appeals a motion for reconsideration on the question of a Brady violation with regard to the original investigative reports prepared by Detective Gary Bailey. The reports were never provided to the defense as required by law. Of course, the "we" in this suggestion translated into another seven-page motion written by Mark and submitted to the court on August 3, 2009.

The court had ruled that the reports were nothing more than the opinion of the first investigators. The court distinguished Gillispie's claim from the similar question regarding missing police reports in *D'Ambrosio* by saying that Gillispie's claim included no new "facts." Godsey's reconsideration brief suggested that the court had overlooked important facts undisclosed to the defense before the trial.

Godsey wrote that Detective Bailey's affidavit said that he remembered doing his due diligence on Gillispie. After nearly two decades, he could not recall all of the details of the investigation, but he remembered concluding that Gillispie was not a "viable suspect."[1] At the time, Sergeant Steve Fritz agreed.

Godsey argued that it was not the burden of the detectives to remember the specific facts of an investigation from so long ago. "The State cannot improperly lose or destroy reports, and then argue that the ensuing Brady claim is not viable because the witness does not remember each and every minute factual detail of the missing reports. Once the reports are deemed missing," Mark wrote, "the burden of overcoming any ambiguity about a 'fact' created by the report's absence is on the State."[2]

Godsey repeated an important fact not available to the defense at the original trials. "By way of one example, Detective Bailey's affidavit said, 'I seem to recall that one of the victims noticed after the perpetrator dropped his pants that she saw the pants size on a tag inside he pants. The pants size did not fit the build of Gillispie.'"[3]

Detective Fritz's affidavit pointed out another fact that went to the heart of Gillispie's defense argument that he had been "charged as a result of Detective Moore's incompetence and recklessness."[4] Fritz and Bailey had actually taught classes on sex crime investigations at the Ohio Basic Police Academy. They developed a profile on the perpetrator of this crime. Fritz said, "I had never seen a sex crime this brazen. This was a rapist who abducted and raped two women simultaneously in broad daylight."[5]

Their profile was of an out-of-control perpetrator with a history of sex crimes. Dean Gillispie simply did not fit this profile.

The defense felt that Moore's failure to hand over the report supported its view that he had been both "incompetent and reckless." Godsey reminded the court, "Defendants have a constitutional right to present police incompetence as a defense at trial."[6] He cited three similar cases in which courts had considered such a failure a Brady violation.

Two days later, on August 11, Prosecuting Attorney Mat Heck submitted a brief arguing that Gillispie had not proved that the supplemental reports ever existed.[7]

On August 25, the court of appeals released its opinion. Gillispie's application for reconsideration was denied. The court did "not find that there was reasonable probability that the result of the proceeding would have been different had the information regarding the pants size been disclosed to the defense." The court added, "...Bailey's statement in this respect is speculative."[8]

The opinion concluded, "Whether or not the information regarding the pants size, or any information allegedly known by Fritz or Bailey, is relevant to the issue which has been remanded is a question for the trial court."[9]

The decision was another disappointment.

We still had the hearing in the trial court, however. We would be returning again to Dayton, home of the trial court and the court of appeals, for another formidable attempt: challenging a trial judge to reverse his opinion. We had left no stone unturned for Dean Gillispie thus far; we would turn over one more as we checked off our dwindling options.

GODSEY AND I DECIDED to try to take the court of appeals' decision on the Brady issue to the Supreme Court of Ohio. Mark would urge the high court to provide guidance on the application of law on what he called "an important sub-point for future application of *D'Ambrosio*." It seemed to us that the appeals court's decision had created a Catch-22 for any defendant or convict who alleged that information supporting his innocence had been withheld. The court of appeals essentially said that you can't claim a Brady violation unless you can show that the information withheld would be relevant to the trial and verdict and could have changed the outcome of the trial. But wait! How can the defendant show this, if the information was withheld from him? Catch-22!

Godsey's memorandum focused on two arguments. The first was that the nondisclosure of the investigative reports should have been deemed a Brady violation. Mark provided examples of how these reports would have enabled the defense to challenge Detective Moore's professionalism.

One example: It was improper in this case to use a photo lineup. Not only because the victims' identification of the suspect occurred two years after the crime but also because so much of their descriptions of the perpetrator "hinged on subtle distinctions such as hair color shade and sound of voice."[10] The fact that Detective Moore was willing to pursue convicting a man by sidestepping the disparities of the victims' descriptions of the suspect through a less comprehensive identification procedure was another example of his subpar handling of the case, if not something worse.

Godsey offered the court a suggested proposition of law, an application of the *D'Ambrosio* decision:

> In a case where the defendant first learns nearly 20 years after his conviction that Brady material was not disclosed prior to trial, and obtains the affidavit of a law enforcement witness stating that exculpatory evidence existed, to the best of that witness's recollection, in written reports that had last been in the possession of the State, the State—who is at fault for not disclosing the report in a timely manner when memories were fresh—bears the burden of proving that the undisclosed report was not exculpatory.[11]

Unfortunately, there was no guarantee that the state supreme court would grant our petition to review the case. In fact, if I were to guess the odds, I had to admit that it was likely that the court would pass on this one.

CHAPTER 36

Pesky Issues

C ONVINCING JUDGE A. J. WAGNER to reverse his own decision on Dean Gillispie would be a formidable challenge. The judge had consistently sided with Prosecutor Mat Heck.

The Heck name was well established in Montgomery County law and politics. Mathias H. Heck Sr. had been county prosecutor when Mathias H. Heck Jr. was a boy. After becoming an attorney, Heck Jr. rose up in the prosecutor's office and eventually became chief trial counsel prosecuting the county's death penalty cases. He became county prosecutor in 1992 and has been re-elected without interruption through this writing.[1]

Mat Heck is a strong personality and political force in his county. When scandals resulted in Democrat Mark Dann's resignation as Ohio attorney general in May 2008, Heck was on Governor Ted Strickland's list of replacement candidates. I've heard it said that in Montgomery County you don't want to cross Mat Heck.

Throughout this long challenge in the courts, I was baffled by Heck's unwavering confidence in Dean Gillispie's guilt. Recognizing the weaknesses in this case based completely on eyewitness identification two years after the crime and utilizing flawed procedures—and in light of what the past twenty years have taught us about memory and eyewitness procedure—I wondered how he could categorically deny the possibility of error with Gillispie.

Some prosecutors were responding to the lessons of DNA by becoming receptive to post-conviction DNA testing in selected cases. When the *Columbus Dispatch's* yearlong investigation of Ohio's experience with requests for post-conviction DNA testing resulted in the paper's naming the thirty cases most worthy of testing (out of more than 313 requests), many Ohio prosecutors were challenged to take a stand on this issue.

Mat Heck chose to oppose the testing. Chris Dillon served twenty years for rape, robbery, and kidnapping, crimes allegedly committed in 1986, when he was twenty-six years old. Even though Dillon was paroled, he wanted to prove his innocence. The *Dispatch* included his case in the batch of thirty recommended for the free DNA testing offered as a public service by DNA Diagnostics Center, a DNA testing lab with sites in all fifty states. The paper found no prior convictions for Dillon and selected his case because it was based "mainly on information by a man already charged with sex crimes" and eyewitness testimony, "possibly mistaken."[2]

Because Ohio's law at that time required that a convict have at least a year left in prison to qualify for testing, Dillon's request was rejected by a judge. Nevertheless, Heck could have followed other prosecutors in permitting testing. Since the *Dispatch* had spent many investigative hours determining the most worthy cases, this would have been a no-brainer for many prosecutors.[3]

However, in denying the testing, Heck said that the evidence in the case was gone. The *Dispatch* observed that Heck "hasn't provided details on where it went."[4] The paper also noted that some involved in the system say that "prosecutors make it nearly impossible for the law to work in favor of the inmates [who seek post-conviction testing]."[5] The Ohio Innocence Project reported that Prosecutor Heck had repeatedly turned down requests for post-conviction DNA testing in Montgomery County.

THE HISTORY OF THE Gillispie proceedings with Judge Wagner had not generated any warmth between the judge and the Ohio Innocence Project.

Knowing this, Godsey felt uncomfortable around the judge. For the first time in his legal career, Mark wondered whether we should ask the judge to recuse himself from the hearing that the court of appeals had granted Gillispie. We were not convinced that the judge was still of an open mind on this case.

I had known Judge Wagner in a different capacity. When I was auditor of state, he was county auditor of Montgomery County. I liked and respected him. I could understand that the decisions required of a trial judge could be sobering.

Under the established procedure, after the court of appeals ordered a hearing for Gillispie, Judge Wagner issued a "docket call." This required that all parties, including Dean, appear in his courtroom so that the court could determine the date and time of the upcoming hearing. The procedure would take all of five minutes, and the entire affair, maybe fifteen—for the other side, that is. The prosecutor's offices (as well as the appeals court offices) and Judge Wagner's courtroom are all located in the Montgomery County Courthouse. I would imagine that these fellows saw each other frequently, working in the same building and living in the same area.

However, for our side, this five-minute court appearance took up a good part of the day. Mark Godsey had to make the 110-mile round trip from Cincinnati, and I had to make the 130-mile round trip from Columbus. Our inconvenience, though, paled compared to what the appearance required of Dean Gillispie: two weeks of boredom, displacement, and accompanying anxieties while he languished in the Montgomery County Jail.

There was a last-minute cancellation of the first of these docket calls, and thereafter we learned that Dean had been transported to the Montgomery County Jail for the hearing anyway. And he was still sitting there. As his attorneys, we had every right to expect that we would be notified that he was to be transported. If we had, we would have asked that he not be. There was no useful reason for him to be there. Even though his cell in prison was small, it was his only home. There he could at least occasionally work on his painting or on the garden displays that had won him accolades. These things kept a man, with a perfect eighteen-year prison record, sane. His stay in the county jail made him increasingly anxious; for one thing, Dean feared that his absence from prison would erode the minimal benefits of good time served.

Those who believe that Gillispie is guilty would, understandably, have no sympathy for him in this situation. However, those of us who saw him as our innocent brother, son, or father were shocked at the lack of respect this action revealed for both Dean Gillispie and his attorneys. Godsey, furious, sent Judge Wagner a letter requesting that our client be returned to his prison cell immediately. He also requested that we be notified if the thought of transporting Gillispie came up again.

Due to the judge's prior decision on the original motion, and his disagreement with Godsey, we were concerned about our opportunity for a fair and impartial hearing. Godsey and I discussed this at length and finally decided that it would be in Dean's best interest to request that Judge Wagner recuse himself. We decided that I would be the one to raise this delicate issue.

At a scheduled docket call a few weeks later, Judge Wagner set the date of the hearing for December 18, 2009. Following this announcement from the bench, I requested a sidebar conference with the judge. The assistant prosecutor and I approached, and I began my request.

My voice was raspy, but I proceeded. "Your Honor," I said in a nonthreatening tone, "as attorney general, I had a few occasions in which I realized that I had made up my mind on an issue, and yet it was still being challenged. I made the decision in those instances to step aside and let a set of fresh eyes and ears consider the issue. You have certainly heard a lot about this case, and it would not be unusual for you to have made up your mind. Yet, as was indicated by the reversal of the court of appeals in enabling this hearing, others may have a different perspective. In the interest of having no one question the outcome, I respectfully request that you consider recusing yourself and allowing a judge less familiar with the case—a judge who has no history with this case—to preside over this important hearing."

"Counselor, that will not be necessary," Judge Wagner responded. "I assure you that I can give a fair opinion in this case."

I had made my pitch. I could see that the judge was not about to voluntarily step aside, and I did not think that pushing this would benefit our cause. The docket call was over. I requested that Gillispie be returned to his prison cell as soon as possible, and then I drove back to Columbus, thinking the entire time about whether, as part of our duty to our client, we should formally petition the Ohio Supreme Court to remove Judge Wagner from the case.

A second issue also weighed heavily on my mind. Between Godsey and me, I had the better rapport with Judge Wagner. However, it was becoming clear that I would not be arguing this case on December 18. My voice still had not returned to full strength, and so my doctor ordered another laser surgery. This time, the pathology report bore bad news: cancer. As a PET scan revealed, a malignant tumor in my neck was restricting my vocal cord.

I immediately began a protocol including chemotherapy and seven weeks of radiation therapy. The doctors told me that I would lose my voice completely within two weeks, and it would not return until at least two weeks following the treatment. If I were lucky, I might speak again sometime before Christmas. The prognosis was very good; my condition was treatable. But my voice would be only a whisper on December 18.

CHAPTER 37

Addressing
Unacceptable Error

IN DISCUSSING HIS WORK in fourteen wrongful conviction cases, private investigator Martin Yant made an interesting observation. While DNA had freed from prison many innocent people, it may have actually raised barriers for innocent inmates who had been convicted of crimes with no DNA evidence. For some prosecutors, no DNA means no second look. Once again, I wondered why my friend Mark Godsey had gotten involved with Gillispie, the case with no DNA.

Godsey and the young Ohio Innocence Project had enjoyed successes following the release of Clarence Elkins on December 15, 2005. On Mother's Day 2006, Chris Bennett walked out of prison after serving four years of a nine-year sentence for vehicular homicide. He was convicted on the theory that he was driving drunk, causing an accident that took the life of his best friend, Ron Young. The Innocence Project team proved through DNA analysis of blood on the passenger side of the van, as well as testimony from a new eyewitness, who had seen Bennett in the car, that Bennett was actually the *passenger*, a new understanding that led to his release.[1] This came as news even to Bennett, who had suffered severe head trauma and therefore had no memory of the crash.

Then in August 2008, in a high-profile case in Ohio, fifty-two-year-old Robert McClendon was exonerated after serving eighteen years, including one year before trial, for the 1990 rape of his ten-year-old daughter. The Innocence Project team was assisted in this win by the *Columbus Dispatch* and, eventually, Franklin County prosecutor Ron O'Brien.

It was the case that would put a face on an emerging reform movement in Ohio. McClendon, who had always proclaimed his innocence, had not qualified to have the crime scene DNA evidence from his case tested. Post-conviction DNA testing for Ohio inmates became possible only with the passing of Ohio Senate Bill 11 in 2003.

It opened the door, but just barely. Because lawmakers feared an avalanche of frivolous applications, the law was restrictive in defining eligibility. If that weren't enough, it also was opposed or not taken seriously by many prosecutors and judges, and it was challenged repeatedly in the courts, delaying and diminishing its impact. In fact, more than four years later, in January 2008, the *Columbus Dispatch* reported that only 313 of more than 50,000 Ohio prisoners had applied for DNA testing.[2]

In nearly two-thirds of these cases, when prosecutors agreed to search for the evidence, it had been lost or destroyed. Ohio had no requirement that evidence be retained or catalogued. In 53 cases, judges did not respond or provide a reason for denial, as the law required. When they did offer a reason, it was often a brief, unexplained denial. In 13 cases, testing had not been performed more than a year after it had been authorized. Bottom line: Testing had been done in only 14 cases in the more than four years since the law passed.[3]

In January 2007, reporters Mike Wagner and Geoff Dutton began the *Dispatch* investigation that included the filing of 150 public records requests and interviews of three-dozen current and former inmates, prosecutors, judges, and victims. It resulted in a series of articles, "Test of Convictions," starting in January 2008, that not only raised awareness of a troubling post-conviction DNA policy but also began to prompt changes in some jurisdictions' handling of DNA evidence and inmates' applications for testing.

Because the law required that a convict be in prison to apply, even parole could lose its appeal for some. "If it means a chance to clear my name and get this test, I would rather stay in prison than be paroled," said McClendon, who had been convicted in 1991 and was eligible for parole in 2007.[4]

He applied to have the evidence of his case tested in 2004. However, McClendon received no response for months and may never have gotten an answer if it hadn't been for the efforts of the Ohio Innocence Project and the *Columbus Dispatch*.

But even in this high-profile situation, nine of the *Dispatch*-selected applicants were denied testing due to opposition by judges or prosecutors or loss of evidence.[5] A convict's fate regarding evidence testing often rests on the luck of the draw: on who happens to be county prosecutor. Initially skeptical that anything could be learned from McClendon's evidence, Franklin County Prosecutor Ron O'Brien had opposed his application for testing in 2004. Nevertheless, this time he agreed to the testing.

The best evidence in the case, cotton swabs from the rape kit, had been destroyed, but O'Brien's office located the victim's underwear for testing. In 1990, the police lab had turned up nothing on the undergarment, but now DNA Diagnostics was able to find and utilize enough scant DNA to make a definitive determination: Robert McClendon was not a match and not the rapist.[6]

Judge Charles A. Schneider released the father of five on August 11 to a large crowd of family including his children and grandchildren. Unfortunately, McClendon's parents and his grandparents were not present for his day of redemption. They had passed away while he was in prison.[7]

When asked about the eighteen years he lost, McClendon demonstrated the same lack of anger observed in Clarence Elkins and Michael Green. Perhaps prison requires that you either banish anger or be tortured by it. "You can't make it up," McClendon said about his lost time. "You just have to move forward."[8]

DNA exonerations are often an awakening for those involved. "Hopefully, after all this, he lives with his family and rejoices," said O'Brien, adding, "I don't want anybody in jail who doesn't belong there."[9] I have known the lanky, likeable, straight-talking Ron O'Brien for more than thirty-five years. As a new Franklin County assistant prosecutor just out of law school in 1973, I became friends with two other new employees in the prosecutor's office: Greg Lashutka and Ron O'Brien. We may not have known it then, but we all had politics and public service in our future. Many years later, Greg was elected mayor of Columbus in 1991 (and 1995), and, in 1996, Ron was elected Franklin County prosecutor. The voters returned him to that office without interruption in 2000, 2004, and 2008.

Occasionally, Ron considered a run for attorney general. I encouraged him, because he would be excellent, but I also cautioned him about the risk of the leap to statewide office. Besides, I told him more than once, "You already have the best job in the state." In the realm of criminal law and public safety, the county prosecutor (in some states known as the *state's attorney* or the *district attorney*) in a populous county with a major urban core, is front and center to both public security and justice.

Just as I had been initiated into a new understanding of wrongful convictions through the Clarence Elkins case, Ron O'Brien had his confidence in the infallibility of convictions shaken by Robert McClendon. Many of O'Brien's prosecutor colleagues had fought or ignored applications from inmates desperate to test evidence. O'Brien felt that much of this was a result of applying the law as it was written. For some, this could be justification for denying testing. But after McClendon, O'Brien said, "We need to look beyond whether they're entitled to it [DNA testing]."[10]

Ron told me that one takeaway for him was that if a suspect is eager to take a polygraph or provide DNA samples, you probably should look carefully at any exculpatory evidence, and if a suspect passes a polygraph, it might be time to broaden the focus of the investigation.

While the *Dispatch* series was raising questions about Ohio's policy regarding post-conviction access to DNA testing and wrongful conviction, I was working with Mark Godsey in advocating new reform legislation that would address the very flaws being exposed in the paper. Ohio's new governor, Ted Strickland, and Attorney General Mark Dann were just getting used to their new offices when the Innocence Project presented them and the Ohio General Assembly a forty-two-page memorandum outlining six suggested reforms:

1. Requiring the preservation of evidence and DNA;

2. Establishing a Criminal Justice Accuracy Commission;

3. Amending the current post-conviction DNA statute to allow for paroled or dead inmates to obtain DNA testing to prove their innocence and find the true perpetrator;

4. Improving police eyewitness identification procedures;

5. Establishing procedures for the videotaping of police interrogations and confessions;

6. Establishing an Ohio Forensic Science Commission.[11]

The main points of the recommended reforms were fairly self-explanatory. An essential improvement in eyewitness identification procedures was the requirement of blind administration, meaning that the officer conducting the lineup could not know which person, if any, was the suspect. The same process gives confidence to the results of testing in consumer products. Whether choosing between Coke and Pepsi, or making a selection that can take a person's freedom for life, blind administration works for both sides because it rules out any concern that the process was purposely or inadvertently prejudiced.

We were striking while the iron was hot. Governor Strickland had recently indicated his understanding of the issues and his probable support. "Even if you don't have any sympathy for the wrongfully convicted, the other side of the coin is a guilty person has gone scot-free," he said after the McClendon exoneration.[12]

The *Dispatch* series and McClendon's release had created some buzz about wrongful conviction and a brief platform for promoting reform. Perhaps the slow drip of DNA exonerations, beginning in Ohio in 1994, was also making a gradual impact on public consciousness:

1994 Brian Piszczek served three years of a fifteen- to twenty-five-year sentence for rape, assault, and burglary before exoneration.

1996 Walter Smith served ten years of a seventy-eight- to one-hundred-ninety-year sentence for rape, kidnapping, and robbery before exoneration.

2001 Anthony Michael Green served thirteen years of a twenty- to fifty-year sentence for rape and aggravated robbery before exoneration. DNA also confirmed the actual perpetrator.

2001 Danny Brown served eighteen and a half years of a life sentence for aggravated murder and aggravated burglary. DNA also identified the actual perpetrator.

2005 Clarence Elkins served six and a half years (seven and a half including his jail time before trial) of a life sentence for murder, attempted aggravated murder, and rape. DNA also identified the actual perpetrator.

2005   Donte Booker served fifteen years of a fifteen- to twenty-five-year sentence for rape, kidnapping, aggravated robbery, and gross sexual imposition. DNA proved his innocence after his parole.

2008   Robert McClendon served seventeen years of a fifteen-years-to-life sentence for rape and kidnapping before exoneration.

2009   Joseph Fears Jr. served twenty-five years of a fifteen- to seventy-five-year sentence for two rapes and aggravated robbery before being exonerated of one of two rapes. DNA evidence survived only from one of the rapes, and the testing also identified the actual perpetrator.[13]

The benefits of new legislation, Senate Bill 77 sponsored by State Senator David Goodman, relating to the expansion of opportunities for DNA testing were highlighted by the McClendon exoneration. As State Public Defender Tim Young observed, "The amount of time and money prosecutors spent around the state fighting whether inmates should get DNA tests was far more expensive than if we'd just done the tests. And then we end up with this," he said, referring to McClendon's long-delayed justice.[14]

"The prosecutors who are still opposing these DNA requests need to do a little soul-searching and rethink their positions," Godsey said.[15]

At the time, I predicted publicly, "Ohio's going to finally do something to create a standard for evidence."[16]

But in Ohio, and across the nation, there were other voices saying, "Not so fast."

It was August 2008. We spent the rest of the year garnering support. We presented and advocated the bill to the Ohio Association of Chiefs of Police, the Buckeye State Sheriffs' Association, and the Ohio Prosecuting Attorneys Association. We knew that the year would end without a new law; it would take more advocacy, compromise, and time to change the rules of Ohio justice.

CHAPTER 38

A Defining Moment for DNA

THE McCLENDON CASE taught me that granting an inmate the right to have post-conviction DNA testing when it can absolutely prove guilt or innocence and perhaps identify the true perpetrator should be a no-brainer. But the U.S. Supreme Court was about to decide how this right of a prisoner stacked up against the rights of a state—specifically the state of Alaska, where no convict had ever been granted the right to have post-conviction DNA testing.

In January 2009, I received a call from Peter Neufeld and Barry Scheck, who created the Innocence Project in 1992. They have been the driving force of a national effort that now numbers more than fifty legal clinics, many of them affiliated with law schools. I knew that this call must be important if both Neufeld and Scheck were on the line.

They were calling to see whether I would be an amicus (friend of the court, a customary means of showing support) in a case that would be argued before the U.S. Supreme Court. *District Attorney's Office for the Third Judicial District v. William G. Osborne*, commonly known as the *Osborne* case, would challenge the high court to clarify a convicted prisoner's rights to post-conviction DNA.

William Osborne was one of two men convicted in 1994 in Alaska of kidnapping, assault, and sexual assault in a brutal crime that included raping, severely beating, and leaving for dead a prostitute. The woman was forced to perform sexual acts on one man while the other raped her, utilizing a condom. Then they beat her, bludgeoned her with an ax handle, shot her (presumably in the head), and kicked snow on what they assumed was a dead body. Remarkably, the woman survived—the bullet had merely grazed her head and had not inflicted a serious wound—and gave police a description of the two men.[1]

Dexter Jackson was arrested after being stopped for a minor traffic incident. His car matched the description that the victim had provided, and items belonging to the woman were found in the car, along with a gun that matched the shell casing found at the crime scene. Jackson confessed that he had been the driver, and he named Osborne as the passenger. Witnesses had seen Osborne leaving an arcade with Jackson the night of the crime. The victim later tentatively identified Osborne in a photo lineup, then made a more certain identification at trial. Osborne's conviction was also supported by the prosecution's DNA testing of the condom found at the crime scene. The genotype of the semen on the condom matched a blood sample from Osborne. DNA testing excluded Jackson and the victim, and it was not a conclusive match to Osborne; it indicated only that he was among 16 percent of the black male population who could have committed the rape.[2]

At the time, more specific DNA analysis was available. However, Osborne's lawyer, unconvinced that he was innocent, made the tactical decision to advise him not to request this testing. For eight years, Osborne sought the DNA testing, which by then was even more sophisticated.[3]

In two decisions, the Alaska Court of Appeals denied Osborne the right to DNA testing. He sued state officials in federal court, claiming that due process and other constitutional guarantees gave him this right, particularly to DNA testing that was not available at the time of his trial. The court dismissed his claim, but the U.S. Court of Appeals for the Ninth Circuit reversed and remanded this decision. The district court later concluded that "there does exist, under the unique and specific facts presented, a very limited constitutional right to the testing sought," and the court of appeals affirmed this decision.[4]

Alaska, one of only six states that did not have a post-conviction DNA testing law, refused to grant Osborne the test, even though it would cost the state nothing (the Innocence Project would pay for it) and even though state officials acknowledged that the test would settle the question of Osborne's guilt or innocence once and for all. The state did not explain its reasons for denying the testing to Osborne, and the district attorney's office appealed the case to the U.S. Supreme Court. The high court accepted the case and scheduled oral arguments for March 2, 2009.

Neufeld and Scheck were seeking amici for the argument that Peter Neufeld would take to the high court. I could not believe that any state would go to such extraordinary expense to deny a person the right to prove his innocence. If Alaska feared a huge demand from other prisoners for testing, it only needed to look at the experience of other states. This demand has not been extraordinary, for the many reasons that have been mentioned in this book.

For me, it was not a difficult decision to respond to Neufeld and Scheck's request to join the amici. I signed on. Nevertheless, the other amici of the brief would have seemed to be strange bedfellows just a few years before. Amicus Janet Reno was U.S. attorney general under President Bill Clinton. Reno may be remembered most for her handling of a string of traumatic events that captured the nation's attention during the administration's first term: the storming of the Branch Davidian compound in Waco, Texas; the investigation of homegrown terrorist Theodore Kaczynski, better known as the "Unabomber"; and the apprehension of Timothy McVeigh and the other perpetrators of the 1995 Oklahoma City bombing.[5] However, Reno leaves a real legacy in the leadership she displayed in responding to the challenges and opportunities in criminal justice as DNA technology was coming of age in the 1990s.

Attorney General Reno directed the National Institute of Justice to look into the spate of wrongful convictions revealed through DNA analysis of crime scene evidence. The resulting report, entitled *Convicted by Juries, Exonerated by Science: Case Studies in the Use of DNA Evidence to Establish Innocence After Trial*, published in 1996, led her two years later to convene the National Commission on the Future of DNA Evidence, which included a wide swath of participants from law enforcement, science, and academia. The commission made ensuing influential guidelines for prosecutors. Our amicus brief recognized that this work had transformed "the state statutory landscape."[6]

While of varied experience and political allegiance, my fellow amici supporting the Innocence Project's Osborne brief had one thing in common: All had been touched by wrongful criminal conviction.

Attorney Thomas M. Breen had defended Gary Dotson, thought to be the first person exonerated by DNA in the United States. Breen represented other wrongfully convicted persons and began to have doubts about a rape case that he had prosecuted more than twenty-five years earlier as assistant state's attorney for Cook County, Illinois. He confided his doubts to the Center on Wrongful Convictions, prompting DNA testing of evidence in the case, which resulted in the exonerations of Michael Evans and Paul Terry. Each had spent twenty-seven years in prison before being freed, a case that the U.S. Court of Appeals called "a tragedy of epic proportions."[7]

Kenneth L. Gillis, former chief of special prosecutions in the Cook County Illinois State's Attorney's Office, recommended that the state allow DNA post-conviction testing for Steven Paul Linscott, who had been convicted of murder based primarily on a dream that prosecutors interpreted as a confession. As a result of the DNA testing, Linscott was exonerated after serving three years in prison.[8]

Carl J. Marlinga, former prosecuting attorney of Macomb County, Michigan, agreed to release evidence for testing in a sexual assault case. This testing exonerated Kenneth Wyniemko, who had served nine years of a forty- to sixty-year sentence, and it identified the true perpetrator, who could not be prosecuted due to the statute of limitations.[9]

Scott D. McNamara, as district attorney of Oneida County, New York, consented in August 2007 to prisoner Steven Barnes's request for DNA testing of evidence from the 1985 rape and murder of a sixteen-year-old. The testing excluded Barnes. McNamara's office and the Innocence Project petitioned for his release and succeeded in 2009. By then, Barnes had served twenty years of a life sentence.[10]

Craig Watkins, district attorney for Dallas County, Texas, established in 2006 a Conviction Integrity Unit charged with the voluntary review of Dallas County cases going back to 1970. In spite of consistent opposition to post-conviction DNA testing by Watkins's predecessor, seven men in Dallas County had been exonerated in the five years prior to Watkins becoming district attorney. In the two years after Watkins established the voluntary approval of testing, nine more persons were exonerated; collectively, they'd spent nearly two hundred years behind bars.[11] Dallas County is the nation's leading county in DNA exonerations, with nineteen through mid-2010.[12]

Andrea L. Zopp, as first assistant state's attorney of Cook County, Illinois, authorized prosecutors to agree to post-conviction testing in a 1978 rape and double murder known as the Ford Heights Four case, which actually involved four men and one woman who were convicted of the crimes.[13] Thanks to the work of law and journalism professors and students from Northwestern University, and DNA analysis, all five of the convicted, including two who had been sentenced to death, were eventually exonerated, and the three actual perpetrators were identified and later convicted of the crimes. The five wrongfully convicted served a combined seventy-two years in prison.[14]

Finally, Peggy A. Lautenschlager, former attorney general of Wisconsin, recognized the value of DNA and championed its use during her term (2002–06) by seeking to facilitate requests of the state's crime laboratory for DNA testing.[15]

These friends of the Innocence Project brief collectively provided ample evidence of the power of post-conviction DNA testing to expose wrongful conviction and identify the true perpetrators of heinous crimes. Without post-conviction testing, it is likely that most of the innocent persons mentioned here would still be in prison.

Neufeld and Scheck not only wanted me to join the amici but also to get other current state attorneys general to join as well. Since leaving the post of Ohio attorney general, I had been very active in the various national attorneys general associations and could call many of the current AGs my friends. However, when I looked into the Osborne case, I discovered that *thirty-one* current attorneys general had signed on as amici for the opposing side! I told Neufeld and Scheck that they were simply too late. It would be highly unlikely for any uncommitted attorney general to sign on to a brief that was opposed by so many of his or her colleagues.

Why would so many attorneys general seemingly oppose the right to access evidence? Did this not fly in the face of the U.S. Supreme Court opinion "that it is far worse to convict an innocent man than to let a guilty man go free"?[16]

Not surprisingly, attorneys general often support states' rights over federal mandates. I probably would have signed on to the states'-rights side myself had I heard only that side of the argument, and had this come at an earlier time in my understanding of how important this issue is to the pursuit of justice. All but six states already had post-conviction testing laws. (At the time of this writing, only two states—Massachusetts and Oklahoma—are without laws granting at least some opportunity for post-conviction DNA testing.)

However, the states' statutes vary widely, and some are very restrictive. For example, in some states, granting DNA testing is limited to those sentenced to death. In Ohio, our reform legislation sought to remove a restriction that convicts who have pled guilty are denied the right to post-conviction DNA testing. Some states have refused testing if the convict had foregone testing during the trial. Most of the attorneys general on the other side of the Osborne case were probably concerned that if the U.S. Supreme Court were to rule in Osborne's favor, states might need to conform to a federal requirement. As a Republican, I am a strong proponent of states' rights, but I also recognize that human rights were being jeopardized—not only in the six states without laws regarding post-conviction DNA but also in others that had overly restrictive requirements for testing. In fact, the brief noted that restrictions in the various state statutes "would have excluded at least 220 of 232 individuals who have been exonerated nationwide by DNA testing."[17]

The attorneys for Osborne argued that while the federal government has supported the *right* to DNA testing, leaving this right to the states and prosecutors had resulted in denial of testing in worthy cases. While many prosecutors agree to testing where it can be exculpatory, fully one-fifth of DNA exonerations nationwide occurred in spite of the opposition and resulting delays from prosecutors.[18]

The brief sought to allay fears of the impact on state laws. *Osborne* was seeking to establish a constitutional right to post-conviction DNA testing, a recourse for those with suitable cases who had been denied testing, and the opportunity to pursue what's referred to as 1983 action in such instances. Section 1983 of Title 42 of the U.S. Code (the general and permanent laws of the U.S.) makes liable in a court of law any person who under the cover of law—under "any statute, ordinance, regulation, custom, or usage of any State, Territory, or the District of Columbia"—subjects a U.S. citizen to any condition that deprives him or her of any of the "rights, privileges, or immunities" guaranteed by the U.S. Constitution and laws.[19]

Part of the Civil Rights Act of 1871, Section 1983 essentially guarantees U.S. citizens their constitutional rights. Osborne's attorneys argued that this federal cause of action would apply "*only* in those cases where the State provides no remedy at all, or where it excludes the application of its statutory remedy to otherwise worthy petitioners based on arbitrary classifications."[20]

I thought that our amicus brief presented a strong argument, but I knew that it would be a close call. The high court would have to make a determination that would consider states' rights, federal mandates from the bench, citizens' rights, and fundamental precepts of the legal system. The court could rule either way, and I suspected that it would be a split decision.

CHAPTER 39

The Supreme Court's Divided Opinion

"U.S. Supreme Court's ruling in Alaska DNA case is a blow to justice."

—Cleveland *Plain Dealer*

O N JUNE 16, 2009, the U.S. Supreme Court ruled, in a 5–4 decision in the Osborne case, that inmates could not use federal civil rights law to obtain post-conviction DNA testing. The majority opinion by Chief Justice John Roberts stated, "We see nothing inadequate about the procedures Alaska has provided to vindicate its state right to post-conviction relief in general, and nothing inadequate about how those procedures apply to those who seek access to DNA evidence."[1]

Later in the opinion, he wrote:

The elected governments of the States are actively confronting the challenges DNA technology poses to our criminal justice systems and our traditional notions of finality, as well as the opportunities it affords. To suddenly constitutionalize this area would short-circuit what looks to be a prompt and considered legislative response.[2]

Establishing a freestanding right to access DNA evidence for testing would force us to act as policymakers, and our substantive-due-process rulemaking authority would not only have to cover the right of access but a myriad of other issues.[3]

Writing in dissent for the minority, Justice John Paul Stevens, said,

...an individual's interest in his physical liberty is one of constitutional significance. That interest would be vindicated by providing post-conviction access to DNA evidence, as would the State's interest in ensuring that it punishes the true perpetrator of a crime. In this case, the State has suggested no countervailing interest that justifies its refusal to allow Osborne to test the evidence in its possession and has not provided any other nonarbitrary explanation for its conduct. Consequently, I am left to conclude that the State's failure to provide Osborne access to the evidence constitutes arbitrary action that offends basic principles of due process.[4]

...a decision to recognize a limited right of post-conviction access to DNA testing would not prevent the States from creating procedures by which litigants request and obtain such access; it would merely ensure that States do so in a manner that is nonarbitrary.[5]

On the record before us, there is no reason to deny access to the evidence and there are many reasons to provide it, not least of which is a fundamental concern in ensuring that justice has been done in this case.[6]

Justice David Souter, in a concurring opinion for the dissent, added, "...taken as a whole, the record convinces me that, while Alaska has created an entitlement of access to DNA evidence under conditions that are facially reasonable, the State has demonstrated a combination of inattentiveness and intransigence in applying those conditions that add up to procedural unfairness that violates the Due Process Clause."[7]

The Cleveland *Plain Dealer* criticized the Supreme Court's decision, in its editorial of June 23, 2009, concluding, "The state of Alaska might not care that it has arbitrarily denied the rights of due process for prisoners, but the U.S. Supreme Court surely should have."[8]

As a states'-rights advocate, I could understand the decision of the Court. Once again, this process had highlighted an important reality: The most effective reform would come by way of the voting booth rather than through the courts, and this required a citizenry that would insist that its legislators, judges, district attorneys, and other elected officials not only commit to justice but also gain a better understanding of how to achieve it.

The Osborne case had a surprise ending for me. I knew that William Osborne was in prison at the time of this Supreme Court challenge in early 2009. However, I later learned that he had actually been paroled in 2007. Although he had claimed innocence, he said that he decided to lie and admit guilt at his 2004 parole hearing to improve his parole prospects. The U.S. Supreme Court justices may have been aware of this, but confessions in this circumstance do not hold much credibility. Besides, the Court was addressing the constitutional questions raised by Osborne's challenge, regardless of the DNA determination of his possible innocence.

Within months of Osborne's parole, he was rearrested for kidnapping and assault "in an armed home invasion in which four victims were bound with duct tape and pistol whipped."[9] That is why he was incarcerated when the Supreme Court case was argued.

It would have been a more satisfying legal effort if Osborne had been a Clarence Elkins or a Michael Green. The Osborne case was a vehicle for obtaining a determination from the high court over the rights of convicts to post-conviction DNA testing. Alaska, having never granted this right to any convict, provided a good opportunity to test this. Ironically, if Alaska had permitted Osborne's DNA testing, the state would have known, conclusively, whether or not he committed the first horrific crime. If the DNA test had proved that he was guilty (and this has happened when prisoners have tried to game the system by requesting DNA testing in the hopes that some glitch may falsely prove innocence), he probably would not have been paroled, and he would not have had the opportunity to be charged with the home invasion and assault for which he now again resides in prison.

PART IV

Dispelling Eight Myths

Nothing is more dangerous to a new truth than an old error.

—Johann Wolfgang von Goethe

JUSTICE DAVID SOUTER, writing his dissenting opinion in the Osborne case said, "It goes without saying that the conception of the reasonable looks to the prevailing understanding of the broad society, not to individual notions that a judge may entertain for himself alone.... On specific issues, widely shared understandings within the national society can change as interests claimed under the rubric of liberty evolve into recognition or are recast in light of experience and accumulated knowledge."

This opinion supports an overriding recognition that resulted from our search for understanding on this issue of American justice: It is conventional wisdom that will define the justice system in this country. Because we live in a democracy, we as a people will have the justice system we demand. We have observed this, for example, with "three strikes" and other mandated sentencing that have reflected a growing "tough on crime" sentiment in this country.

A lifetime of legal and political work has taught me that real change can occur only when "widely shared understandings within the national society" change. And this happens in America "as interests claimed under the rubric of liberty evolve into recognition, or are recast in light of experience and accumulated knowledge."[1]

The insightful German-born Hugo Münsterberg, who moved to the United States to pursue his pioneering research in applied psychology, revealed his keen understanding of how things get changed in this nation when he suggested that "if the time is ever to come when even the jurist is to show some concession to the spirit of modern psychology, *public opinion will have to exert some pressure*."[2] (Italics added by authors.)

Nancy and I believe that eight commonly held beliefs are actually myths that hinder justice in the United States. One definition of a myth is "an unproved or false collective belief that is used to justify a social institution."[3] These collective beliefs need to be recast in light of the experience and accumulated knowledge of this age of DNA. Most are now clear to the reader of this book; others require some additional discussion.

None of these myths will be disarmed of its destructive power until we as a people replace all eight of them with truth and a commitment to the work of perfecting our criminal justice system.

CHAPTER 40

MYTH NO. 1

Everyone in Prison Claims Innocence

W HEN I HAVE SAID, "I am providing legal services for a convicted rapist who has consistently maintained his innocence," a common response is, "Aren't they *all* 'innocent'?" The implication is that all in prison claim innocence. Is this true?

My sense is that people who believe this haven't talked to many people in prison. Frankly, *I* haven't talked to many people in prison. So Nancy and I decided to ask someone who has. Conversations with those in the trenches can often be enlightening.

Lauren McGarity never planned to spend nearly ten years traveling weekly to prisons to work with convicted felons. A professional mediator, she had a successful traditional practice mediating disputes between companies, families, and individuals. McGarity's particular focus was conflict resolution. As founder of WinWin, a nonprofit organization chartered to provide tools and education to advance nonviolent conflict management, she often worked in schools. Occasionally colleagues who had practices that included service to inmates in Ohio prisons asked her to assist in those venues. A busy working mother of three children, she consistently declined, but one day she agreed to help a colleague in a pinch: McGarity substituted as a presenter in a class of high-level felons at Ohio's Marion Correctional Institution.

Knowing nothing about the environment and culture of prisons, McGarity violated every unwritten rule about working with convicts. Even though inmates were known in prison only by a number, Lauren called them by name. She had the class sit in a circle, not in traditional rows, and she taught from inside the closed circle. She later learned that circular seating creates vulnerability in an environment that ordinarily permits no hint of it. McGarity's willingness to teach from inside the circle revealed her trust, rarely extended from one in a position of authority in a prison.

It took only one class for Lauren to be hooked. She knew that she could open the door to a better life for these men. In the ten years that followed, McGarity developed the Institute for Response-Able Re-Entry. Believing that preparation for successful reentry to society should begin the first day of incarceration, through integrated curricula and tools, she seeks to transform convicted felons from reacting instinctively to life's daily challenges to responding thoughtfully.

McGarity has created a charter school (now called "community schools" in Ohio), in partnership with the Ohio Department of Rehabilitation and Correction. Pending expected legislative approvals, the schools will be launched in two Ohio prisons and with corresponding campuses around Ohio. Classes located inside the prisons will offer the opportunity of a high-school diploma and enhanced life-coping skills for selected inmates ages eighteen to twenty-two.

Lauren has known hundreds of convicts on a first-name basis. She has helped them repair damaged relationships, restore respect, and establish roles as responsible fathers in families who had given up any hope or desire for such a restoration.

When Nancy and I wanted to know what convicts really say about their guilt or innocence, McGarity was a credible resource. We asked her, "Of the nearly one thousand convicted felons that you have known, how many have said that they are innocent of the crime?"

McGarity replied, "Only two."

If Lauren McGarity's experience with felons is representative of the nation's inmates, the vast majority do not claim innocence. Those who do often have turned down opportunities to plead to lesser crimes and have forgone opportunities for parole. They have paid a heavy price for maintaining innocence.

Contrary to conventional wisdom, it is my belief that a very small minority of inmates claim innocence. This is a reassuring indication that most in prison are guilty. Nonetheless, we now know that there are exceptions, and each one of these has a devastating impact not only on the families of the wrongfully convicted but also on future victims (and their families), as the actual perpetrators continue their criminal activity.

The notion that everyone in prison claims innocence has a companion belief. When we posed the question of wrongful conviction, a very accomplished defense attorney assured us that the number was very low, but "even if we get it wrong in rare cases, believe me, these are bad guys." He confidently implied that these are career criminals, even if the system doesn't get the conviction right every time.

It may be easier to live with an error if the outcome is somewhat justified in the big picture. But are most of the wrongfully convicted career criminals? Clarence Elkins, Michael Green, and Dean Gillispie had no prior convictions when they were convicted of major felonies. They are not alone.

Professor Samuel Gross of the University of Michigan Law School and Assistant Professor Barbara O'Brien of Michigan State University College of Law compared two distinct groups of persons who were sentenced to death in the United States from 1973 through 2003: 133 defendants who were executed, and 96 who were exonerated and released because they had been wrongfully convicted. Only 9 percent of those who were executed had *no* prior felony convictions of any sort, but 38 percent of those who were exonerated had no felony convictions prior to their wrongful capital conviction. Conversely, more than half of the executed convicts, 53 percent, had prior violent felony convictions (homicide, rape, robbery, arson, or felonious assault), while only 32 percent of the exonerated capital defendants had prior violent felony convictions. (Another 38 percent of those executed and 30 percent of the exonerated had prior convictions for misdemeanors—offenses such as disorderly conduct, simple assault, petty theft, or driving under the influence—or for nonviolent felonies such as criminal possession or sale of a controlled substance, forgery, or theft.)[1]

At least in the niche of convicted murderers, significantly more of those exonerated had no felony convictions when compared to those executed. It is not surprising that just under a third of the exonerated had a prior violent felony conviction. A criminal record can increase the likelihood of coming under suspicion, and it can bolster a theory of guilt. In spite of this greater potential for wrongly convicting a person with a record, 38 percent of the convicted murderers later exonerated had no prior felony criminal record.

Reality: Research and experience suggest that most in prison do not claim innocence, and a significant percentage of persons wrongfully convicted had no criminal record.

CHAPTER 41

MYTH NO. 2

Our System Almost Never Convicts an Innocent Person

I always thought—my whole life I've been practicing law, especially as a criminal defense attorney—that 98 percent, 99 percent, of the people convicted by juries and judges must be guilty. And now I look at this new data which shows that with DNA testing they're exonerating 25 percent of the people accused in sexual assault cases, and I'm completely freaked out by the number, because it tells me that the number of people who are unjustly convicted in our system is extraordinarily high, is a number that we as a democracy can't live with, is a number that I want to do everything that I can to change.

—Peter Neufeld, cofounder, Innocence Project,
Benjamin N. Cardozo School of Law[1]

THIS STATEMENT MADE by Peter Neufeld in an interview on *Frontline*'s "What Jennifer Saw" mirrored our own response to the fact that public and private laboratories have consistently shown a 25 percent error rate in the identification of rapists by police authorities and prosecutors.[2]

The good news is that DNA is now reducing wrongful conviction by excluding people *before* they are indicted. Once again, we must ask why there would be opposition to post-conviction testing for those who were convicted before DNA, if evidence survives that could provide certainty. Today, many persons in prison would have been eliminated as suspects if the science had been available.

Unfortunately, in the vast majority of cases—an estimated 90 percent or more of all crimes—there is no biological evidence. Perhaps there is a higher error rate in rape cases, where DNA primarily has been used in exonerations, because of the likelihood of eyewitness identification, with all of its fallibility, in this crime. But, then again, perhaps not: Eyewitness identification is often used in crimes such as robbery and even drive-by shootings, where the time to view the perpetrator may be much shorter, and the distance from the perpetrator greater than in a rape. One has to assume that the factors that contribute to wrongful convictions in rapes impact other crimes as well.

We have reported many estimates of wrongful conviction. In Lauren McGarity's sample, let's assume that the two prisoners who claimed innocence in approximately one thousand are actually innocent. If that low number of two in one thousand is representative of the nation's prison population, then nearly five thousand inmates in the United States are innocent.

Several researchers and professionals in the justice system have indicated much higher numbers than this. In any case, the number of innocent Americans in prison is certainly more than we as a nation would agree to abandon in any similar dangerous, life-threatening circumstance.

The reader of this book has seen what it takes to correct an injustice once a jury has spoken. The Innocence Project is reporting 253 exonerations, primarily for rape and murder/rapes, as we write this. This number will soon be obsolete; for the latest statistic, visit www.innocenceproject.org.

Exonerations represent a very fortunate turn for those who have had the worst luck imaginable. Their convictions were likely for crimes that fall into the 10 percent minority of crimes in which there is biological evidence. By chance, they learned about DNA; the evidence in their case was not thrown away; and someone cared enough to track down the evidence, pay the costs, and pursue the long legal road to possible exoneration. By chance, the crime was prosecuted in a state that permits post-conviction DNA testing, and their case met the specific requirements for testing in that state. By chance, their county prosecutor did not stand in the way of testing. By chance, they received acknowledgment from the justice system and were released from prison.

Not many hard-luck people have this extraordinarily good fortune.

Innocent people in prison number in the thousands (our belief) because they have been misidentified by a witness. Or because a snitch saw an opportunity to improve his or her own situation. Or because they confessed in order to bargain for a better sentence or because they were psychologically beaten down or were a juvenile or were of diminished cognitive capacity. Or because they pled to a lesser crime rather than gamble away most or all of their lives with a jury. Or because a past mistake put them on a permanent list of go-to suspects. Or because they had a worthless lawyer, or even just one who was overly busy or underpaid. Or because they drew a county prosecutor who was particularly rigid or arrogant or superficial—or up for re-election that year. Or because a forensic scientist was lazy or incompetent or fudged the numbers to help make the case.

Because our prison population is so large, the absolute numbers of imprisoned innocents can be high even though those who claim innocence are relatively rare. As the late Robert Dawson, cofounder of the Actual Innocence Clinic at the University of Texas at Austin's School of Law, observed, the work of exoneration requires finding the "needle in the haystack—a claim of actual innocence that can be proved."[3]

Reality: There are many more innocent people in prison than most Americans believe, and we are capable of doing better.

CHAPTER 42

MYTH NO. 3
Only Guilty People Confess

B RAINWASHING, MIND GAMES, false promises, trickery, lies, abuse. I like to think that these are not practiced by professionals in the American criminal justice system. But there are reasons that people confess to crimes they did not commit, and there are reasons that 25 percent[1] of wrongful convictions involved a false confession, admission, or statement treated as a confession.

Readers remember the long interrogation in Manchester, Vermont, of Steven Boorn shackled in the local jail and told that he was a "gone goose,"[2] but it is easy to dismiss an event that occurred in 1819, an earlier time in our history and justice system.

Christopher Ochoa, another man convicted of murder based on a false confession, explained what prompted him to incriminate himself. He was interrogated for two days about the murder of a fellow Pizza Hut employee because he and his friend Richard Danzinger were seen toasting two beers at the Austin, Texas, Pizza Hut where the murder had occurred. He claimed that he was repeatedly threatened during long hours of interrogations. "This is where the needle's gonna go in if you don't cooperate," the detective said.[3]

Ochoa was denied an attorney, and when he tried to call one, he said he was told that this attempt proved that he was guilty of rape and murder. "You're not gonna be able to hug your mom or your family anymore; you're gonna die in the death chamber," the detective told him.[4] According to Ochoa, "At one point, the sergeant got up and threw the chair he was sitting on at my head. He missed, but he threw it with such force, and I was really scared 'cause those guys were really big."[5]

Ochoa confessed and implicated Danzinger. Both were convicted and spent twelve years in prison before DNA exonerated them, and they were released. While in prison, Danzinger was brutally beaten and kicked repeatedly in the head by another prisoner who confused him with someone else. The young man underwent surgery to remove part of his brain, with lasting complications.

The City of Austin settled with the two men in 2003. Ochoa received $5.3 million; Danzinger, $9 million.[6] This happened in contemporary America.

ON OCTOBER 5, 1999, Keith Longtin learned that his estranged wife had been brutally raped and murdered when detectives showed him the horrifying photos of her corpse during a thirty-eight-hour interrogation. Even though Longtin and his wife had separated, the photos devastated him. As he sobbed with his head on the table, he alleged the detectives mocked him and accused him of phony grief.[7]

After spending hours in the room with detectives, he said that he was going to go home. One of the detectives said that he was going to handcuff Longtin to the wall "and beat the crap out of me if I didn't sit down," Longtin recalled.[8] After many more hours, the forty-four-year-old Maryland man began to question his own mind.[9] Detectives came and went. They talked about the crime in detail. They suggested to Longtin that he had a split personality. Could his "other self" have done this? Longtin says the detectives described to him the hypothetical possibilities of how the crime could have occurred.

He doesn't remember sleeping at all, but the detectives' log says he slept for only fifty minutes in more than thirty-eight hours in the interrogation room.[10] He recalls a detective thanking him for his confession, even though Longtin never wrote or signed anything to incriminate himself.

In the months that Longtin sat in jail, a string of rapes and assaults in the area led to the eyewitness identification by several victims of Antonio D. Oesby, a retail clerk. His DNA matched that of the semen from the rape of Longtin's wife. Oesby was convicted and sentenced to two life sentences for this crime.[11]

After eight months in jail, Keith Longtin was released, and all charges against him were dropped. In 2001, he was awarded $6.4 million for this violation of his civil rights.[12] This happened in contemporary America.

THESE CASES MAY SEEM extreme, but they illustrate tactics that have shown up again and again in cases of false convictions. *True Stories of False Confessions*, edited by Rob Warden and Steven A. Drizin, is a collection of dozens of cases of wrongful convictions involving false confessions. They were selected from a much larger pool of such cases, because they exemplified the important role of investigative journalism in revealing not only wrongful convictions but also the factors that contribute to them. (The book credits *Salon* for coverage of the Ochoa case in "Texas Justice" and April Witt and the *Washington Post* for coverage of the Longtin case in "Allegations of Abuses Mar Murder Cases.") Nancy and I learned that there are recurring factors and conditions prevalent in these counterintuitive decisions to self-incriminate.

For example, we were surprised to learn about interrogation tactics that are sanctioned and recommended, within limits. Many jurisdictions in the United States and Canada utilize the same training playbook. *Criminal Interrogations and Confessions,* by Professor Fred Inbau of Northwestern University and John Reid, a former police officer, was first published in 1962. Often referred to as the Reid Technique (a registered trademark) or the Reid manual, it was developed by John E. Reid and Associates. Thousands of law enforcement, government, and private-sector investigators are trained with this resource. A survey of two thousand randomly selected graduates of the Reid training program showed that 95 percent of the respondents said that using the Reid Technique helped them improve their confession rates.[13]

In response to the questions raised by false confessions in DNA-proven exonerations, John E. Reid and Associates prepared a position paper indicating that four factors have repeatedly appeared in confirmed false confessions. We have mentioned these as well: (1) Juveniles or (2) the mentally or psychologically impaired appear to be especially vulnerable to tactics—especially (3) illegal tactics or techniques—that can produce false confessions, and false confessions are often given during (4) exceedingly long interrogations.[14]

These cautionary conditions would appear to be a matter of common sense and human decency, if the risk of a court reversal is not enough to curtail abuses. However, subtler tactics that can easily become improper are admissible. For example, it is permissible to use "themes," a tactic in which an interrogator may suggest a moral excuse for the crime: "It's understandable why anyone so unfairly harassed the way you were...." However, it becomes improper if the suspect is misguided into thinking that this kind of characterization can somehow minimize the punishment.[15]

Another area of concern acknowledged in the Reid paper is the improper use of alternatives such as "Do you want to be charged with first-degree murder, which will mean life in prison, or was this just manslaughter?"[16] The use of improper threats or promises has also contributed to false confessions: "If you don't tell the truth, I will get your children turned over to protective services, and you'll never see them again."[17]

Under conditions of duress, such as long interrogations, suspects have been subjected to role-playing exercises, hypothetical crime scenarios, and dream analysis that can lead a worn-down person to believe that he somehow forgot that he did, in fact, commit the crime. Brainwashing techniques can deliver false confessions.

Lies—for example, about accomplices confessing and implicating the suspect; or a "failed" polygraph test that was not actually failed; or a phony lab report—are permitted in the United States, and this kind of deception has been utilized in some of the false confessions proven by DNA. (Such practices are illegal in England and most European nations.) Some states have drawn the line on the use of fake *written* documentation of accomplice confessions and lab reports in interrogations.[18]

The recording of all custodial interrogations, from the reading of Miranda rights on, improves integrity in interrogations. Moreover, a commitment by law enforcement to make certain that the suspect understands the importance of the rights ensured by Miranda, decreases the likelihood of false confessions. In the meantime, we share what we have told our loved ones: If you are ever picked up for questioning involving a criminal act, do not waive your Miranda rights.

Reality: Known interrogation techniques have contributed to the eliciting of false confessions. Embracing the spirit of Miranda, utilizing fair interrogation procedures, and video recording interrogations lead to confessions that are more likely accurate and less apt to be challenged in trial and appellate courts.

CHAPTER 43

MYTH NO. 4

Wrongful Convictions Are the Result of Innocent Human Error

S ADLY, GOVERNMENT MISCONDUCT (prosecutorial and police misconduct) has been demonstrated in many DNA-proven exonerations. While innocent human error can lead to wrongful conviction, we also now know that many abuses, misrepresentations, and improper tactics are often involved. Negligence, ineptitude, laziness, callousness, excessive pride or arrogance, and other human failings contribute to conviction error, and the persons responsible usually go blameless and without sanctions. Many of these cannot properly be categorized as "human error."

Among the intentional abuses most concerning to me is the failure of prosecutors to comply with *Brady v. Maryland*, and the failure of the courts to consistently enforce the *Brady* requirement: namely, that prosecutors must disclose to defendants any evidence known to be favorable, whether it is "material either to guilt or to punishment."[1] In light of the growing number of proven convictions of innocent people, we have fallen short of the fundamental tenet that *Brady* sought to uphold: "Society wins not only when the guilty are convicted but when criminal trials are fair; our system of the administration of justice suffers when any accused is treated unfairly."[2]

As I believe has been demonstrated in the Dean Gillispie case, the prosecutor (or police detective working with the prosecutor) has a distinct opportunity to skirt the obligation of *Brady* because the defense doesn't know what exculpatory evidence the prosecution may have until (and usually only if) the prosecutor reveals it. This significant disadvantage for the defense is compounded when courts determine that even if exculpatory evidence was not disclosed, it may not be a Brady violation if it is deemed "immaterial" to the outcome of the trial.

While *Brady* has reversed many verdicts, it has nevertheless been emasculated. *Brady* cannot do what it was intended to do—ensure fairness in the courtroom—if it is relegated to an after-the-verdict, on-appeal, rearview appraisal of whether or not the undisclosed evidence would have been material to the outcome of the trial. As in the Gillispie case, this post-trial appraisal is subjective and debatable. As long as the courts refrain from exercising a strong response to Brady violations, some prosecutors will take the limited risk of nondisclosure. Our courts can and should give *Brady* more muscle.

Some states have taken any guesswork out of what should be disclosed by adopting "open discovery" in their rules of criminal procedure. Open discovery requires prosecutors and defense attorneys to freely share all relevant information for a full and fair opportunity for both sides to find truth and justice. The American Bar Association approved expanded open discovery in 1994. Many states have now followed the lead of Florida, which established open discovery rules in 1968.

Reality: Exonerations have revealed police and prosecutorial misconduct that go well beyond "human error." We in a democracy must be ever diligent in requiring that our standards of fairness in criminal justice are never relaxed, because a fair and level playing field provides the best opportunity for finding truth.

CHAPTER 44

MYTH NO. 5

An Eyewitness Is the Best Evidence

B Y NOW, THE READER KNOWS that despite its compelling nature and importance as a criminal identification tool, mistaken eyewitness testimony is the largest contributor to conviction error. Eyewitness testimony, as it is often utilized, cannot be considered the most reliable testimony. DNA exonerations have proven this. The consistent exclusion of more than 25 percent of rape suspects whose DNA is now checked with crime scene biological evidence *before* indictment has proven this. Hundreds of research experiments involving memory and eyewitness testimony have proven this. Police detectives have learned this through the significant error rate of eyewitnesses in lineups: About 30 percent of the time, witnesses who make a selection choose a "filler," one of the nonsuspects included in the lineup.[1]

Reforms that incorporate what we now know about memory are gradually being adopted so that the valuable tool of eyewitness testimony can become more reliable. These reforms seek to keep the witness's memory as untainted as possible by avoiding any suggestiveness.

However, even as procedural reforms are slowly gaining ground through legislation or voluntary operational change in some jurisdictions, the courts have been slower in considering this new knowledge. We challenged the courts in Gillispie to recognize as "new evidence" research findings from the past fifteen years about memory and eyewitness identification...especially in this case, which utilized a seriously flawed procedure in capturing the eyewitness evidence. In fact, given the blatant procedural errors, eyewitness experts would suggest that identification error in this case was predictable!

We previously mentioned that the U.S. Supreme Court's latest guidance for eyewitness procedure, *Manson v. Braithwaite*, reveals a lack of understanding of eyewitness research findings. The court set forth a two-pronged test for excluding an eyewitness's testimony in a trial. First, the Court held that the eyewitness identification process should not be overly suggestive. However, in *Manson*, the Court opined that even if overly suggestive, the eyewitness testimony is admissible if it meets five criteria, known as the *reliability test*:

> ...the opportunity of the witness to view the criminal at the time of the crime, the witness's degree of attention, the accuracy of his prior description of the criminal, the level of certainty demonstrated at the confrontation, and the time between the crime and the confrontation. Against these factors is to be weighed the corrupting effect of the suggestive identification itself.[2]

One of the criteria, as an example, is the witness's level of confidence. However, we now know that even when an eyewitness is totally confident, she or he can be dead wrong, and that there is no reliable relationship between confidence and eyewitness accuracy. *Manson v. Braithwaite* was written in 1977, more than ten years before the first DNA-proven exoneration in the United States. The progress made in memory and eyewitness research since then is similar to that seen in other fields in a particularly dynamic period, such as this same period for technology. Sadly, our understandings about eyewitness testimony are significantly ahead of the courts, and these will not change until the Supreme Court agrees to hear challenges to the dated understandings reflected in *Manson*.

Gary Wells, a researcher and distinguished professor of psychology at Iowa State University, and author of more than 150 articles and chapters and two books, served as co-chair of the panel that wrote the Department of Justice's training manual for law enforcement on the collection and preservation of eyewitness evidence. He has noted concerns with the way in which *Manson* is applied and a possible explanation for why *Manson* has failed to prevent the significant eyewitness errors proven in DNA exonerations.

Wells points out that three of the criteria in *Manson*'s reliability test—view, attention, and certainty—are based on retrospective evaluations by the witness. Psychologists have learned that this kind of rear-view-mirror self-assessment is often inconsistent with reality. Moreover, self-evaluations are vulnerable to the very suggestibility that has brought the testimony into question in the first place.[3]

One by one, researchers can reveal findings that would enlighten the court's evaluation of the reliability criteria. Looking at the issue of certainty (confidence), for example, here is one of Wells's studies that demonstrates how suggestibility impacts witness certainty:

> ...fewer than 15 percent of eyewitnesses who had mistakenly iden-
> tified someone stated that they were positive or nearly positive in
> their identification. However, when given a suggestive statement that
> appeared to confirm their identification ("Good, you identified the
> actual suspect"), a full 50 percent of the mistaken eyewitnesses said
> that they were positive or nearly positive in their identification.[4]

Virtually everyone agrees that suggestibility should be avoided in capturing eyewitness evidence. However, the courts rarely exclude eyewitness testimony that has been overly suggestive! Instead, they generally allow the testimony based on a reliability test that utilizes criteria that can be tainted by the same suggestibility in the case.

Manson did not prevent hundreds of DNA-proven wrongful eyewitness identifications and untold thousands (our estimate) of unidentified eyewitness errors. The courts should acknowledge what research reveals about eyewitness testimony. They should rule more aggressively on the first, all-important test of eyewitness reliability: whether or not the procedure was overly suggestive. A more informed judicial branch would ask whether or not any criteria can reestablish reliability once a memory has been tainted.

Reality: Mistaken eyewitness testimony is the most frequent contributor to wrongful conviction. The lessons of DNA and psychological research on human memory and eyewitness testimony should inspire law enforcement to embrace recommended reforms that reduce suggestion in the collection of eyewitness evidence, and the courts should be less forgiving in cases where suggestive procedures have been employed.

CHAPTER 45

MYTH NO. 6

Conviction Errors
Get Corrected on Appeal

THE JURY HAS THE formidable responsibility of determining whether the case presented for conviction proves beyond a reasonable doubt that the accused is guilty. A common belief is that if the jury makes a mistake, the error will get corrected in the appeal process. The reader now knows how difficult it is to reverse a jury's decision.

What can be reconsidered in the appeal process is limited to what was raised in the trial. The only alternative route is to uncover new evidence that must meet difficult requirements in the quest for a new trial. The system's justifiable commitment to finality in the process resists reconsideration at every step, as illustrated by the Gillispie case.

Devastated by a verdict that sent her son to prison for a crime that she was certain he did not commit, Juana Gillispie telephoned the jurors after the verdict. The calls revealed a troubling misunderstanding by several jurors of the concept of "guilty beyond a reasonable doubt" or of the finality of their decision.

Recall that the jury had come back split, the majority believing that Gillispie was not guilty. The judge did not rule this a hung jury. Instead, he sent them back into deliberations and urged them to understand their responsibility, to see one another's viewpoints and to reach a decision.

When the jury came back soon thereafter, the decision had turned the other way: guilty. Juana Gillispie asked a juror, "What made the jury change their minds?"

"...it goes back to when they realized or when they became comfortable with the fact that they had to make a decision," was one answer.

"I did not see clear-cut proof either way, guilt or innocence," said another. "I think the police should have had a better lineup. I hope down the line that he [Gillispie] is proven innocent."[1]

Nineteen years later, we are still working on that.

Reality: Opportunities to reverse a verdict are limited. Jurors need to understand the enormous authority and finality of their decision; the system succeeds when we get verdicts right the first time.

CHAPTER 46

MYTH NO. 7

It Dishonors the Victim to Question a Conviction

I T IS INEXPLICABLE TO ME that DNA testing is opposed and denied by prosecutors in cases where the test could unequivocally prove guilt or innocence. The often-expressed reason for this is that revisiting the case somehow dishonors the victim.

"We think it would be devastating to victims everywhere, not just this victim," said Fairfield County (Ohio) assistant prosecutor Gregg Marx. He told the *Columbus Dispatch* that he had opposed testing for a paroled rapist "out of confidence in and respect for the jury, the appeals court, and the victim."[1]

Another case selected for free DNA testing (semen-stained underwear from a child rape) by the *Dispatch* was opposed by the Fairfield County prosecutor, David Landefeld. "The victim in this case, we wanted her to get closure on this matter," he said. "I think it would be devastating for her. It just dredges up a lot of memories. She was a brave little girl to come in and testify."[2]

Let's break down this reasoning. Recognizing the barriers to reversing a wrongful conviction, the 253 exonerations proven by DNA most likely represent many more cases that have not had the same opportunity for correction. No one can now deny that errors happen. Prosecutors and judges who deny access to DNA in worthy cases where definitive biological evidence has survived either reveal an arrogance that says, "No errors happen in my county," or they are willing to allow injustice to steal or ruin a person's life and put others at risk for victimization in order to protect a mistake.

"It's not honoring the victim to take the chance that an innocent person is paying the price for victimizing them, because the flip side of the coin is that means the guilty party has escaped justice," Ohio Governor Ted Strickland said in the wake of another exoneration in Ohio.[3]

In fact, in at least two of the three cases explored in this book, the real perpetrator continued to victimize others while the innocent person sat in jail. Earl Mann raped his three daughters and perhaps more children. Rodney Rhines burglarized. KC, a potential suspect in the crimes for which Dean Gillispie languishes in prison, was arrested for abducting a young woman and apprehended by police while in the act of this crime.

The Innocence Project reports that of 253 exonerations since it began its work with DNA, the true perpetrators or suspects have been identified in 111 cases.[4] In the report *Reevaluating Lineups: Why Witnesses Make Mistakes and How to Reduce the Chance of a Misidentification,* released on July 16, 2009, the Innocence Project said, "In at least 48 percent of the misidentification cases where a real perpetrator was later identified through DNA testing, that perpetrator committed (and was convicted of) additional violent crimes (rape, murder, attempted murder, etc.), while the innocent person was serving time in prison for the real perpetrator's crime."[5]

A relatively small number of cases even qualify for DNA testing. So the excuse that an avalanche of requests will choke the system is unsubstantiated. Excuses for denying access to DNA testing in worthy cases are dwindling.

Reality: Denying DNA testing in worthy post-conviction cases does not dishonor victims. It just increases the number of them.

CHAPTER 47

MYTH NO. 8

If the Justice System Has Problems, the Pros Will Fix Them

"**I** **AM REALLY SORRY**. You have to understand that I was just doing my job."

What a multitude of sins this disclaimer has tried to cover in the history of mankind. Many of the exonerated have not even gotten an apology from those who had worked to convict them. We have noted several cases in which the exonerated received significant compensation, but these are relatively rare. There are many states—just under half at the time of this writing—that have *no* provision for compensating those who have spent years in prison for crimes they did not do. And even among states that do compensate are those that fall short of reasonable compensation or have restrictive requirements or pursue a resistive stance that precludes prompt or full compensation.

For many, a few words of apology are all they will get from a state that stole years from them. These inadequate words reveal a lot about the criminal justice system. Wrongful convictions often result from the unlikelihood of stopping an erroneous course once it builds steam. Like the train that has left the station, a single-track effort focused upon one suspect makes its stop at each station until delivery to the jury.

By now, the reader knows that it is likely that thousands of mistakes have gotten past many professionals in the criminal justice system. Ours is a system that has many players, and therefore rarely is any one person held accountable for error. As in all human experience, if many people agree that the course is correct, a lone skeptic is reluctant to express reservations, and he or she may not have the proof, ability, time, or authorization to try to find the truth.

This is just one reason that it is erroneous to believe that we can rely on professionals within the justice system to correct the system. To be sure, leaders within the system will rise to champion reform, but it is unlikely that they will or can effect change alone. Likewise, the courts contribute greatly to the evolution of the criminal justice process. However, as Justice David Souter stated in his dissenting opinion in the Osborne case, "the conception of the reasonable looks to the prevailing understanding of the broad society, not to individual notions that a judge may entertain for himself alone."[1]

Yes, even the U.S. Supreme Court takes its cues from the conventional wisdom of the broad society.

We, the American people, ultimately must be responsible for understanding our justice system and demanding improved outcomes. We must do this with the recognition that the criminal justice environment may not always be receptive to considering alternative methods. As Nancy and I studied wrongful convictions, we witnessed defensiveness from police and sheriffs' organizations as well as prosecutors, as if suggested change indicated criticism or invasion of someone's territory—an us-versus-them mentality. We observed an unwillingness to consider alternatives: an alternative suspect, an alternative procedure, a new look at evidence with new capabilities (such as a new DNA technology). This was so apparent that, without prodding, some along the way volunteered explanations, for example, that a black-and-white view is not just anecdotal; it shows up frequently in police organizations.

I have been involved in the justice system for nearly a lifetime and therefore feel that I have earned the right to make this critique: DNA-proven wrongful conviction should humble us all. Our performance does not justify arrogance! I believe that the vast majority of people in the justice system are professional, well-intentioned, capable public servants deserving of our respect and appreciation, but we in the system need to always enthusiastically seek ways to perfect our understanding and our processes in the pursuit of truth in justice.

As a former prosecutor, and one who has made the kinds of decisions that prosecutors make—questions of whether or not evidence supports a criminal charge—I, and many others along the way, recognize that much of the responsibility for the effectiveness and accuracy of our criminal justice system rests with the prosecutor. With college and law school degrees, the prosecutor is charged with weighing the evidence presented by law enforcement and correcting the course of the case at critical moments. Law enforcement officers are so focused on the details of the case they are building that they may not recognize their own tunnel vision. The prosecutor must insist on more evidence when appropriate before proceeding and must raise questions about inconsistencies in the case's theory.

For example, in the Elkins case, the only evidence that pointed to Clarence Elkins was testimony from a six-year-old who saw the perpetrator briefly in the dark of night before a vicious attack that left her unconscious. Because this was an identification of a known relative, at first glance it seemed open and shut. But, where was the supporting evidence in this case? How could this bloody murder be committed without any evidence in Clarence Elkins's cars or home or on him? Since numerous friends and family were with him that evening, how could Clarence have driven nearly an hour to the crime scene, and an hour back, without disturbing his family in their mobile home? Why did Tonia Brasiel act so strangely in not calling police or an ambulance when she became aware of a horrific crime a couple doors away?

The prosecutor has the responsibility to ask these kinds of questions. And if such questions, tragically, were not asked, prosecutors and judges must be receptive to, and cooperative with, post-conviction efforts that challenge truly questionable outcomes and seek to correct resulting injustices.

The mandate that we, the American public, have placed on prosecutors to win convictions—paired with the competitive nature of the courtroom—challenges prosecutors daily to find the proper balance between their roles as their state's advocates seeking to convict criminals and as "ministers of justice"[2] pursuing truth.

The U.S. Supreme Court has made the importance of this difficult balance clear:

> The United States Attorney is the representative not of an ordinary party to a controversy, but of a sovereignty whose obligation to govern impartially is as compelling as its obligation to govern at all; and whose interest, therefore, in a criminal prosecution is not that it shall win a case, but that justice shall be done. As such, he is in a peculiar and very definite sense the servant of the law, the twofold aim of which is that guilt shall not escape or innocence suffer. He may prosecute with earnestness and vigor—indeed, he should do so. But, while he may strike hard blows, he is not at liberty to strike foul ones. It is as much his duty to refrain from improper methods calculated to produce a wrongful conviction as it is to use every legitimate means to bring about a just one.[3]

I believe that many prosecutors struggle with this, consciously or not, and that we, as citizens, bear much responsibility when our courtrooms become error prone.

Reality: We—everyday Americans—are best positioned to change the system. We get the judges and the prosecutors we elect; we set the expectations and the priorities; and we ultimately determine the justice system that serves us.

EPILOGUE

WHEN WE BEGAN this book two years ago, Nancy and I anticipated that resolution in the Gillispie case would have come before publication. As it turns out, the Gillispie case reflects the usual reality. It just continues....

After much deliberation and believing that it would be in the best interest of our client, we submitted a motion seeking the replacement of Judge Wagner for the hearing for Dean Gillispie. This motion was denied by the Ohio Supreme Court. The hearing was scheduled for July 9, 2010. (Please see a late postscript on this hearing following this epilogue.)

Having exhausted all state remedies regarding Dean Gillispie's constitutional claim, in February 2010 we filed a habeas corpus action in United States District Court. The authors will seek to update readers on this case at www.falsejustice.com.

It must be noted that KC has not been convicted or indicted for anything relating to this case. While the legal arguments I have made on behalf of Gillispie point to KC as a more likely suspect, he remains innocent until proven otherwise.

Senate Bill 77, criminal justice reform legislation we actively advocated was signed into law by Governor Stickland in April 2010. Calling Ohio a "model state," Rebecca Brown, national policy advocate for the Innocence Project," said, "...no other state has adopted an omnibus bill of this magnitude."[1]

Ohio Innocence Project client Ray Towler became the nation's 254th DNA exoneration on May 5, 2010. Towler, who steadfastly maintained his innocence and had no prior convictions, served nearly 29 years for a 1981 kidnapping and rape he did not commit. He was one of thirty selected as most worthy of DNA testing by the *Columbus Dispatch*.

In *False Justice,* Nancy and I have shared our experiences and insights from many who have committed their life's work to solving the mysteries of guilt and innocence. With the grace of God, this book will be another voice prodding our nation's conscience. We must utilize the knowledge that DNA and scientific research have revealed to institute reforms that lead to greater conviction accuracy. We must provide access to post-conviction DNA testing and a stance of cooperation, not stonewalling, where claims of innocence accompany select cases in which there was little or no real evidence or none other than eyewitness identification. It is up to us, everyday Americans, to call upon our prosecutors, judges, and public safety officials to always be mindful of their awesome responsibility: to lead this noble democracy in ever-improved methods of pursuing truth; and to be our true, fair ministers of justice for all.

POSTSCRIPT

THE LAST-EDIT DEADLINE for this book was technically yesterday, Friday, July 9, 2010, but that was also the date of the Gillispie hearing before Judge Wagner. We include this eleventh-hour update on the case....

The day before the hearing, Thursday, July 8, Nancy and I joined Mark Godsey and two University of Cincinnati law school students in a downtown Dayton hotel. Godsey had just finished a grueling pre-hearing meeting with the prosecutors and Judge Wagner. The prosecutors were objecting to evidence and didn't seem to acknowledge the purpose of the hearing. Godsey had argued that the court of appeals had ruled that the information on our new suspect met that illusive standard of "new" evidence. It was now the judge's responsibility to determine if it also met the standard for a new trial, namely, that if it had been presented to the jury, the probability was strong that the verdict would have been different.

Godsey vented: The prosecutors were fighting the very evidence the court of appeals had found worthy of evaluating! Godsey had sought to give the judge his best lecture ever on the rules of evidence, tried to explain that the hearing was about proving that a pattern of very uncommon statements (about being a contract killer; about past sexual abuse; the repeated false use of the name "Roger") expressed by the rapist to his victims and also by our suspect to his girlfriend, was reason enough, especially in light of new findings on eyewitness testimony—to grant a new trial for Dean Gillispie.

Based on the illogical objections of the prosecutors, the preliminary meeting with the judge had been a disaster.

It would be a long night. Godsey and the students worked into the morning hours preparing the evidence items. But would we be permitted to present them?

Nancy and I couldn't sleep, and finally got up before the sun. We left the hermetically sealed hotel in search of fresh air, a brisk walk, and coffee. Downtown Dayton was dead at this hour. Nancy's phone GPS directed us to a locked building that may have contained a Starbucks. We ended up an hour later waiting for a local coffee shop to open at 7:00 and then hurried back to the hotel to shower and drive to the hearing.

Apparently we weren't the only ones who didn't get much sleep. Judge Wagner had done his homework. When the attorneys met in his office, he acknowledged that "the professor," Mark Godsey, had been correct the day before. The judge would hear the evidence.

The courtroom filled up quickly with Gillispie supporters, law students from the Ohio Innocence Project, the press, and others. Just before the judge was about to come in, a door near the bench opened and two armed sheriff deputies escorted Dean Gillispie into the hushed room. Totally white haired, he was dressed from neck down in canary yellow with large block letters on his shirt that said MONTGOMERY COUNTY JAIL.

"You look good, Deanie," a friend from his high school days called out.

"Yeah, yellow is my color!" Dean quipped, scanning the room and nodding to family and friends. A nervous chuckle came from the crowd, which quickly became quiet again in anticipation of the judge's entrance. The only sound was the breathy sobbing of Juana Gillispie.

It was the first time Nancy had seen Dean and his family in person. "They are attractive, warm, impressive people," she said. Dean, his mother, and sister had snow white hair and the fairest skin Nancy had ever seen. "They're Irish," I explained.

Dean's balding spot was deep pink. "There's no way that he could ever have a tan," Nancy said. "Let alone a deep tan," she added, referencing the victims' description of the rapist twenty-two years ago.

From the outset Judge Wagner seemed engaged in the testimony of our witnesses, ruling more often than not in our favor over the prosecutors' numerous objections.

Steve Clark, an eyewitness expert from the University of California, Riverside, testified on new findings in eyewitness research. Often counterintuitive, the research nevertheless revealed how, under circumstances such as those in which Dean was identified, errors can be nearly predictive and multiple eyewitnesses can finger some innocent person.

The judge was attentive. At times he gently waved off the prosecutor's objections as if they were an irritating fly. Was it possible that this testimony was shaking Judge Wagner's assumptions?

The judge allowed all but one of our witnesses to testify. Then he called the attorneys into his chambers. The prosecutors were attempting to block the submission of KC's police records of the copycat abduction and other arrests consistent with the behavior of an out-of-control criminal. "You mean that you are not going to stipulate *police reports*?" I asked. "The prosecutor's sworn duty is to seek the truth," I added, chiding one of the prosecutors directly.

Godsey had been masterful throughout the entire witness testimony in court that day. I had been the "bad guy" in the sidebar discussions. This reminder to the prosecutor had an impact. His objections became noticeably more subdued.

We returned to the courtroom, and Judge Wagner apologized for the time this would take. He asked for briefs on legal issues from both sides to be submitted by September 2. He scheduled time for responses and set the continuation of the hearing for November 22, Thanksgiving week.

I turned to Dean Gillispie and said, "I am so sorry that this is taking so long."

"I have been waiting twenty years," he said with a weak smile. "I can wait a few more months." Once again, he thanked me for working on his behalf.

"I believe in you, Dean," I responded.

Dean's parents, family, high-school friends, neighbors, and former fiancée (now married with two children) had spent another day with him in a courtroom. As I patted Dean's shoulder in a goodbye gesture, my heart again ached for him.

Just days before, I had presented the myths in this book to a conference of judges at Ohio's Miami University. Numerous judges I truly respect expressed appreciation for the message. It was as if much about wrongful conviction was new to them!

The judges' responses, back-to-back with Judge Wagner's attentive handling of the Gillispie hearing, brought yet another epiphany in this string of life lessons. This difficult effort to find true justice really isn't about good people in the system verses bad, or smart verses dumb. By the hand of

God my life's trajectory had an unlikely intersection with Clarence Elkins, Michael Green, and Dean Gillispie. Prosecutor Ron O'Brien experienced his unexpected awakening to wrongful conviction with Robert McClendon and Joseph Fears. Could it be that Judge Wagner was having a similar jarring of his assumptions with Dean Gillispie?

From all appearances Judge Wagner was keeping his word made to me personally: He would look at this case with an open mind.

Roger and Juana Gillispie watched attentively as their son was escorted out by two armed deputies. They hung back until everyone had left the courtroom to ask how I thought it went. As we walked out, I responded, "Better than I thought it would when we started this morning."

I felt good about the day and said that I thought the odds of our getting a new trial had improved significantly. The Gillispies needed some hope. My appraisal no doubt sprang from my own cautious hope. On reflection, however, I have to admit that I really haven't a clue. It is difficult to know the human heart.

ACKNOWLEDGMENTS

WRITING THIS BOOK was a collaborative effort that relied upon support and guidance from many over our lifetime. My late parents, Lila and William J. Petro, provided a loving home, encouragement to follow in my father's footsteps as a lawyer, and a belief that public service is a noble calling. My late brother Bill dragged me into many political campaigns, providing an important education in politics. Dorothy and Don Bero, Nancy's parents, are kind, generous, loving, and inspirational. Our son, John, and daughter, Corbin, are blessings in our lives. Nancy's sister Sally, her husband Mark and our niece Jane as well as my late brother's children, our niece Jessica and nephew Ben, round out our immediate loved ones in our larger, supportive family.

I was blessed with outstanding mentors. The late U.S. senator and attorney general Bill Saxbe provided my first political staff position, which helped pay for my law school education. While in law school, my work on Ralph Perk's uphill race for mayor of Cleveland catapulted me into an active role in politics. Perk taught me the importance of staying resolute in uphill battles.

Mayor Earl Martin guided me with his example of solid competence. He and his wife Beth led a loyal group of friends in a tradition of more than twenty years: the Petro Pancake Breakfast, held the Sunday before November elections in Rocky River.

Cuyahoga County Republican Chairman Bob Hughes and Bob Bennett, Ohio's legendary State Republican Chairman, guided my political efforts. Jon Hughes managed my first two statewide campaigns, followed by John Conley, Mitch Givens, and Bob Paduchik. Bob Klaffky and Rex Elsass were essential advisors.

I will always be grateful for the campaign county chairs, financial supporters, and political advocates who made possible each campaign victory.

I consider Democrat Cuyahoga County Commissioner Tim Hagan a cherished friend. Along with Commissioner Mary Boyle, we provided county leadership during a Greater-Cleveland renaissance, proving the power of bipartisanship.

I am so grateful for friendships and gracious support from political and community leaders of both parties. I was often inspired by their political courage and sacrifice.

My election as Auditor of State presented an opportunity to select an outstanding management team. Lana Rueble was one of the most capable Chiefs of Staff I have known. Chief Deputy Auditor Dan Shultz and Chief Counsel Mike Grodhaus brought private sector leadership to our operations. Jon Hughes guided the staff in the Auditor's office in our early "aggressive reform" years; and Kim Norris proved to be the most effective communicator in Ohio state government. My executive assistant, Melissa Vasil, kept my days orderly and efficient, and senior managers Mary Cool and Chris Hansen steadfastly advanced our technology goals.

As Attorney General, I augmented the management team with attorneys Doug Cole, Jim Canepa, Elizabeth Smith, Lisa Iannotta, Stephanie McCloud, Brian Cook, Stephen Carney, and John Guthrie.

I count many of these true-blue friends. We add Don and Sandy Dobos; Marty and Lynnie Erbaugh; Dr. Bob and Barbara McVicker; George and Denise Ramonas; Nancy's nearly lifelong friendships of Sharon Wilbert; Penny Pritchard; Francoise Devuyst Boden; and Nancy Scott Beren; as well as many cherished friends from Rocky River, Cleveland, and Columbus.

We thank many writers, researchers, attorneys, judges, legislators, and scholars. We hope that we have done justice to their important work and that this book expands awareness of it. We acknowledge numerous journalists for their leadership, particularly Mary McCarty, Laura A. Bischoff, Connie Schultz, Regina Brett, Geoff Dutton, and Mike Wagner.

We are grateful to private investigator Martin Yant and attorneys Jim Canepa and Mark Godsey for assisting with accuracy and insight. We thank Clarence Elkins; Melinda Elkins; Barry Scheck; Vanessa Potkin; Dean Gillispie; Roger and Juana Gillispie; Jim Wooley; Samuel Gross; Rob Warden; and others who spoke with us.

We acknowledge the guiding work of Robert M. Bloom, Edwin Borchard, Robert Buckhout, James Doyle, Steve Drizen, Brandon L. Garrett, Bennett L. Gershman, C. Ronald Huff, Edward J. Imwinkelried, Saul Kassin, Richard Leo, Elizabeth Loftus, Gerald McFarland, Hugo Münsterberg, Peter Neufeld, Nancy Steblay, Thomas Sullivan, Gary Wells, John Henry Wigmore, and many others.

We thank fellow Denison alumna Sara Fritz for her guidance and gift of the book *Thinking Like Your Editor* by Susan Rabiner and Alfred Fortunato; Susan Rabiner for suggesting that we send our book proposal to Don Fehr of Kaplan Publishing; Don Fehr for recognizing its potential; Kaplan for purchasing the book; Kaplan editor Kate Lopaze, for her editing expertise and guidance; and production editor Kim Bowers.

We thank the amazing doctors and medical staff at the James Cancer Center at The Ohio State Medical Center, for their caring treatment of my malignancy diagnosed during the writing of this book. (After completing chemotherapy and radiation treatments, my follow-up PET scan revealed that my tumor is gone. I view myself a cancer survivor.)

Finally, Nancy and I thank God for our lasting friendship and marriage; for the blessing of our children; for the love of family and friends; and for divine guidance in our lives.

SOURCE NOTES

A WORD ABOUT SOURCES:
What Nancy and I learned over a seven-year period about wrongful criminal conviction was an awakening like none we had ever experienced. We became driven to provide for others the same learning experience and process. The result was a narrative of my past seven years.

However, if the narrative were to cover only my most recent direct experiences, it would fall short on two levels. First, there would be no sense of the transformation that comes with a true shaking up of one's assumptions. We needed to reveal who I was before this period of my life to demonstrate how these events and lessons changed Nancy and me. Second, my experience alone would still lack important context of the fuller stories of which I was just a small part.

To provide the full detail of this journey, Nancy and I relied on primary sources such as trial and hearing transcripts, legal memoranda, motions, replies, court decisions, lab reports, investigative reports, police reports, scientific reports, and professional opinions. However, as we focused on three Ohio cases for the book, we became aware of the rich details of the human context through the work of Ohio journalists who conducted original research and interviews. Their writing informed our work.

I was directly involved in two of the three Ohio cases explored in detail. I heard from the principals and studied the records and histories of them as part of my work. Nancy and I subsequently interviewed many of the people involved. Without the published newspaper and magazine articles, we may well have learned of the incredible stories that put a human face on these cases; however, we give full credit to the superb work of the journalists who informed our information gathering. The result is that much of this information has two or more sources. While many journalists reported on these cases, we are especially indebted to those who wrote multi-article series: Mary McCarty and Laura A. Bishoff of the *Dayton Daily News,* on the Clarence Elkins case; Connie Schultz, of Cleveland's *Plain Dealer,* on the Anthony Michael Green case; Laura A. Bischoff, of the *Dayton Daily News,* on the Dean Gillispie case; and Geoff Dutton and Mike Wagner, of the *Columbus Dispatch,* on the coverage of Ohio's DNA policies and criminal justice reform. Regina Brett's writing in the *Plain Dealer* on the Elkins case from the perspective of Prosecutor Sherri Bevan Walsh was also an important contribution to the Elkins coverage in our book.

We believe that we have read virtually everything written about these three cases, viewed every available television program, and learned from every available radio report on them. We pored over the same trial and sentencing transcripts as other writers, and the most pertinent and dramatic points surface in any detailed account. While we have sought to specifically credit exact wording and other details to their proper sources and have worked with others involved to reconstitute conversations that occurred over many years, if we have erred in any way or used without accreditation words or a turn of words—that may have come from latent memory or simply be coincidence—this was certainly inadvertent.

We stand on the shoulders of other writers, scientists, academics, researchers, legislators and other public office holders, lawyers, judges, law enforcement officers, and other professionals, many of whom have made the issues in this book their life's work. Their work and discoveries became part of our story. Detailing the shared factors that contributed to these wrongful convictions; delineating the myths that enabled them; and advocating the reforms that have evolved to improve outcomes have been the goals and, hopefully, the contributions of *False Justice.*

ENDNOTES

PROLOGUE

[1] Edward Connors, Thomas Lundregan, Neal Miller, and Tom McEwen, *Convicted by Juries, Exonerated by Science: Case Studies in the Use of DNA Evidence to Establish Innocence After Trial* (message from the Attorney General) (Washington, D.C.: U.S. Department of Justice, Office of Justice Programs, National Institute of Justice, June 1996), p. iii.

[2] Deborah Rieselman, "Wrongfully Imprisoned Man Thanks UC Students for Freedom," *University of Cincinnati* magazine, www.magazine.uc.edu/exclusives/elkins.htm Copyright University of Cincinnati, 1999-2008.

[3] Innocence Project, "Understand the Causes: Government Misconduct," accessed online March 19, 2010, www.innocenceproject.org/understand/Government-Misconduct.php.

CHAPTER 1

The authors acknowledge the comprehensive coverage of the Elkins case by Mary McCarty and Laura A. Bishoff in the *Dayton Daily News*. The authors interviewed Mark Godsey, Jim Canepa, Clarence Elkins, Melinda Elkins, and Martin Yant, all of whom informed the writing of the Elkins story. Description of the morning of the arrest was primarily from trial transcript and interview with Melinda Elkins.

[1] *State of Ohio v. Clarence A. Elkins,* transcript of proceedings, Court of Common Pleas, Volume 1, 932; also, interview with Melinda Elkins.

[2] *Ohio v. Elkins*; also, interview with Melinda Elkins.

[3] Bill Hewitt and Mary Lopez, "My Husband Was No Killer," *People*, October 9, 2006, p. 88; also, interview with Melinda Elkins.

[4] Mary McCarty and Laura A. Bischoff, "Traumatized Child Hid Her Doubts," *Dayton Daily News*, August 7, 2006.

[5] Ibid.; also, interview with Melinda Elkins.

[6] *Ohio v. Elkins*, transcript of trial, Case No. 98- 06-1415, p. 1397 (Testimony of Clarence: "...It was so devastating, I said, well, yes, I will consent.").

[7] Memorandum from Brent E. Turvey, MS, to Martin D. Yant; also, transcript of trial, *Ohio v. Clarence A. Elkins*, Case No. 98-06-1415, Index and pp. 298–328.

[8] *Ohio v. Elkins*, transcript of trial, Index and pp. 298–328.

[9] Memorandum from Turvey; also, *State of Ohio v. Clarence A. Elkins*, transcript of sentence, pp. 16–17.

[10] Ibid. Transcript of Sentence, *Ohio v. Elkins*, p. 6.

11 Ibid., p. 8.

12 Ibid., pp. 9–10.

13 Ibid., p. 11.

14 Ibid., pp. 15–16.

CHAPTER 2

1 *State of Ohio v. Clarence A. Elkins*, transcript of sentence, in the Court of Common Pleas, County of Summit, pp. 16–17.

2 McCarty and Bischoff, "Child Hid Doubts."

3 *Ohio v. Elkins*, transcript of trial, Case No. 98-06-1415, p. 1518 (a reference to the cassette from the answering machine).

4 Ibid., p. 605.

5 Ibid., p. 117.

6 Transcript of 807 hearing, testimony of April, pp. 13–18; also, testimony of Dr. Richard Daryl Steiner, pp. 228–29.

7 *Ohio v. Elkins*, transcript of trial, Case No. 98-06-1415, p. 1238 (quotes in trial testimony).

8 Ibid., p. 603 (testimony of Tonia Braziel).

9 Ibid., pp. 526 (testimony of Lab Corp's Anita Matthews) and 520 "excluded"; also, Memorandum to Jim Petro, state of Ohio attorney general, and James V. Canepa, chief deputy attorney general, from Elizabeth Benzinger, Ph.D., October 28, 2005 ("Clarence Elkins is not the source of the DNA from the pink panties…, the vaginal swab from Judith Johnson or the right hand thumb fingernail clipping from Judith Johnson").

10 Memorandum from Brent E. Turvey to Martin D. Yant, Investigator, June 24, 2002, Forensic Solutions, LLC, www.corpus-delicti.com (author's summary of and direct quotes from memorandum).

11 Interview with Melinda Elkins.

12 Ibid.

13 Decision and Journal Entry Filed From Court of Appeals—Judgment Affirmed #19684, Web site of Summit County Clerk of Courts, accessed March 25, 2010; also *Ohio v. Elkins*, Appeal from Judgment, in the Court of Appeals, Ninth Judicial District ("The Supreme Court of Ohio declined Jurisdiction to hear the matter."); also Clarence Elkins's Case History, copyright 2003 by FreeClarence.com.

14 Interview with Martin Yant (description of reunion); also, Mary McCarty and Laura A. Bischoff, "'My God, This Thing Is Horrifying,'" *Dayton Daily News*, August 8, 2006 (date of reunion, reference to sentencing confrontation).

15 Interview with Martin Yant.

16 Ibid.

17 *Ohio v. Elkins*, Motion for Leave to Amend (Supplement), Court of Common Pleas, Summit County, Ohio, August 9, 2002.

18 Interview with Martin Yant.

19 Phil Trexler, "Hypnosis Session Criticized in Court," *Akron Beacon Journal*, August 20, 2002 ("Elkins's attorney, Elizabeth Kelley, said the 30-minute hypnosis session brought no new

revelations and only confirmed her suspicion that authorities influenced the girl's testimony four years ago"); also, interview with Martin Yant.

20 *State of Ohio v. Clarence Arnold Elkins*, Findings of Fact and Conclusions of Law, Judge John Adams, December 9, 2002, p. 48; also, McCarty and Bischoff, "'This Thing Is Horrifying.'"

CHAPTER 3

1 Interviews with Melinda Elkins and Martin Yant.

2 *Ohio v. Elkins*, transcript of hearing, Court of Common Pleas, Case No. 98-06-1415, July 30, 2002, p. 10.

3 Ibid., pp. 10–11.

4 Ibid., p. 10; also, interview with Martin Yant.

5 *Ohio v. Elkins*, transcript of hearing, p. 11.

6 Interview with Martin Yant.

7 McCarty and Bischoff, "'This Thing Is Horrifying'" ("Melinda continues to investigate the suspects on her improvised list, injecting herself into their lives so that she can pick up their pop bottles, beer glasses and cigarette butts—places they would likely leave their DNA").

8 Interviews with Mark Godsey and Martin Yant.

9 Donna J. Robb, "Noted Forensic Scientist Doubts Murderer-Rapist's Guilt," *Plain Dealer*, July 5, 2002 ("More than 50 friends and relatives of Elkins gathered outside the county courthouse this month on the anniversary of Johnson's murder").

10 Rebecca Leung, "Star Witness," *48 Hours*, copyright © CBS Worldwide Inc, September 13, 2003.

11 Interview with Mark Godsey.

12 *Ohio v. Elkins*, Hearing on Motion for Retrial, 1998-06—1415, p. 89 (Orchid Labs's forensic analyst: "I concluded that Ryal Rush was also excluded as a contributor to the evidence items that we were able to obtain a result."); also, interviews with Mark Godsey and Martin Yant.

13 *Ohio v. Elkins*, Hearing on Motion for Retrial, 1998-06—1415, 62 (Orchid Labs's forensic analyst: "I found that Clarence Elkins was excluded as a contributor to the DNA that was detected on these items of evidence") p. 237, and p. 76 (Orchid Labs technician: "For a Caucasian male, these four markers were compared to our database of 580 males. In the Caucasian population, it was 15 out of 272 Caucasians." Godsey: "So is it fair to say that, based on your database, essentially one in a little more than 18 men, somewhere between 18 and 19 men, Caucasian men, would have these four markers?" Johnson: "Yes."). Authors' note: This would be a 94.5 percent chance that the male DNA on the six-year-old girl's underwear and Judy Johnson's vaginal swab were from the same male. However, this calculation assumes that the perpetrator was Caucasian. Since Elkins was excluded, the race of the perpetrator was unknown. Therefore, the odds for all of the evidence should have been calculated on the entire database, resulting in even higher odds of these being from the same male. Godsey made this correction in his closing argument on pp. 236–37: "Because we have no idea what race that person would have been, we have to use their [Orchid Labs's] entire database.").

14 Judge Judy Hunter, *Ohio v. Elkins*, Findings of Fact and Conclusions of Law, Court of Common Pleas, Summit County, Ohio, July 14, 2005, p. 50.

15 Interview with Martin Yant.

16 McCarty and Bischoff, "'This Thing Is Horrifying'"; also, interview with Martin Yant.

CHAPTER 4

Recollections of Jim Petro.

CHAPTER 5

Recollections of Jim Petro.

CHAPTER 6

[1] Finley Peter Dunne (1867–1936), author of the Mr. Dooley sketches.

CHAPTER 7

[1] www.dna.gov/basics/biology/Department of Justice, DNA Initiative—Advancing Criminal Justice Through DNA Technology, Basic Biology of DNA ("DNA is the abbreviation for deoxyribonucleic acid, which is the genetic material present in the cells of all living organisms.").

[2] Dictionary.com, "DNA," in *The American Heritage Stedman's Medical Dictionary*. Source location: Houghton Mifflin Company. http://dictionary.reference.com/browse/DNA. Available: http://dictionary.reference.com. Accessed: February 25, 2010 ("it carries the cell's genetic information and hereditary characteristics…").

[3] Dr. John Butler, *Forensic DNA Typing: Biology, Technology, and Genetics of STR Markers* (2d ed.), Burlington, Mass./London: Elsevier Academic Press, (authors' summary of history accessed February 25, 2010, at www.dna.gov/basics/analysishistory/ Department of Justice.

[4] Ibid. ("The RLFP method was first used to help in an English immigration case and shortly thereafter to solve a double homicide case.")

[5] Elizabeth Benzinger, Ph.D., memorandum to Petro and Canepa ("The statistical estimates of profile frequency obtained for full STR profiles are often in excess of one in several quadrillion.").

[6] Ibid. (quote verbatim).

[7] www.dna.gov/dna-databases/codis Department of Justice, DNA Initiative (authors' summary from "Combined DNA Index System").

[8] Press release, Orange County Sheriff's Department, Orange County District Attorney's Office, November 2004, p. 1 ("DNA evidence warms up a cold case, solving one of the oldest kidnap/murder/rape cases in Orange County").

[9] Mark Miller, "DNA Pegs Killer After 13 Years," *Columbus Dispatch*, September 24, 2007 ("The murder…shocked the OSU campus, and spurred the university to improve safety on and around campus").

[10] Jim Petro's recollection; also, Bruce Cadwallader, "Student's Killer Takes Plea Deal," *Columbus Dispatch*, September 21, 2007.

CHAPTER 8

[1] McCarty and Bischoff, "'This Thing Is Horrifying.'"

[2] Mark Godsey, Jana DeLoach, and Pierre H. Bergeron, letter to Summit County prosecutor Sherry Bevan Walsh, September 21, 2005.

[3] Ibid.

[4] Editorial, *Akron Beacon Journal*, September 23, 2005.

[5] Mary McCarty and Laura A. Bischoff, "'We Can All Start to Heal,'" *Dayton Daily News*, August 9, 2006 ("Since the results from the cigarette butt DNA became public, Elkins has been in 'the

hole,' locked up for his own protection in case Earl Mann's friends at the Mansfield Correctional Institution might want to do him harm. He is treated like any other inmate in solitary confinement: shackled and separated from his visitors by glass partitions, released from his cell for only minutes each day. The single bed takes up most of the space, forcing Elkins to sleep with his head next to the toilet"); also, interview with Melinda Elkins.

[6] Details of attempts to meet with Summit County prosecutor and conversation with Mary Ann Kovach from interview with Jim Canepa.

[7] *Ohio v. Elkins*, transcript of proceedings, March 23, 2005, p. 106 (Michael Carol: "And how about clothing that commingles the father's, the brother's..." and quote of forensic analyst, verbatim).

[8] Benzinger, memorandum to Petro and Canepa (quote verbatim).

[9] News from the Criminal Division, Summit County Prosecutor's Office, "Message from Prosecutor Walsh," the *Rap Sheet*, November 2005, p. 1 (Sherri Bevan Walsh: "My office contends the DNA evidence presented several times about other possible suspects in the case is inconclusive").

[10] Ibid., p. 3 (Sherri Bevan Walsh: "The current state of the DNA evidence is partial and incomplete").

[11] Ibid., p. 1 (Sherri Bevan Walsh quote verbatim).

[12] Ibid., p. 1 (Sherri Bevan Walsh: "My criticism is based on the fact that the Attorney General made this conclusion without ever reviewing our file, the police reports, the decisions of the judges, the transcripts of the trial testimony, and without ever speaking to the Barberton Police or the prosecutors").

[13] Ibid., p. 3 (Sherri Bevan Walsh quote verbatim).

[14] Ibid., p. 3 (Sherri Bevan Walsh quote verbatim).

[15] Petro's recollection; also, Karen Farkas, "Summit Prosecutor Rips Petro for Saying Prisoner Is Innocent," *Plain Dealer*, November 1, 2005.

[16] Petro's recollection of assessments from Cellmark and the Ohio Bureau of Criminal Investigation; also, McCarty and Bischoff, "'This Thing Is Horrifying,'" ("With both the maternal and paternal lines matching, Godsey's experts handicap the odds that Earl Mann isn't the attacker: about 19 million to one").

[17] Petro's recollection; also, Shane Hoover, "DNA Could Clear Man Convicted of Murder," CantonRep.com, December 10, 2005 (Jim Petro quote verbatim).

[18] Petro's recollection; also, Hoover, "DNA Could Clear Man" (Mary Ann Kovach quote verbatim, and "The defense has not made their charts and DNA analyst available to prosecutors, and until prosecutors can review the evidence, the office will not support Elkins' release," the statement said).

[19] Ibid., Hoover ("Ohio Innocence Project Director Mark Godsey said that he has given prosecutors copies of the evidence and offered to arrange interviews with the analyst"); also, Mark Godsey quote verbatim, and Petro's recollection.

[20] Petro's recollection; and McCarty and Bischoff, "'Start to Heal.'"

[21] Petro's recollection; and McCarty and Bischoff, "'Start to Heal.'"

[22] Petro's recollection; and McCarty and Bischoff, "'Start to Heal.'"

CHAPTER 9

1 Daniel Shorn, "Wife's Detective Work Frees Hubby," Louisville, Ohio, December 20, 2005, CBS News, *The Early Show*, accessed February 26, 2010, www.cbsnews.com/stories/2005/12/20/earlyshow/main1140199.shtml (Clarence Elkins quote verbatim).

2 Ibid. (Melinda Elkins quote verbatim).

3 Interview with Melinda Elkins (quote verbatim).

4 Interview with Melinda Elkins; also, McCarty and Bischoff, "'Start to Heal'" ("I immediately felt this connection.").

5 Interview with Melinda Elkins (quotes verbatim).

6 Ibid.

7 Bob Gilmartin, *Dateline NBC* producer, *Inside Dateline*, "About Covering the Elkins Case," MSNBC, March 11, 2007; accessed February 25, 2010.

8 Ibid.

9 James Ewinger, "Whatever Happened to...? Wrongly Imprisoned Man Still Seeks Justice," PD Extra, *Plain Dealer*, August 15, 2008 ("...he files a civil-rights suit in U.S. District Court against the Summit County Prosecutor's Office, the county and Barberton police for his arrest and imprisonment.").

10 *The Prosecutor*, Civil Case Review, Summit County Prosecuting Attorney, Spring 2008, p. 5 ("The Court held that not only was the Prosecutor and her employees immune from liability for their actions as Prosecutors regarding his case, but also that the settlement, which he obtained from the State of Ohio, precluded claims against said parties regarding the same matter").

11 Interview with Clarence Elkins.

12 Ibid.

13 "Imprisoned Rapist Is Indicted in New Case," Vindy.com, July 1, 2007 (Clarence Elkins quote verbatim).

14 Dave Sereno, "Killer's Family Hopes for Sentence Reversal or New Trial," Cantonrep.com, June 23, 2002 (Elkinses' son's quote verbatim).

15 Interview with Melinda Elkins (Melinda Elkins reflects on the case's impact on her sons).

16 McCarty and Bischoff, "Start to Heal" (quote verbatim).

17 Interview with Melinda Elkins.

CHAPTER 10

1 Message from Prosecutor Sherri Bevan Walsh (press release), June 29, 2007.

2 *State of Ohio v. Earl Mann*, journal entry, in the Court of Common Pleas, County of Summit, Case No. CR 07 06 2079, January 10, 2008.

3 *Ohio v. Elkins*, hearing in front of Judge Judy Hunter, March 23, 2005, pp. 76–77 (testimony of forensic analyst).

4 Ibid., p. 33 (Opening remarks, Michael Carroll: "I'll start with the chain [of evidence] issue first... I don't think anyone is claiming tampering. I think the word used in the order is 'alteration.'").

5 Tony Bosma, "Personal Motivations Aid Walsh, Summit County Prosecutor Sherri Bevan Walsh Prepares Case Against Christopher Butts," *Buchtelite*, November 12, 2009 ("Daylight Rapist," and "...he threatened the women with a knife, placed duct tape over their eyes and put sunglasses on them as he walked them to a vehicle.").

[6] Ibid. (Summary of crime, and statement of Sherri Bevan Walsh verbatim: "'He opened the driver's side door and grabbed me,' Walsh said. 'I screamed and screamed and screamed, and he was freaking out, screaming at me to shut up. He was looking around, and then he'd choke me again and then look around again.'").

[7] Ibid. ("He was charged and found guilty of 31 charges that included 12 counts of rape, 10 counts of kidnapping, one count of aggravated burglary, three counts of aggravated robbery and five counts of felonious assault. Before he could be sentenced, McRoy hanged himself with a bed sheet in his jail cell.").

[8] Regina Brett, "Summit County Prosecutor Sherri Bevan Walsh Fought to Convict Clarence Elkins, Then to Free Him," *Plain Dealer*, August 24, 2008 ("Later in the fall, investigators gave Mann 10 hours of polygraph tests over three days...Mann said he hadn't been to Brasiel's home in three months before the murder...He said he was at Johnson's the night of the murder but only briefly... finally, Mann said that he had sex with Judy...How did his DNA end up on the little girl?").

[9] *State of Ohio v. Clarence Arnold Elkins*, State's Motion to Dismiss Indictment with Prejudice, Vacate All Convictions, and to Discharge the Defendant, December 15, 2005.

[10] Brett, "Walsh Fought to Convict Clarence Elkins" ("May 2007," "30 pieces of evidence," and "The match was 1 in 96,990,000.").

[11] *Ohio v. Mann,* journal entry, August 19, 2008 ("It is further ordered that the Defendant will not be eligible for parole until serving over 55 years of his sentence.").

[12] "Message from the Prosecutor," Sherri Bevan Walsh, Summit County Prosecutor Newsletter, End of Year Wrap up—2008, p. 1 ("I want to begin by commending the outstanding prosecutors that work in my office. As of the release of this newsletter, our conviction rate is up to 96% on our disposed cases, that is defendants who pled guilty or were found guilty at trial. Our trial results are also impressive, with 79% of the defendants being found guilty by a jury.").

[13] Ibid. (Sherri Bevan Walsh quote verbatim).

CHAPTER 11

[1] Connors, Lundregan, Miller, and McEwen, *Convicted by Juries, Exonerated by Science*, pp. 51–52 (summary of case, including, "The lab performed PCR DQ alpha tests that showed that the semen on the victim's undergarments could not have come from Dotson but could have come from the victim's boyfriend." And "Dotson's conviction was overturned on August 14, 1989, after he had served a total of 8 years.").

[2] Michael Sneed, "Gary Dotson Pardon Likely—Falsely Accused of Rape, DNA Analysis Cleared His Name," *Chicago Sun-Times*, May 13, 1985 (summary of case, including "Sweet Savage Love" and "high school dropout." "In fact, Crowell later confessed, she made up the entire story because she feared the premarital sex she had a few days earlier with her boyfriend might result in pregnancy and cause trouble with her parents").

[3] Ibid. ("She went to her minister, confessed her sin, unloaded her guilt, and hired a lawyer in an effort to redeem herself and free Dotson.")

[4] Connors, Lundregan, Miller, and McEwen, *Convicted by Juries, Exonerated by Science* ("The governor stated that he did not believe the victim's recantation and refused to pardon Dotson. On May 12, 1985, however, the governor commuted Dotson's sentence to the 6 years he had already served, pending good behavior. In 1987 the governor revoked Dotson's parole after Dotson was accused by his wife of assaulting her. The Appellate Court of Illinois affirmed Dotson's conviction on November 12, 1987 [516 N.E.2d 718]. On Christmas Eve 1987, the governor granted Dotson a 'last chance parole.' Two days later, Dotson was arrested in a barroom fight, and his parole was revoked.").

5 University of Texas at Austin website feature story: "A Passion for Justice," www.utexas.edu/features/archive/2005/innocence.html.

CHAPTER 12

The authors acknowledge the comprehensive coverage of the Green case by Connie Schultz and the Cleveland *Plain Dealer*. The authors interviewed Vanessa Potkin, Barry Scheck, and Jim Wooley in addition to utilizing trial transcripts.

1 Connie Schultz, "An Unfair Burden," *Plain Dealer*, May 22, 2003.

2 Petro's recollection; also, Gabriel Baird, "State Reconsiders, Pays Green," *Plain Dealer*, July 31, 2003.

3 Ibid., Petro's recollection; also, Baird, "State Reconsiders."

4 *The State of Ohio v. Anthony Green*, transcript of trial proceedings, Court of Common Pleas, County of Cuyahoga, Case No. CR 228250, p. 34 (West Virginia, nurse).

5 Ibid., p. 38.

6 Ibid., p. 40.

7 Ibid., p. 42.

8 Ibid.

9 Ibid., p. 43.

10 Ibid.

11 Ibid., p. 44.

12 Ibid., pp. 44–46.

13 Ibid., pp. 44–47.

14 Ibid., p. 48.

15 Ibid., p. 49.

16 Connie Schultz, "Long Road to Justice," *Plain Dealer*, October 13, 2002 (38-year-old, seven years).

17 *Ohio v. Green*, p. 49.

18 Ibid., pp. 146, 148.

19 Ibid., pp. 132–33.

20 Ibid., p. 176.

21 Ibid., p. 180.

22 Ibid., pp. 179–80.

23 Ibid., p. 196.

24 Ibid., p. 149.

25 Ibid., pp. 192–93.

26 Ibid., p. 62.

27 Ibid., pp. 61–62.

28 Ibid., p. 117.

29 Ibid., p. 63.

30 Ibid.

CHAPTER 13

[1] *Ohio v. Green*, p. 223.

[2] Ibid., p. 225.

[3] Ibid., p. 227.

[4] Ibid., 232–33.

[5] Ibid., pp. 236–37.

[6] Ibid., p. 235.

[7] Ibid., p. 237.

[8] Ibid., p. 220.

[9] Ibid.

[10] Ibid., p. 221.

[11] Ibid., p. 264.

[12] Ibid., pp. 273–74.

[13] Ibid.

[14] Ibid., p. 310.

[15] Ibid., pp. 361, 354.

[16] Ibid., p. 294.

[17] Ibid.

[18] Ibid., p. 314.

[19] Ibid., p. 328.

[20] Ibid., p. 335.

[21] Ibid., pp. 336–37.

[22] Ibid., p. 338.

[23] Ibid., p. 339.

[24] Ibid., pp. 341–42.

[25] Ibid., pp. 343–45 (note that there is reference to both $25,000 and $35,000 bond in this testimony).

[26] Ibid., p. 375.

[27] Ibid., pp. 376–77.

[28] Ibid., pp. 369–70.

[29] Ibid., pp. 351–52.

CHAPTER 14

[1] Ibid., p. 398.

[2] Ibid., p. 400.

[3] Ibid.

[4] Ibid. p. 402. (summary of defense summation on the evidence), p. 407 ("Mr. McGinty went on almost twenty minutes, and he didn't talk about any evidence."); p. 412 ("…and try as he may through his experts, no way this man is going to get on the stand and say a pubic hair," and "Well, what would be consistent with taking a cloth and washing yourself in the pubic area? A pubic hair."); p. 413 ("Where are the panties, Mr. Serowick?"); p. 416 ("But for sure there was no

evidence of anybody taking fingerprints."); p. 417 ("He is looking for sperm, mobile or otherwise. Absolutely none.").

5 Ibid., p. 423.

6 Ibid., p. 435.

7 Ibid., p. 462.

8 Ibid., p. 463.

9 Ibid., p. 464.

10 Ibid., p. 467.

11 Ibid., p. 482.

12 Schultz, "Long Road" ("Michael Green stood motionless as his mother, Annie Green, screamed. 'Not my son! He didn't do it! He didn't do it! He wouldn't rape anyone!' She continued to sob. 'Michael!' She cried. 'Michael!'").

13 *Ohio v. Green*, p. 482.

14 Ibid.

15 Ibid., p. 483; also, Schultz, "Long Road," ("Draper noticed that juror No. 1, Lucille Poindexter, was crying, too.").

16 Ibid. Schultz, "Long Road," ("None of the jurors budged," "'We all have jobs to get back to,'" "Within the hour, Poindexter folded").

17 *Ohio v. Green*, p. 483.

18 Schultz, "Long Road" ("That night at her home, Lucille Poindexter prayed: 'Dear God I don't believe that poor boy did it'"); also, Schultz, "'Thank you. Thank you for believing in me,'" *Plain Dealer,* October 24, 2002 ("Mrs Poindexter, the mother of seven and a seamstress," and "'That's right. All these years, I never stopped praying for him.'").

CHAPTER 15

1 *Ohio v. Green*, p. 496.

2 Ibid., pp. 496–97.

3 Ibid., pp. 497–98.

4 Schultz, "Long Road" ("[He] had been at Lima 12 years when Michael arrived. In 1976, [he] shot a man to death in a bar on Cleveland's East Side.").

5 Ibid. ("In November 1996, at age 54, she married Robert Mandell..." and "Mandell's nights grew longer and longer in the year after he responded to Michael's plea for help.").

6 Ibid. (summary of search), and interview with Vanessa Potkin.

7 Connie Schultz, "Knowledge Is Power," *Plain Dealer,* October 14, 2002; also, interview with Potkin.

8 Schultz, "Knowledge Is Power" ("Forensic Science Associates in California" and "Mandell drew on his retirement fund to pay the $3,000 down payment on the nonrefundable $6,700 needed for testing."); also, interview with Potkin.

CHAPTER 16

[1] Schultz, "Long Road" ("Three times the parole board told him confessing to the 1988 rape and enrolling in the prison's sex offenders program was the only way he'd get out before 2013" and "If he served the entire sentence, Michael would be 48 years old.").

[2] *Ohio Parole Board Guidelines Manual*, 3d ed., July 1, 2007, p. 51.

[3] Shultz, "Knowledge Is Power" ("I'm not confessing to something I did not do.").

[4] "DNA Testing May Set Man Free," 90.3 WCPN, www.wcpn.org/WCPN/news/6935, Thursday, October 4, 2001.

[5] Innocence Project, "Know the Cases: Anthony Michael Green," www.innocenceproject.org/Content/163.php ("Anthony Michael Green was released on October 9, 2001, and exonerated based on postconviction DNA test results on October 18, 2001.").

[6] City Mission website, www.thecitymission.org ("Hurting, homeless, and hungry.").

[7] Schultz, "Remorseful Man Details How He Raped Clinic Patient," *Plain Dealer*, October 11, 2002.

[8] Schultz, "DNA Confirms Rape Confession," *Plain Dealer*, November 17, 2002 ("swabs of saliva," DNA confirmed guilt).

[9] Schultz, "Remorseful Man Details How He Raped Clinic Patient," (summary of crime, including "...He had worked briefly in the kitchen at the Cleveland Clinic Center Hotel, and so he knew where the employees' entrance was and how to navigate the route to the hotel" and "Before he left, he lied and told the victim his name was Tony. 'It was just a name I threw out.'").

[10] Schultz, "Man Who Did the Time: 'I Harbor No Bitterness,'" *Plain Dealer*, January 24, 2003 (summary of sentencing of Rodney Rhines, including, "I didn't come out of prison with a bitter heart, and I won't leave here with a bitter heart," he said. "I harbor no bitterness toward you, and I hope you can continue to walk the path you're on now.").

[11] Ibid. ("'I commend you for the kindness in your heart for this man'" and, "'I'm sorry,' she told Michael. 'You don't look alike.'").

[12] Ibid. ("She then sentenced Rhines to five years in prison.").

CHAPTER 17

[1] Exhibit A in the United States District Court for the Northern District of Ohio Eastern Division, *Anthony Michael Green v. City of Cleveland* ("A condition of that settlement agreement is the City's commitment to conduct an audit of files from the City's forensic laboratory involving serology and/or hair analysis.").

[2] "Professional Biography—Profile", Jones Day, www.jonesday.com/lawyers/bio.aspx?attorneyID=S4099.

[3] Exhibit A, *Green v. Cleveland* (summary of settlement including "The City will retain James Wooley as Special Master" and other mentioned stipulations of the audit).

[4] Mark Gillispie, "Experts Fault Job Done by Police Lab Tech, Boss," *Plain Dealer*, June 16, 2004 ("'[Serowick] was poorly trained, and even more poorly supervised.'").

[5] Ibid. ("Without his faulty assumptions, Blake wrote, Serowick should have concluded that no man could have been excluded as a possible source of the semen on the washcloth, rendering it meaningless in the Green prosecution.").

[6] Ibid. ("...another expert hired by Green's attorneys said Serowick should not have made that assertion because hair analyses aren't precise enough to calculate probabilities.").

[7] Joe Malicia, "Lab Audit: Cleveland Juries Not Misled," Foxnews.com, February 17, 2007 ("...the AP review of retired FBI agent Robert Spalding's reports on Serowick's lab records and trial transcripts shows that Spalding concluded Serowick did not mislead any juries with his trial testimony.").

[8] Ibid. ("I haven't sent [prosecutors] a single thing that made me think they [should] act on this," said Jim Wooley.").

CHAPTER 18

[1] Jennifer Warren and Susan Urahn, "One in 100: Behind Bars in America 2008," the Pew Center on the States, p. 5 (in chart entitled "Prison Count Pushes Up: Between 1987 and 2007, the national prison population has nearly tripled"; also in chart: based on the Bureau of Justice Statistics, the 1987 year-end prison count was 585,084; the Pew Public Safety Performance Project count as of January 1, 2008 was 1,596,127).

[2] All statistics in this section: ibid. pp. 5, 35, table A-7, entitled International Comparisons; note that the source for the European comparison information is the International Centre for Prison Studies at King's College, London, "World Prison Brief." Data downloaded January 2008.

[3] Ibid., p. 33, table A-5, State Employees in Corrections Workforce, 2006, source: Reanalysis of U.S. Census Bureau, State Government Employment and Payroll data

[4] Ibid., p. 30, table A-3, State Spending on Corrections and Higher Education, FY 1987–2007.

[5] C. Ronald Huff, "Wrongful Conviction: Causes and Public Policy Issues," *Criminal Justice Magazine* 18, no. 1 (Spring 2003) in section "Wrongful conviction in the United States," American Bar Association, Criminal Justice Section, www.abanet.org/crimjust/spring2003/conviction.html.

[6] Ibid., in section "How Often Does It Happen" ("In carrying out our research, we utilized a very conservative criterion in defining 'wrongful conviction'—that is, only those convicted of a felony and later officially cleared were included in our database," and, later, "In our database, we include cases involving official acknowledgment of error based on the following criteria: [1] a new trial was permitted and the defendant was found not guilty; [2] a pardon was granted due to new evidence; [3] innocence was established on the basis of overwhelming evidence; or [4] appellate court review proved innocence," and "Based on the responses to our survey, we used 0.5 percent as our estimate," and "in the year 2000, there were 2.2 million arrests in the United States for index crimes alone. We also know that about 70 percent of those arrested for felonies are ultimately convicted of either a felony or a misdemeanor. This means that if we assume that the system was 99.5 percent accurate in those cases and made errors in only one-half of 1 percent [0.5 percent] of those convictions, that rate of error would have produced about 7,500 wrongful convictions among those 2.2 million arrested for index crimes.").

[7] "Crime in the United States, 2008," United States Department of Justice, Federal Bureau of Investigation (September 2009) (retrieved January 13, 2010, from www.fbi.gov/ucr/cius2008/data/table_29.html).

[8] Samuel R. Gross, Kristen Jacoby, Daniel J. Matheson, Nicholas Montgomery, and Sujata Patil, "Exonerations in the United States, 1989 Through 2003," *Journal of Criminal Law & Criminology* 95, no. 2 (2005), p. 524.

[9] Samuel R. Gross, "Convicting the Innocent," University of Michigan Public Law Working Paper no. 103, *Annual Review, 2007.* Available at http://ssrn.com/abstract=1100011.

[10] Ibid., p. 2.5.

[11] Ibid., p. 2.5.

[12] Ibid., p. 2.6.

[13] *Kansas v. Marsh* (No. 04-1170) 278 Kan. 520, 102 P. 3rd 445, reversed and remanded (Souter dissenting) ("...and the total shows that among all prosecutions homicide cases suffer an unusually high incidence of false conviction, id., at 532, 552, probably owing to the combined difficulty of investigating without help from the victim, intense pressure to get convictions in homicide cases, and the corresponding incentive for the guilty to frame the innocent, id., at 532).

[14] Ibid. (Scalia concurring).

[15] Gross, Jacoby, Matheson, Montgomery, and Patil, "Convicting the Innocent," p. 2.7 (authors have summarized the report's factors supporting the opinion that homicide cases may be more error prone than other crime investigations).

[16] Joseph Marquis, "The Innocent and the Shammed," *New York Times*, Op-Ed, January 26, 2006.

[17] Gross, "Convicting the Innocent," p. 2.4.

[18] Governor George H. Ryan, *Report of the Governor's Commission on Capital Punishment,* state of Illinois, April 15, 2002, p. 7.

[19] Clemency Report, State of Ohio Parole Authority, Richard E. Fox, January 15, 2003, p. 5.

CHAPTER 19

[1] *Kansas v. Marsh* (Scalia concurring).

[2] Scott Turow, *Ultimate Punishment: A Lawyer's Reflections on Dealing with the Death Penalty* (New York: Picador, 2003), p. 58.

[3] Governor's Statement Regarding Clemency Application of John G. Spirko, Office of the Governor Press Releases, January 9, 2008, www.governor.ohio.gov/Default.aspx?tabid=578.

[4] Gross, Jacoby, Matheson, Montgomery, and Patil. "Exonerations 1989 Through 2003," p. 527.

[5] *Kansas v. Marsh* (Scalia concurring); also, Adam Liptak, "Consensus on Counting the Innocent: We Can't," *New York Times,* March 25, 2008 ("A couple of years ago, Justice Antonin Scalia, concurring in a Supreme Court death penalty decision...pronounced himself satisfied. The rate at which innocent people are convicted of felonies is, he said, less than three-hundredths of 1 percent—.027 percent, to be exact. 'One cannot have a system of criminal punishment without accepting the possibility that someone will be punished mistakenly,' he wrote. 'That is a truism, not a revelation'").

[6] Gross, Jacoby, Matheson, Montgomery, and Patil, "Exonerations in the United States," p. 551.

[7] Connors, Lundregan, Miller, and McEwen, *Convicted by Juries, Exonerated by Science*, p. xxviii.

[8] Ibid. p. xxix ("It must be stressed that the sexual assault referrals made to the FBI ordinarily involve cases where [1] identity is at issue [there is no consent defense], [2] the non-DNA evidence linking the suspect to the crime is eyewitness identification, [3] the suspects have been arrested or indicted based on non-DNA evidence, and [4] the biological evidence [sperm] has been recovered from a place [vaginal/rectal/oral swabs or underwear] that makes DNA results on the issue of identity virtually dispositive").

[9] Ibid., p. xxx ("...before convicted prisoners have been released, ...the prosecution has insisted upon independent testing of samples by their own experts and elimination samples from other possible sperm donors [husbands or boyfriends] even if it was the prosecution's position at trial that the sperm came from the perpetrator").

[10] Ibid., p. xxix (private lab 26 percent exclusion rate).

[11] Ibid., p. xxix ("State conviction rates for felony sexual assaults average about 62 percent").

¹² Ibid., p. xxviii–xxix.

CHAPTER 20

The Boorn murder story is a well-known historical event. The authors credit Rob Warden, executive director of the Center on Wrongful Convictions, who posted a comprehensive summary of the case on May 1, 2002, on the website of the Bluhm Legal Clinic, Northwestern University School of Law, and authored *Wilkie Collins's* The Dead Alive: *The Novel, the Case, and Wrongful Convictions* (Evanston, Ill.: Northwestern University Press, 2005). The authors referenced *True Stories of False Confessions*, which Warden edited with Steve Drizin; Edwin M. Borchard's *Convicting the Innocent, Errors of Criminal Justice*, University Libraries, University at Albany, State University of New York, (a presentation online of the original book published by Yale University Press in New Haven, 1932) http://library.albany.edu/preservation/brittle_bks/Borchard_Convicting/titlepage.pdf; *The Counterfeit Man* by Gerald McFarland (New York: Pantheon Books, 1990); and the minutes of testimony taken at trial by Judge Dudley Chase, *Journals of the General Assembly of the State of Vermont, at their Session begun and held at Montpelier in the County of Washington, on Thursday, the Fourteenth of October, A.D. 1819.*

¹ Center for Wrongful Convictions, Northwestern Law, Bluhm Legal Clinic, Meet the Exonerated www.law.northwestern.edu/wrongfulconvictions/exonerations/vtBoornSummary.html, "America's First Wrongful Murder Conviction Case," and "The exoneration of the Boorns received prominent play in newspapers throughout New England."

² Ibid. ("The Boorn brothers made no secret of their disdain for their sister's spouse" and "[Colvin] was sloughing off on the job and freeloading off the family.").

³ McFarland, *Counterfeit Man*, p. 35 ("Stephen had complained to Wyman about his obnoxious sister, her incompetent husband, and their many children, who, since they were living with his parents, were draining off money.").

⁴ Minutes of testimony taken at trial by Judge Dudley Chase, *Journals of the General Assembly of the State of Vermont, at their Session begun and held at Montpelier in the County of Washington, on Thursday, the Fourteenth of October, A.D. 1819*, p. 194, used by permission of NewsBank/Readex and the American Antiquarian Society (testimony of Sally Colvin: "He used to get up, take the boy on his back, and go off and stay a day or two, without saying anything about it. Once I understood he went off and staid [sic] eight or nine months"); also, Borchard, *Convicting the Innocent*, p. 15 ("...he [Russell] was noted particularly for his habit of suddenly disappearing, to be gone for as much as eight or nine months at a time.").

⁵ Borchard, *Convicting the Innocent*, p. 16 (summary of events described in this source, including "In the dream, Russell Colvin appeared...He told the old man that he had been murdered...The tomb was described as an old cellar hole" and "Fire destroyed an old barn on the Boorn place... it was gossiped that perhaps the barn had been burned to conceal evidence of Colvin's murder" and "...a large knife, a penknife, and a button"); also, Chase, *Journals of the General Assembly*, p. 186 ("I attended the court of examination, the knife, and button, and some bones were found in the cellar hole..." and testimony of Thomas Johnson: "One day at night the children brought in a hat—I observed it was that of Russell Colvin—...it was very mouldy and rotten.").

⁶ Borchard, *Convicting the Innocent*, p. 16 ("Finally, Thomas Johnson's children came home one afternoon with an old, dilapidated hat they found in the field near the Boorn place. Johnson recognized it as the hat he had seen on Colvin the day of the argument in the field.").

[7] Borchard, *Convicting the Innocent*, p. 17 ("A lad and his dog were walking near the Boorn place… the dog stopped and began digging furiously into the earth under an old stump. Bones were unearthed and summarily pronounced human.").

[8] McFarland, *Counterfeit Man*, p. 60 ("Four physicians were called in to examine the charred bones" and "At first the four doctors agreed that the bones were remnants of a human foot.").

[9] Borchard, *Convicting the Innocent*, p. 17 ("…on Saturday, Jesse Boorn charged his brother, Stephen, with the murder" and "On Monday a warrant was issued for Stephen's arrest. He had gone to New York some time before this.").

[10] McFarland, *Counterfeit Man*, p. 60 ("…a man named Salisbury who lived about four or five miles from Manchester Village had lost a leg through amputation. A delegation was sent to the neighboring town where Salisbury's leg was buried, the remains of the limb were exhumed, and the bones were compared with those found in East Manchester. All four doctors now agreed that the East Manchester bones were not of human origin.").

[11] Borchard, *Convicting the Innocent*, p. 16 ("People began to recall certain peculiar remarks they had heard the Boorn boys, or members of the family, make from time to time concerning the missing Colvin. Someone said he had heard one of the boys say that Colvin was dead.").

[12] Chase, *Journals of the General Assembly*, p. 191 (testimony of Silas Merrill: "he [Jesse] said that it was true…that Stephen struck Colvin with a club and brought him to the ground—that Colvin's boy run, that Colvin got up and Stephen gave him a second blow above his ear and broke his skull…the old man cut his throat."); also, McFarland, *Counterfeit Man*, pp. 65–66 (summary of author Gerald McFarland's account of Silas Merrill's version of Jessie's "confession" to Merrill).

[13] Chase, *Journals of the General Assembly*, p. 194 ("Mr. Skinner proposed to show that Merrill, previous to his disclosure before the grand jury, was confined to chains, and afterwards was freed from them, and has been permitted to walk about the streets. Objected to by Mr. Attorney, but admitted by the court."); also, Borchard, *Convicting the Innocent*, p. 18 ("Needless to say, the jury was impressed by this gruesome recital. And it did not suffer from attempts of the defense to break it down by showing that Merrill had been promised leniency if he would tell it in court. [After telling the story he was allowed freedom to roam about the town."]).

[14] Borchard, *Convicting the Innocent*, p. 18 ("…Stephen admitted his guilt and blamed Colvin for initiating the fatal quarrel.").

[15] Chase, *Journals of the General Assembly*, p. 191 ("Stephen said that he would kill me if I said anything about striking.").

[16] Ibid., p. 191.

[17] Warden, *Wilkie Collins's* The Dead Alive, p. 125 (*The Dead Alive* was published in 1874 by Shepard and Gill; "Skinner inexplicably did not play the ace he was holding: he failed to call any of the physicians who had unanimously agreed that the bones recovered from the stump were not human.").

[18] Chase, *Journals of the General Assembly*, 192–94.

[19] Ibid., p. 196.

[20] Borchard, *Convicting the Innocent*, p. 19 ("After a petition for pardon had been presented to the Legislature, Jessie's sentence was commuted to life imprisonment.").

[21] Warden, *Wilkie Collins's* The Dead Alive, p. 127 ("What actually happened was recounted by Gerald W. McFarland, a professor of history at the University of Massachusetts.").

[22] McFarland, *Counterfeit Man*, pp. 122–24 (summary of story of how Russell Colvin was found, including Tabor Chadwick's letter).

²³ Ibid., pp. 125–32.

²⁴ Borchard, *Convicting the Innocent,* pp. 20-21 ("To set the brothers free by due process of law, the case was reopened, they were allowed to plead again, and the state's attorney entered a *nolle prosequi.*"); also, McFarland, *Counterfeit Man,* p. 140 ("He suggested that he petition the Court for a new trial on the grounds of newly discovered evidence... As State's Attorney, Calvin Sheldon responded nolle prosequi...and the tribunal declared the Boorns free men.").

CHAPTER 21

¹ Innocence Project, "Know the Causes: False Confessions," www.innocenceproject.org/understand/False-Confessions.php.

² Rob Warden and Steven A. Drizin, *True Stories of False Confessions* (Evanston, Ill.: Northwestern University Press, 2009), p. 167 ("Stephen was moved to a dark, windowless room and placed in triple chains—he had shackles on his hands and feet and was also chained to the floor.") Note that this account was adapted with permission from McFarland, *Counterfeit Man.*

³ Warden and Drizin, *True Stories,* p. 169 ("Raymond told Stephen that he had 'no doubt of his guilt,'" and Burton chimed in that Stephen was 'a gone goose.'").

⁴ Richard A. Leo, "Inside the Interrogation Room," *Journal of Criminal Law & Criminology* 86, no. 2 (Winter 1996), pp. 266–303; see also Leo, "Miranda's Revenge: Police Interrogation as a Confidence Game," *Law and Society Review* 30, no. 2 (1996), p. 260 ("The most recent empirical study of police interrogation found that 78% of custodial suspects studied waived their Miranda rights and 64% of the suspects questioned provided incriminating statements, admissions of guilt, or full confessions to their interrogators.").

⁵ Saul M. Kassin and Rebecca J. Norwick, "Why People Waive Their Miranda Rights: The Power of Innocence," *Law and Human Behavior* 28, no. 2 (April 2004), p. 212: "As previously observed by researchers in Great Britain (P. Softley, 'Police Interrogation: An Observational Study in Four Police Stations,' London: Home Office Research Study, Royal Commission on Criminal Procedure Research Study, 1980), Leo found that people who have no prior felony record are far more likely to waive their rights than are those with criminal justice 'experience' [Leo, "Miranda's Revenge," pp. 259–88].

⁶ Ibid., p. 212 ("One possible reason for the high waiver rate is that police employ techniques designed to obtain waivers just as they do confessions"; also, "minimizing the process as a mere formality.").

⁷ Thomas P. Sullivan, *Police Experiences with Recording Custodial Interrogations*, a Special Report Presented by Northwestern University School of Law, no. 1, Summer 2004, p. 6.

⁸ Ibid. (summary of benefits delineated in this report, including enabling detectives to focus on the interview instead of note taking), p. 15 (Juneau, Alaska, Police Department); p. 10 (fewer frivolous lawsuits and claims of interrogation abuse and less detective time spent in witnessing in the courtroom—International Association of Chiefs of Police); p. 18 (the opportunity to review the interrogation for important details that may have been overlooked and the improved training tool provided by the recordings).

⁹ Saul M. Kassin, Steven A. Drizin, Thomas Grisso, Gisli H. Gudjonsson, Richard A. Leo, and Allison D. Redlich, "Police-induced Confessions: Risk Factors and Recommendations," published online, 2009, p. 74 ("30 minutes to two hours") Note that Kassin, et al. credit M. Wald, R. Ayres, D.W. Hess, M. Schantz, and C.H. Whitebread (1967). "Interrogations in New Haven: The impact of Miranda." *Yale Law Journal,* 76, 1519–1648. And for "16.3 hours," S.A. Drizin and R.A. Leo

(2004), "The problem of false confessions in the post-DNA world," *North Carolina Law Review*, no. 82, pp. 891–1007.

[10] Jim Trainum, "I took a false confession—so don't tell me it doesn't happen," ACLU of Northern California, www.calitics.com/showDiary.do?diaryId=3831; also, Kassin, et al., "Police-induced Confessions," p. 69 ("no yelling, no cursing, and no physical abuse").

[11] Ibid., Trainum; also, Kassin, et al.

[12] Sullivan, "Police Experiences with Recording" (full Hennepin County, Minnesota, state attorney quote).

[13] Innocence Project, "Understand the Causes: Informants/Snitches," www.innocenceproject.org/understand/Snitches-Informants.php.

[14] Rob Warden, *The Snitch System, How Snitch Testimony Sent Randy Steidl and Other Innocent Americans to Death Row*, a report from Northwestern University School of Law Center on Wrongful Convictions (2004), p. 3 (statistics of 51 death-row exonerations in cases with snitch testimony, 45.9 percent of death row exonerations, "leading cause" in U.S. capital case exonerations).

[15] Robert Reinhold, "California Shaken Over an Informer," *New York Times*, February 17, 1989.

[16] Ibid. ("a bail bondsman, a prosecutor, and a police officer").

[17] Ibid. ("money, furloughs" and "a letter recommending parole").

[18] *Snitch System*, p. 2 ("Don't go to the pen, send a friend.").

[19] Robert M. Bloom, "Jailhouse Informants," *Criminal Justice Magazine* 18, no. 1, Spring 2003, American Bar Association (1999, *Chicago Tribune*, 300/46, summary of results leading to Governor Ryan's moratorium, establishment of commission, and commutation of death sentences).

[20] Bloom, "Jailhouse Informants" ("pretrial discovery, jury instructions, cross-examination, and the use of experts").

[21] Ibid. ("The only effective way to deal with this problem is to provide a pretrial exclusion process to ensure the reliability of an informant's testimony.").

[22] Warden, *Wilkie Collins's* The Dead Alive, p. 125 ("Perhaps, in the face of the overwhelming public opinion against the Boorns, the physicians were reluctant to help them. And perhaps the Boornses' lawyers, in turn, chose not to offend the physicians by compelling them to testify.").

[23] Innocence Project, "Understand the Causes, Bad Lawyering," www.innocenceproject.org/understand/Bad-Lawyering.php.

[24] Innocence Project, "Know the Cases: Charles Chatman," www.innocenceproject.org/Content/1216.php ("Chatman has said he saw his attorney only once before trial, and eventually called him after waiting seven months in jail without any news. He said the attorney told him at that point that the trial was set for the next day."); also, Megan Feldman, "Life After DNA Exoneration," *Dallas Observer*, February 6, 2008.

[25] Feldman, "Life After DNA" (quote of attorney).

[26] Ibid.

CHAPTER 22

[1] Innocence Project, "Understand the Causes: Unvalidated or Improper Science," www.innocenceproject.org/understand/Unreliable-Limited-Science.php.

[2] Brandon L. Garrett and Peter J. Neufeld, "Invalid Forensic Science Testimony and Wrongful Convictions," *Virginia Law Review* 95, no. 1 (March 2009), pp. 1–2, 14 ("Trial transcripts were sought

for all 156 exonerees identified as having trial testimony by forensic analysts, of which 137 were located and reviewed. These trials most commonly included testimony concerning serological analysis and microscopic hair comparison, but some included bite mark, shoe print, soil, fiber, and fingerprint comparisons, and several included DNA testing. This study found that in the bulk of these trials of innocent defendants—82 cases or 60%—forensic analysts called by the prosecution provided invalid testimony at trial—that is, testimony with conclusions misstating empirical data or wholly unsupported by empirical data.").

[3] Ibid., p. 34.

[4] Ibid., p. 2 (In the few cases in which invalid forensic science was challenged, judges seldom provided relief.).

[5] Ibid., p. 17 (verbatim).

[6] Gillispie, "Experts Fault Job" ("Without his faulty assumptions, Blake wrote, Serowick should have concluded that no man could have been excluded as a possible source of the semen on the washcloth.").

[7] Garrett and Neufeld, "Invalid Forensic Science Testimony," p. 18.

[8] Ibid. (Book authors summarized study report, which includes, as an example, statistics from the Perry Mitchell case.)

[9] *Ohio v. Green* ("I recall a study that said one in 40,000 would be a pretty good estimate").

[10] Garrett and Neufeld, "Invalid Forensic Science Testimony," p. 19.

[11] Ibid., fn. 46.

[12] *Strengthening Forensic Science in the United States: A Path Forward*, National Academy of Sciences (Washington, D.C.: National Academies Press, 2009), p. 160.

[13] Ibid., p. 161.

[14] Ibid., p. 20.

[15] Maurice Possley, Steve Mills, and Flynn McRoberts, "Scandal Touches Even Elite Labs," *South Florida Sun-Sentinel*, October 21, 2004 ("Zane" and "Gilchrest," "at least ten exonerations," and "millions in settlement costs").

[16] Garrett and Neufeld, "Invalid Forensic Science Testimony," p. 24.

[17] Interview with James Wooley.

[18] *Daubert v. Merrill Dow Pharmaceuticals* (92-102), 509 U.S. 579 (1993), (b).

[19] Garrett and Neufeld, "Invalid Forensic Science Testimony," *Virginia Law Review*, p. 32, fn. 93; David L. Faigman, "Anecdotal Forensics, Phrenology, and Other Abject Lessons From the History of Science," *Hastings Law Journal*, 59 (2005) 979, 991–92 ("An analysis of the application of *Daubert* in its first decade reveals that while it was used frequently to exclude questionable scientific evidence in civil cases, it almost never resulted in the exclusion of forensic evidence proffered by the prosecution in criminal cases."); also, Peter J. Neufeld, "The (Near) Irrelevance of Daubert to Criminal Justice and Some Suggestions for Reform," *American Journal of Public Health*, 95, Supplement 1 (2005), p. S107, S109; also D. Michael Risinger, "Navigating Expert Reliability: Are Criminal Standards of Certainty Being Left on the Dock?" *Albany Law Review*, 64, 99, 149 (2000).

[20] Ibid., Garrett and Neufeld, authors have summarized the material on page 33, which reads: "At least in criminal cases, having found that the underlying discipline is satisfactory and the evidence admissible following the Frye—or now the Daubert—standard, courts do not typically examine conclusions experts reach on the stand regarding whether statistical claims or other inferences drawn from the data are supported by the evidence. (Footnote 94: See Cole, *supra*

note 16, at 819, "[J]udges assume that their work is done once they have ruled proffered evidence admissible or inadmissible." There is no screening of the case-specific inferences and opinions before the jury hears them. Yet it is precisely while the expert testifies that, as Simon Cole puts it, "the rubber meets the road," and the jury hears claims about the actual evidence in the case (see footnote 95: Id. at 818.). In the few cases where the exonerees' defense counsel raised objections to invalid forensic testimony, judges rarely limited it. When appellate attorneys challenged faulty forensic testimony, courts rarely granted relief, often finding any error to be harmless. (See footnote 96: *infra* Subsection III.A.3.)

Thus, if an expert overstates the evidence or presents it in a misleading fashion, cross-examination is relied upon to test the evidence. Yet, in a criminal case, the defense is typically an unarmed adversary that lacks expert assistance. Also of crucial importance, the presentation of forensic science during criminal trials is usually one-sided, provided only by analysts testifying for the prosecution. Most states do not routinely fund the provision of forensic experts for indigent defendants, though there are strong arguments that under *Ake v. Oklahoma* defendants should be entitled to expert assistance as a matter of due process, at least in some types of cases. (See footnote 97: See *Ake v. Oklahoma*, 470 U.S. 68, 83 (1985); 1 Giannelli and Imwinkelried, *supra* note 78, § 4-5; Paul C. Giannelli, *Ake v. Oklahoma*: The Right to Expert Assistance in a Post-Daubert, Post-DNA World, 89 *Cornell L. Rev.* 1305, 1338–41 (2004); Gross and Mnookin, *supra* note 18, at 189 ("In many criminal cases, there is only one side on expert issues: the prosecution. The result is a national scandal. We have seen case after case of systematic fraud and incompetence by prosecution experts and police crime laboratories, with no end in sight.").

[21] "Badly Fragmented Forensic Science System Needs Overhaul; Evidence to Support Reliability of Many Techniques Is Lacking," National Research Council, press release, February 18, 2009.

[22] Ibid. (All quoted information from citations 26 and 27 is verbatim directly from this press release.)

CHAPTER 23

[1] Innocence Project, "Understand the Causes: Government Misconduct," www.innocenceproject.org/understand/Government-Misconduct.php.

[2] Nina Totenberg, "Can Prosecutors Be Sued by People They Framed?" NPR, November 4, 2009 (details of this case): "Back in 1977, Harrington, captain of his Omaha high school football team, was applying to college and being recruited for a possible scholarship at Yale"; also, "just over the state line" and "all-white jury").

[3] The details of this crime are reported in the U.S. Court of Appeals decision captioned *Curtis W. McGhee Jr., v. Pottawattamie County*, 07-1453, (U.S. District Court for Southern District of Iowa), February 1, 2008, p. 5, and the Iowa Supreme Court decision *Terry J. Harrington v. State of Iowa*, No. 122/01-0653, February 23, 2003.

[4] *McGhee Jr. v. Pottawattamie County*, pp. 4–5 ("Detectives Larsen and Brown traveled to Lincoln to interview Hughes, telling Hughes they knew he was involved in the car theft ring and the… murder, but promised: (1) he would not be charged with the murder, (2) he would be helped with his other criminal charges, and (3) there was a $5,000 reward available if Hughes helped the detectives with the…murder. Hughes agreed to help.").

[5] *Harrington v. Iowa* ("Hughes, the primary witness against Harrington, was by all accounts a liar and a perjurer"); also, "The Right Not to Be Framed—Can Prosecutors Be Sued?" Editorial, *Washington Post*, November 2, 2009 ("a liar and a perjurer").

[6] *McGhee Jr. v. Pottawattamie County*, p. 7 (Only after…began an independent investigation did the extent of the Brady violations committed by Hrvol and Richter come to light. Footnote 4:

[She] was an employee at the prison where Harrington was incarcerated. [She] got to know Harrington and his family.").

7 *McGhee Jr. v. Pottawattamie County*, p. 4 ("A witness saw a man with a dog and a shotgun around the time of the murder, a man Detective Larsen determined was [the suspect]. Richter personally interviewed another witness who positively identified [the suspect] as the person seen walking dogs in the vicinity of the murder. Two more witnesses also placed [the suspect] near the scene of the murder in the relevant time frame" and "Richter had been appointed as County Attorney in 1976 and would stand for election, for the first time, in 1978. Richter was campaigning in the face of [the victim's] unsolved murder.").

8 *Harrington v. Iowa* ("All but one of the eight reports documented the police department's investigation of another suspect in [the victim's] homicide" and "One of the reports also references a polygraph test administered to [the suspect] by Confidential Polygraph Service in Omaha. This test was interpreted to show [the suspect] was 'not truthful in his denial of owning a shotgun or having shot [the victim]'" and "The reports that were found showed that [he] was a suspect in a fourteen-year-old unsolved murder in Omaha." Also, "We hold, therefore, that Harrington's due process right to a fair trial was violated by the State's failure to produce the police reports documenting their investigation of an alternative suspect in [the] murder." See *Mazzan*, 993 P.2d at 74–75 (finding Brady violation where withheld "police reports provided support for [the defendant's] defense that someone else murdered the victim"), *McGhee Jr. v. Pottawattamie County*, and Mark Siebert, "Free Man," *Des Moines Register*, October 25, 2003, pp. 4–5.

9 *McGhee Jr. v. Pottawattamie County*, pp. 7–8 (Wilber quotes verbatim).

10 Ibid. (We find immunity does not extend to the actions of a county attorney who violates a person's substantive due process rights by obtaining, manufacturing, coercing and fabricating evidence before filing formal charges, because this is not "a distinctly prosecutorial function.").

11 Lee Rood, "$12 Million Wrongful Conviction Settlement Is Hailed," DesMoines.com, January 5, 2010 ($12 million: $7.03 million to Harrington and $4.97 million to McGhee).

12 Ibid. ("Current Pottawattamie County Attorney Matt Wilber noted that the settlement, approved Wednesday, 'involves no admission of wrongdoing by the county, by Dave Richter, by Joe Hrvol, or myself.'" Also, verbatim quote from Rob Warden.)

13 Jennifer Emily and Steve McGonigle, "Dallas County district attorney wants unethical prosecutors punished," *Dallas Morning News*, May 4, 2008.

14 Ibid.

15 Innocence Project, "Understand the Causes: Government Misconduct," www.innocenceproject.org/understand/Government-Misconduct.php (verbatim from list provided on website).

16 *United States v. Modica*, 663 F.2d 1173, 1178-79 (2d Cir. 1981); also, Gershman, "Misuse of Scientific Evidence," p. 20.

17 *Berger*, 295 U.S.; also, Gershman, "Misuse of Scientific Evidence," p. 20.

CHAPTER 24

This high-level look at selected highlights in the history of psychological research, law, and eyewitness testimony was informed by James M. Doyle, *True Witness: Cops, Courts, Science, and the Battle Against Misidentification* (New York: Palgrave Macmillan, 2005). The authors' summary of the burglary of Hugo Münsterberg's home is from his book *On the Witness Stand*, with page references indicated.

[1] Hugo Münsterberg, *On the Witness Stand: Essays on Psychology and Crime* (Whitefish, Mont.: Kessinger Publishing, 2007), p. 25.

[2] Ibid., pp. 25–27 ("During the last eighteen years, I have delivered about three thousand university lectures. For those three thousand coherent addresses, I had not once a single written or printed line or any notes whatever on the platform; and yet there has never been a moment when I have had to stop for a name or for the connection of the thought").

[3] Ibid., p. 25.

[4] Doyle, *True Witness*, p. 13 ("father of industrial psychology" and "father of applied psychology").

[5] Doyle, *True Witness*, p. 13; also, Münsterberg, *Witness Stand*, p. 31 ("…no subjective feeling of certainty can be an objective criterion for the desired truth" and "'On the Witness Stand'": Professor Hugo Münsterberg Inquires into the Reliability of Human Testimony—Astonishing Fallibility of Eye, Ear, and Memory," *New York Times*, April 25, 1908 ("…they still cling to the delusion that an honest witness necessarily can and always does tell the truth about things he has seen with his own eyes and heard with his own ears. Prof. Münsterberg's chapters on 'Illusions' and 'The Memory of the Witness' prove how grotesquely false this assumption is.").

[6] Münsterberg, *Witness Stand*, p. 28.

[7] Münsterberg, *Witness Stand*, p. 86. ("The untrue confessions from hope or fear, through promises and threats, from cunning calculations and passive yielding thus shade off into others which are given with real conviction under the pressure of emotional excitement or under the spell of overpowering influences"); also, "On the Witness Stand," *New York Times*).

[8] "On the Witness Stand," *New York Times*.

[9] Münsterberg, *Witness Stand*, p. 9.

[10] Ibid., pp. 9–10.

[11] John H. Wigmore, "Professor Muensterberg and the Psychology of Testimony," *University of Illinois Law Review* 3, no. 7 (February 1909), p. 415.

[12] Doyle, *True Witness*, p. 25 ("He set up the country's first forensic crime laboratory at Northwestern.").

[13] Wigmore, "Professor Muensterberg," p. 433.

[14] William Stern, "Hugo Munsterberg: In Memoriam," *Journal of Applied Psychology* 1, no. 2 (June 1917), pp. 186–88.

[15] Stern, "Hugo Munsterberg," p. 10 ("…by the time of his death in 1916, he was in such thorough eclipse that no memorial notice appeared in any of the Association's publications.").

[16] Doyle, *True Witness*, p. 33.

[17] Doyle, *True Witness*, pp. 55–58 (summary of Buckhout's testimony and contribution to the Davis trial and verdict).

[18] Solomon M. Fulero, Katherine Ellison, and Justin L. Anderson, "Robert Buckhout (1935–1990)," *Law and Human Behavior* 15, no. 5 (October 1991), p. 568.

[19] Ibid.

[20] Doyle, *True Witness*, p. 68; also, Brian Cutler and Steven Penrod, *Mistaken Identification: The Eyewitness, Psychology and the Law* (New York: Cambridge University Press, 1995), p. 41.

[21] *Manson v. Braithwaite*, 1997 (Justice Harry Blackman for the majority).

[22] *Neil v. Biggers*, 409 U.S. 188, 200; also *Manson v. Braithwaite*; also, Doyle, *True Witness*, p. 79.

[23] Doyle, *True Witness*, p. 79 ("In 1983, the Arizona Supreme Court became the first state supreme court to find that a trial judge had abused his discretion by refusing to allow Loftus to testify as an expert on eyewitness identification"); also, Cutler and Penrod, *Mistaken Identification*, pp. 21–25 (history of criteria for admitting eyewitness testimony); also, *Frye v. United States,* 54 App. D.C. 46, 293 F. 1013 No. 3968, Court of Appeals of District of Columbia, submitted November 7, 1923, decided December 3, 1923 ("...while the courts will go a long way in admitting expert testimony deduced from well-recognized scientific principal or discovery, the thing from which the deduction is made must be sufficiently established to have gained general acceptance in the particular field in which it belongs").

[24] Book review: *Eyewitness Testimony,* www.hup.harvard.edu/catalog/LOFEYE.html ("poor viewing conditions, brief exposure, and stress" and "witness's expectations, biases").

[25] Elizabeth F. Loftus, *Eyewitness Testimony* (Cambridge, Mass.: Harvard University Press, 1979), pp. 77–78.

[26] Loftus, *Eyewitness Testimony,* p. 78.

CHAPTER 25

[1] Edward J. Imwinkelried, commentary to *Convicted by Juries, Exonerated by Science,* by Connors, Lundregan, Miller, and McEwen, p. xii ("abandoned," "a more flexible validation standard," "However, the Court decided *Daubert* on statutory rather than constitutional grounds, and, consequently, each State remains free to fashion its own standard for admitting scientific evidence," and "the conservative general acceptance test"); also, *Frye v. United States,* 293 F. 1013 (D.C. Cir. 1923); Id. at 1014 ("gained general acceptance in the particular field in which it belongs;" also, Joseph R. Meaney, "From *Frye* to *Daubert*: Is a Pattern Unfolding?" *Jurimetrics Journal* 35 (1994), pp. 191, 193 (on "22 states committed to Frye").

[2] Imwinkelried, commentary, p. xii ("mystic infallibility"); also, *United States v. Addison,* 498 F.2d 741, 744 (D.C. Cir. 1974) "mystic infallibility."

[3] Imwinkelried, commentary, p. xii ("...when we subject new scientific techniques such as DNA typing to special admissibility rules, we force the courts to rely on inferior types of evidence, such as eyewitness testimony.").

[4] Loftus, *Eyewitness Testimony,* p. 21.

[5] Gary Wells, Amina Memon, and Steven D. Penrod, "Eyewitness Evidence," *Psychological Science in the Public Interest* 7, no. 2 (November 2006), p. 45 ("A subset of the variables that affect eyewitness accuracy fall into what researchers call system variables, which are variables that the criminal justice system has control... We also review estimator variables, variables that affect eyewitness accuracy but over which the system has no control.")

[6] Wells, Memon, and Penrod, "Eyewitness Evidence," p. 55.

[7] Developed and Approved by the Technical Working Group for Eyewitness Evidence, *Eyewitness Evidence: A Guide for Law Enforcement* (Washington, D.C.: U.S. Department of Justice, Office of Justice Programs, National Institute of Justice, October 1999), p. 6.

[8] Ibid., p. 11.

[9] www.innocenceproject.org/fix/Eyewitness-dentification.php?phpMyAdmin=52c4ab7ea46t7da4197.

[10] Nancy Steblay, presentation and presentation handouts at "Strengthening Prosecutions: Improving Eyewitness Identification Procedures in Ohio," sponsored by the University of Cincinnati College of Law, Oct. 2, 2009.

[11] Ibid.

[12] Ibid.

CHAPTER 26

The authors acknowledge the comprehensive coverage of the Gillispie case by Laura A. Bischoff in the *Dayton Daily News*. The authors interviewed or had discussions with Mark Godsey, Dean Gillispie, Juana and Roger Gillispie, Jim Canepa, Steve Fritz, Dennis Leiberman, and Martin Yant, all of whom informed the writing of the Gillispie story. The story of the crime is based primarily on the trial transcript, the police record of the statements of witnesses, briefs, court opinions, and other investigative and official records.

[1] Statement of Witness, Miami Township Police Department, August 21, 1988, pp. 12–13 ("I said I was buying a friend a bridal shower gift.").

[2] Ibid., p. 1 (red Camaro).

[3] Ibid. (conversation with abductor in witness's words).

[4] Statement of Witness, Miami Township Police Dept., August 21, 1988, pp. 1–2 (conversation with abductor in witness's words).

[5] Statement of Witness, p. 11 (conversation: "Give it here, bitch.").

[6] Ibid., p. 6 (conversation: "One sister said that she was scared to death.").

[7] Ibid., p. 12 (conversation in witness's words: "Columbus").

[8] Ibid., p. 13 (conversation in witness's words: "32 automatic with nine rounds" and "close range").

[9] Offense report number 88-1819, Miami Township Police, p. 2 ("possibly near Bear Creek bridge and stopped near a wooded area.").

[10] Statement of Victim, p. 4 (conversation in witness's words).

[11] Offense report 88-1819, p. 2 ("…with some of the semen dropping onto her grey T-shirt.").

[12] Statement of Victim, p. 5 (crime in witness's words).

[13] Ibid., p. 6 (bandannas, "I was scared he was going to shoot us.").

[14] Statement of Witness, p. 10 (crime in witness's words).

[15] Ibid., p. 14 ("He had alcohol on his breath when he got in the car. We both smelled it.").

[16] Ibid., p. 8 (statement in witness's words: "He said his name was Roger.").

[17] Offense report 88-1819, p. 3 (…"he stated…that he was from Columbus and then said he was from Corpus Christi, Texas.").

[18] Statement of Witness, p. 9 (conversation in witness's words: "He said he kills people for a living; $1,000 per person. He said he didn't mind because he never sees them again.").

[19] Ibid., p. 13 ("He also said he was raped when he was twelve years old by his grandfather. 'I have to live with this every day,' he said.").

[20] Ibid., p. 10 ("After two songs on the radio [about ten minutes], we could get up" and "He said if we bob our heads up before that, that he would kill us.").

[21] Affidavit of Steven Fritz, *State of Ohio v. Roger Dean Gillispie*, Case No. 90 CR 2667, February 25, 2007, p. 5 (quotes verbatim).

[22] Offense report 88-1819, pp. 2, 5.

[23] *Ohio v. Gillispie*, trial transcript, Case No. 90-CR-2667, vol. 2 at 412 (witness testimony: Q. Except that you did notice some light blemishes around his jaw line, is that correct? A. Yes).

[24] *Ohio v. Gillispie*, p. 412 (witness testimony: Q: "…you've never said that there was any distinguishing marks about his body; wasn't real hairy or nothing like that, right?" A. "Correct").

[25] Police Offense Report, November 25, 1988, p. 1 (suspect information: "Wearing a gold chain with unknown object attached to same," and "6′0″, 200 lbs., somewhat stocky, short light colored blondish hair, light colored mustache, blue eyes with light complexion with some tanning, strong odor of cologne and smoke," and "small chrome hand gun").

[26] *Ohio v. Gillispie*, pp. 723–24 (testimony of Brian "Otis" Poulter: "About as long as I've known him, he's always had grey. You know, he's always had grey here [indicating the temple area]." and "…and the name that we called him [Dean Gillispie] about his hair was the Silver Fox.").

[27] Ibid., pp. 251, 641 ("…we always made fun of him because he was also blistered all the time" and "…all poor Spiz [Gillispie] does is burn, blister, peel off, and burn again.").

[28] Ibid., p. 734 ("…he has a pickup and he's got a metal magnet sticker that says no smoking; and he's completely against smoke.").

[29] Ibid., p. 747 ("He [Gillispie] was a light drinker.").

[30] Ibid., pp. 764–65 (Q: "Did you ever see him wear jewelry specifically around his neck or throat?" A: "No…He had lots of hair.").

[31] *State of Ohio v. Roger Dean Gillispie*, Case No. 90-CR-2667, affidavit of Steven Fritz, p. 7.

[32] J. D. Caudill, polygraph Examination Report, Area Wide Investigative Consultants, December 10, 1990.

[33] *Ohio v. Gillispie*, affidavit of Fritz, p. 8 (quote verbatim).

[34] Laura A. Bischoff, "'Sometimes I Wonder if Death Ain't Better,'" *Dayton Daily News*, June 3, 2007.

[35] *Reevaluating Lineups: Why Witnesses Make Mistakes and How to Reduce the Chance of a Misidentification*, Innocence Project Report, Benjamin N. Cardozo School of Law, Yeshiva University, p. 12. (Download report at www.innocenceproject.org/Content/2080.php.)

[36] *Ohio v. Gillispie*, declaration of Steven E. Clark, attachment to petition for postconviction relief and motion for a new trial, November 19, 2007, p. 174. (Clark references the study by John W. Shepherd, Hadyn. D. Ellis, and Graham. M. Davies, (Aberdeen: Aberdeen University Press, 1982).

[37] *Ohio v. Gillispie*, trial transcript, p. 418 ("I was 90 percent sure.").

[38] Ibid. (Witness: "He told us we both picked the same person, and that was the suspect that they had, or that was their suspect.").

[39] Ibid., p. 421 (Q: "Remember any conversation [with Detective Moore] about the coloring of the hair?" A: "Yes." Q: "And the conversation about how he might have dyed his hair?" A: "I believe so.").

[40] Ibid., p. 618 (Barber Connie Trent—Q: "Have you ever applied any coloring or dye to his hair?" A: "No") and p. 595 (Forensic scientist Kipling D. Williams: "No, there was no evidence of any artificial treatment to any of those hairs [pulled as samples from Dean Gillispie]").

CHAPTER 27

[1] Bischoff, "Sometimes I Wonder" ("But after reading Godsey's brief to the parole board, the twins' father said, 'It looks to me like the man is innocent.'").

[2] Mark Godsey, memorandum to Ohio Parole Board, February 28, 2007, p. 20.

[3] Ohio Parole Board Decision, Inmate Roger Gillispie, Inmate 246292, April 18, 2007.

[4] Ohio Innocence Project, UC College of Law, staff, Mark A. Godsey, faculty director and professor of law, University of Cincinnati College of Law (www.law.uc.edu/institutes/rosenthal/staff.shtml).

[5] Ibid. (authors' summary of online biography).

[6] University of Cincinnati College of Law Rosenthal Institute for Justice/Ohio Innocence Project 1, no. 2, Summer 2009, p. 3.

[7] *Ohio v. Gillispie*, affidavit, pp. 1–2 (authors' summary).

[8] Ibid. (authors' summary).

[9] *Ohio v. Gillispie*, affidavit of Fritz, p. 9.

[10] Fairfield Police Department record of arrest, docket No. 90M961, September 27, 1990.

[11] Ibid.

[12] *Ohio v. Gillispie*, affidavit of Fritz, p. 8, item 10.

[13] Fairfield Police Department record of arrest, September 27, 1990.

[14] *Ohio v. Gillispie*, affidavit of Fritz, p. 9, item 10.

CHAPTER 28

Jim Petro's recollection.

CHAPTER 29

Jim Petro's recollection.

CHAPTER 30

[1] *State v. Petro*, 76 N.E. 2nd 370 (Ohio App. 1947) syllabus; also, *Ohio v. Gillispie*, petition for post-conviction relief and motion for a new trial, p. 55.

[2] *City of Dayton v. Martin*, 539 N.E. 2nd 646 (Ohio App. 2nd Dist. 1987) syllabus; also, *Ohio v. Gillispie*, petition for post-conviction relief and motion for a new trial, p. 55.

[3] *State v. Petro*, syllabus; also, *Ohio v. Gillispie*, petition, p. 55.

[4] *Ohio v. Gillispie*, petition, p. 4.

[5] *State of Ohio v. Roger Dean Gillispie* in the Court of Appeals of Ohio, Second Appellate District, Montgomery County, Ohio, February 20, 2009, pp. 5–8.

[6] *Ohio v. Gillispie*, petition, p. 4.

[7] Editorial: "Our View—Wagner Sided with Prosecutor Too Fast on Gillispie Case," *Dayton Daily News*, Sunday, July 20, 2008.

[8] Ibid.

[9] Ibid. ("Judge Wagner does not take note of these statements.").

[10] Ibid. (verbatim).

CHAPTER 31

[1] *Ohio v. Gillispie*, in Court of Appeals, brief of appellant Roger Dean Gillispie, p. 11, referencing *D'Ambrosio v. Bagley* (N.D. Ohio 2006).

[2] *State of Ohio v. Roger Dean Gillispie*, petition for post-conviction relief and motion for new trial, February 4, 2008, p. 20 (tr. vol. I at p. 154).

[3] *State of Ohio v. Roger Dean Gillispie*, p. 24, (Ibid. at 3; Exhibit 18 at 3 ¶ 11).

[4] *State of Ohio v. Roger Dean Gillispie*, p. 24 (Exhibit 21 at 5).

[5] *State of Ohio v. Roger Dean Gillispie*, p. 51, fn. 16: "In addition, the Court of Appeals in its 1993 opinion, which resulted from Gillispie's direct appeal, overruled Gillispie's assignment of error that the jury's verdict was against the manifest weight of the evidence relying in part that the 'assaults on the twins took place on Sunday, August 20, 1988.' *State v. Gillispsie*, 1993 WL 10927 at *5 (Ohio App. 2nd Dist. 1993). The actual day of the twins' rape was Saturday, August 20, 1988, not Sunday."

[6] Petro's recollection; also, *Ohio v. Gillispie*, appellee's brief, p. 4 (verbatim material in quotes).

[7] *Ohio v. Gillispie*, Appellee's Brief, May 13, 2009, pp. 5–6 (authors' summarized case history, pp. 1–6).

CHAPTER 32

Petro's recollection.

CHAPTER 33

Petro's recollection.

CHAPTER 34

[1] *State of Ohio v. Roger Dean Gillispie*, final entry, opinion of the Court of Appeals of Ohio, Second Appellate District, July 24, 2009, p. 21–22.

[2] Ibid., p. 23 (referencing *Vinzant, supra*).

[3] Ibid., p. 24.

[4] Ibid., p. 32.

[5] Ibid., p. 34.

[6] *State of Ohio v. Roger Dean Gillispie*, final entry, opinion of the Court of Appeals of Ohio, Second Appellate District, July 24, 2009, pp. 35–36.

[7] Ibid., p. 37 ("[She] asserted that Moore turned the tape recorder on and off during their conversations" and "According to [her], the transcript is not an accurate reflection of their conversation.").

[8] Ibid., p. 39.

[9] Ibid., p. 43.

[10] Ibid.

[11] Ibid., pp. 43–44.

[12] Ibid., p. 46.

[13] Ibid., pp. 48–49.

[14] Lou Grieco, "Roger Dean Gillispie to Get Hearing Concerning New Evidence About an Alternative Suspect," *Dayton Daily News*, Friday, July 24, 2009.

CHAPTER 35

[1] *State of Ohio v. Roger Dean Gillispie*, motion for reconsideration of *Brady* issue surrounding supplemental reports and memorandum of law in support, Court of Appeals, Second Appellate District, Montgomery County, Ohio, August 3, 2009, p. 2 (author's summary of Detective Bailey's affidavit, "due diligence," and "Gillispie was not a viable suspect.").

[2] Ibid., p. 3.

[3] Ibid., p. 2.

[4] Ibid., p. 4.

[5] Ibid., p. 4, referencing affidavit of Fritz, at paragraph 6.

[6] Ibid., motion for Reconsideration, 5

[7] *State of Ohio v. Roger Dean Gillispie*, memorandum contra appellant's motion for reconsideration, in the Court of Appeals of Ohio, Second Appellate District, p. 2.

[8] *State of Ohio v. Roger Dean Gillispie*, decision and entry, August 25, 2009, pp. 3–4.

[9] Ibid., p. 4.

[10] *State of Ohio v. Roger Dean Gillispie*, memorandum in support of jurisdiction of appellant Roger Dean Gillispie, in the Supreme Court of Ohio, p. 11.

[11] Ibid., p. 12.

CHAPTER 36

[1] National District Attorneys Association, www.ndaa.org/ndaa/profile/mat_heck_nov_dec_2003.html (author's summary of Heck bio).

[2] "Test of Convictions: Christopher Dillon," *Columbus Dispatch*, www.dispatch.com/live/content/special_reports/stories/project1/dillon.html.

[3] Geoff Dutton and Mike Wagner, "DNA Tests OK'd for 7 Inmates," *Columbus Dispatch*, March 16, 2008 ("Prosecutors so far have been receptive.").

[4] "Test of Convictions: Christopher Dillon," *Columbus Dispatch*.

[5] Geoff Dutton and Mike Wagner, "Lost Hope," *Columbus Dispatch*, January 27, 2008.

CHAPTER 37

[1] "Significant Cases, Ohio Innocence Project," University of Cincinnati, http://www.law.uc.edu/institutes/rosenthal/SignificantCases.shtml (authors' summary of online article).

[2] Geoff Dutton and Mike Wagner, "Lost Hope."

[3] Ibid. (authors' summary of the *Columbus Dispatch*'s findings).

[4] Wagner and Dutton, "Out of Time: Ohio Restricts Convicts Who Try to Prove Innocence," *Columbus Dispatch*, January 28, 2008 (quote of Robert McClendon).

[5] "Test of Convictions," *Columbus Dispatch*, www.dispatch.com/live/content/special_reports/stories/2008/dna/index.html (interactive page with updated information on this investigation).

[6] Mike Wagner and Geoff Dutton, "Hello, Freedom: Robert McClendon Rejoins his Family as a Free Man," *Columbus Dispatch*, August 12, 2008 ("DNA Diagnostics discovered faint traces of semen in the underwear that the Columbus police crime lab had missed in 1990.").

[7] Ibid. ("father of five," "Both of his parents and grandparents died when he was in prison.").

[8] Ibid. (Robert McClendon quote verbatim).

[9] Ibid. (Ron O'Brien quote verbatim).

[10] Geoff Dutton and Mike Wagner, "New Bill Would Expand DNA Testing for Convicts," *Columbus Dispatch*, August 17, 2008.

[11] Memorandum to Governor Ted Strickland, Attorney General Marc Dann, and the Ohio General Assembly from the Ohio Innocence Project (OIP) at the University of Cincinnati College of Law

regarding proposed legislative reforms in light of the recent *Columbus Dispatch* series on DNA and wrongful convictions in Ohio, February 20, 2008, p. 1.

[12] Dutton and Wagner, "New Bill" (Governor Strickland quote verbatim).

[13] Innocence Project, "Know the Cases," http://www.innocenceproject.org/Content/Joseph_Fears_Jr.php.

[14] Dutton and Wagner, "New Bill" (Tim Young quote verbatim).

[15] Ibid. (Mark Godsey quote verbatim).

[16] Petro's recollection; also, Dutton and Wagner, "New Bill."

CHAPTER 38

[1] *William G. Osborne v. District Attorney's Office*, opinion, April 2, 2008, p. 3365 (authors' summary of description of sentence and case, including "…she heard the gun fire and felt a bullet graze her head.").

[2] *District Attorney's Office for the Third Judicial District et al. v. Osborne*, certiorari to the United States Court of Appeals for the Ninth Circuit, No. 08-6. I A, argued March 2, 2009, decided June 18, 2009.

[3] Ibid., certiorari, B ("He claimed that he had asked his attorney, Sidney Billingslea, to seek more discriminating restriction-fragment-length-polymorphism (RFLP) DNA testing during trial, and argued that she was constitutionally ineffective for not doing so.").

[4] Ibid., certiorari, B, history of appeals in this case.

[5] Biography of Janet Reno, www.washingtonpost.com/wp-srv/politics/govt/admin/reno.htm.

[6] In the Supreme Court of the United States, *District Attorney's Office for the Third Judicial District, et al., Petitioner v. William G. Osborne, Respondent*, brief of current and former prosecutors as amici curiae in support of respondent, pp. 3–4.

[7] "Meet the Exonerated," Northwestern University, Northwestern Law, Bluhm Legal Clinic, Center on Wrongful Convictions, www.law.northwestern.edu/wrongfulconvictions/exonerations/ilEvansTerrySummary.html ("They were convicted of the crime by a jury and languished behind bars for 27 years before DNA exonerated them in what the U.S. Court of Appeals labeled 'a tragedy of epic proportions'"; also, *District Attorney's Office v. Osborne* (Supreme Court of the United States), brief of current and former prosecutors as amici curiae in support of respondent, p. 4 (authors' summary of brief biography of Thomas M. Breen).

[8] Ibid., brief of current and former prosecutors as amici curiae, p. 5 (authors' summary of brief biography of Kenneth L. Gillis).

[9] Ibid., pp. 5–6 (authors' summary of brief biography of Carl J. Marlinga).

[10] Ibid., p. 6 (authors' summary of brief biography of Scott D. McNamara).

[11] Ibid., pp. 7–8.

[12] "DNA Exonerations," *Dallas Morning News*, February 24, 2010 (Introduction: "The *Dallas Morning News* spent most of this year investigating Dallas County's 19 DNA exonerations as well as current felony cases to document flaws in the witness identification process").

[13] *District Attorney's Office v. Osborne* (Supreme Court of the United States), brief of current and former prosecutors as amici curiae in support of respondent, p. 8 (authors' summary of brief biography of Andrea L. Zopp).

[14] Innocence Project, "Know the Cases: Kenneth Adams," www.innocenceproject.org/Content/46.php ("With the help of David Protess, Rob Warden, and a team of journalism students from

Northwestern University, the four men gained access to the evidence for DNA testing. They also discovered that the police had been tipped to the identity of the actual perpetrators but did not pursue the lead. Eventually DNA testing exonerated all four men and implicated three other men, two of whom confessed and pleaded guilty to the crimes in 1997"; also, authors calculated combined 72 years from individual cases at www.innocenceproject.org).

[15] *District Attorney's Office v. Osborne* (Supreme Court of the United States), "brief of current and former prosecutors as amici curiae in support of respondent," p. 5 (authors' summary of brief biography of Peggy A. Lautenschlager).

[16] *In re Winship*, 397 U.S. 358, 372 (1970) (Harlan, J. concurring: "In this context, I view the requirement of proof beyond a reasonable doubt in a criminal case as bottomed on a fundamental value determination of our society that it is far worse to convict an innocent man than to let a guilty man go free"); also, *District Attorney's Office v. Osborne* (Supreme Court of the United States), brief of current and former prosecutors as amici curiae in support of respondent," p. 33.

[17] *District Attorney's Office v. Osborne* (Supreme Court of the United States), brief of current and former prosecutors as amici curiae in support of respondent, pp. 21–22.

[18] Ibid., pp. 9–10.

[19] 42 U.S.C. § 1983: U.S. Code—Section 1983: Civil action for deprivation of rights.

[20] *District Attorney's Office v. Osborne* (Supreme Court of the United States), brief of current and former prosecutors as amici curiae in support of respondent, February 2, 2009, p. 28.

CHAPTER 39

[1] *District Attorney's Office v. William G. Osborne*, Supreme Court of the United States, opinion of the Court (Roberts), June 18, 2009, p. 16.

[2] Ibid., p. 22.

[3] Ibid., p. 20.

[4] Ibid. (Stevens dissenting, pp. 13–14, verbatim).

[5] Ibid., pp. 15–16 (verbatim).

[6] Ibid., p. 17 (verbatim).

[7] Ibid. (Souter, concurring dissenting, p. 7, verbatim).

[8] Opinion, *Plain Dealer*, Tuesday, June 23, 2009.

[9] William Richey, "What Impact Will Supreme Court Decision of DNA Evidence Have?" *Christian Science Monitor*, June 18, 2009.

PART IV (INTRODUCTION)

[1] *District Attorney's Office for the Third Judicial District (Alaska), et al., Petitioners v. William G. Osborne*, 557 U.S.—(2009) Supreme Court of the United States (Souter dissenting), p. 3. (Full text: "It goes without saying that the conception of the reasonable looks to the prevailing understanding of the broad society, not to individual notions that a judge may entertain for himself alone, id., at 542, 544, and in applying a national constitution the society of reference is the nation. On specific issues, widely shared understandings within the national society can change as interests claimed under the rubric of liberty evolve into recognition, see *Griswold v. Connecticut*, 381 U.S. 479 (1965) (personal privacy); *Lawrence v. Texas*, 539 U.S. 558 (2003) (sexual intimacy); see also *Washington v. Glucksberg*, 521 U.S. 702, 752 (1997) (Souter, concurring in judgment), or are recast in light of experience and accumulated knowledge, compare *Roe v. Wade*, 410 U.S. 113 (1973), with

Planned Parenthood of Southeastern Pa. v. Casey, 505 U.S. 833 (1992) (joint opinion of O'Connor, Kennedy and Souter)."

[2] Hugo Münsterberg, *On the Witness Stand,* Ams Pr Inc., June 1927, downloaded from all-about-psychology.com January 19, 2010, pp. 9–103.

[3] http://dictionary.reference.com/browse/myth Dictionary.com unabridged.

CHAPTER 40

[1] Samuel R. Gross and Barbara O'Brien, "Frequency and Predictors of False Conviction: Why We Know So Little and New Data on Capital Cases," *Journal of Empirical Legal Studies* 5, no. 4 (December 2008), p. 956.

CHAPTER 41

[1] "What Jennifer Saw," *Frontline,* Peter Neufeld interview, website WGBH Educational Foundation, http://www.pbs.org/wgbh/pages/frontline/shows/dna/interviews/neufeld.html.

[2] Connors, Lundregan, Miller, and McEwen, *Convicted by Juries, Exonerated by Science,* pp. xxviii–xxix. (Specifically, FBI officials report that out of roughly ten thousand sexual assault cases since 1989, about two thousand tests have been inconclusive—usually insufficient high molecular weight DNA to do testing—about two thousand tests have excluded the primary suspect, and about six thousand have "matched," or included, the primary suspect. The fact that these percentages have remained constant for seven years, and that the National Institute of Justice's informal survey of private laboratories reveals a strikingly similar 26 percent exclusion rate, strongly suggests that post-arrest and post-conviction DNA exonerations are tied to some strong, underlying systemic problems that generate erroneous accusations and convictions.)

[3] Robert Dawson, "A Passion for Justice," University of Texas at Austin website, updated October 9, 2008, www.utexas.edu/features/archive/2005/innocence.html.

CHAPTER 42

[1] Innocence Project, "Understand the Causes: False Confessions," www.innocenceproject.org/understand/False-Confessions.php ("In about 25 percent of DNA exoneration cases, innocent defendants made incriminating statements, delivered outright confessions or pled guilty.").

[2] Chase, *Journals of the General Assembly,* p. 195 (testimony of Mr. Pettibone: "Burton once said to Stephen, 'You are a gone goose and had better state the facts than not'"); also, Warden and Drizin, *True Stories,* p. 169 ("…and Burton chimed in that Stephen was 'a gone goose.'").

[3] Christopher Ochoa, "My Life Is a Broken Puzzle," in *Surviving Justice, America's Wrongfully Convicted and Exonerated,* a Collection of Oral Histories, ed. Lola Vollen and Dave Eggers (San Francisco: Voice of Witness, McSweeney's Books, 2005), p. 19. (Authors read many accounts of the Ochoa case including these credited sources.)

[4] Ibid., p.19 (storyline and quote: "You're not going to be able to hug your mom or your family anymore.").

[5] Ibid., p. 23 (storyline and quote: "At one point the sergeant got up and threw the chair he was sitting on, at my head. He missed, but he threw it with such force, and I was really scared 'cause those guys were really big.").

[6] Warden and Drizin, *True Stories,* (based on "Texas Justice," *Salon,* October 31, 2000, © Salon) p. 148 ("The City of Austin settled the suits in 2003 with payments of $5.3 million to Ochoa and $9 million to Danziger.").

[7] Ibid.; *True Stories of False Confessions*, based on writings of April Witt, *Washington Post*, June 23, 2001 (storyline for this case, pp. 291–96, including [p. 292] "...when a detective flipped the photographs. They showed the brutalized body of his once-beautiful wife" and "As he laid his head on the table and wept, two detectives began accusing him and taunting him. While one detective shoved the hideous photos in his face, the other mocked his grief as phony and said he'd killed her.").

[8] Ibid., p. 293 ("He said he was going to handcuff me to the wall and beat the crap out of me if I didn't sit down," Longtin said.).

[9] Ibid., p. 293 ("Longtin said he began to question his own sense of reality.").

[10] Ibid., p. 294 ("The police log indicated he slept about fifty minutes in more than thirty-eight hours in the interrogation room. He said he hadn't slept at all.").

[11] Ibid., pp. 295–96 (storyline including eyewitness identification of Antonio D. Oesby, DNA match, conviction and sentence).

[12] Ibid., p. 296 ("In 2001 a civil jury in St. George's County awarded Keith Longtin $6.4 million for the violation of his civil rights.").

[13] John E. Reid & Associates, www.reid.com/success_reid/r_sresults.html.

[14] "False Confession Cases—The Issues," John E. Reid and Associates (white paper) www.reid.com/educational_info/pdfs/Falseconfessioncases.pdf ("...there are four factors that appear with some regularity in false confession cases: the suspect is a juvenile; and/or the suspect suffers some mental or psychological impairment; and/or the interrogation took place over an inordinate amount of time; and/or the interrogators engaged in illegal tactics and techniques.")

[15] Ibid. ("During the presentation of any theme based upon the morality factor, caution must be taken to avoid any indication that the minimization of the moral blame will relieve the suspect of criminal responsibility.") Note: This is an excerpt from *Criminal Investigations and Confessions* (4th edition, 2001, Inbau, Reid, Buckley, and Jayne).

[16] Ibid. "In the Reid Technique, the alternative question should never threaten consequences or offer promises of leniency. The following are improper alternative question examples:

- 'Do you want to cooperate with me and tell me what happened, or spend the next five to seven years behind bars?' (improper)
- 'Do you want to be charged with first-degree murder, which will mean life in prison, or was this just manslaughter?' (improper)
- 'Are you going to get this straightened out today, or do you want to spend a few days in jail to think about it?' (improper)."

[17] Ibid., "False Confession Cases" (quote is one of several provided that are indicative of threats that were made in actual exoneration cases).

[18] Kassin, et al., "Police-Induced Confessions," p. 43 ("...studies of actual cases reveal that the false evidence ploy, which is not permitted in Great Britain and most other European nations, is found in numerous wrongful convictions in the U.S., including DNA exonerations in which there were confessions in evidence [Drizin and Leo 2004; Leo and Ofshe, 1998]); p. 75 ("In *Frazier v. Cupp* [1969], the U.S. Supreme Court reviewed a case in which police falsely told the defendant that his alibi had confessed and sanctioned this type of deception—seeing it as relevant to voluntariness but not disqualifying. Although some state courts have distinguished between mere false assertions, which are permissible, the fabrication of reports, tapes, and other evidence, which are not, the Supreme Court has not revisited the issue.").

CHAPTER 43

[1] *Brady v. Maryland*, 373 U.S. 83 (1963).

[2] Ibid.

CHAPTER 44

[1] Gary L. Wells and Deah S. Quinlivan, "Suggestive Eyewitness Identification Procedures and the Supreme Court's Reliability Test in Light of Eyewitness Science: 30 Years Later," American Psychology-Law Society/Division 41 of the American Psychological Association, published online February 27, 2008, p. 6 (archival studies of actual eyewitnesses to serious crimes show that, among eyewitnesses who select someone from a lineup, they select a known innocent filler 30 percent of the time, on average [Behrman and Davey 2001; Behrman and Richards 2005; Slater 1994; Valentine, et al., 2003; Wright and McDaid, 1996; Wright and Skagerberg 2007]).

[2] *Manson v Braithwaite*, 432 U.S. 98 (1977) No. 75-871, p. 114.

[3] Wells and Quinlivan, "Suggestive Eyewitness Identification Procedures," p. 9. (Authors summarize the fuller discussion. Key points: "...three of the five Manson criteria, namely view, attention, and certainty, are what psychological scientists call retrospective self-reports. Psychological scientists are highly skeptical of retrospective self-reports because of well-known tendencies for such reports being at odds with objective facts" and "At another level, psychological scientists find it somewhat odd that an eyewitness, whose credibility as a witness is being assessed, would be asked to report on his or her own credibility." Also, "...at least three of the Manson factors are not independent of the suggestive procedure itself. In other words, the use of suggestive procedures can lead the eyewitness to enhance [distort] his or her retrospective self-reports in ways that help ensure the witness's high standing on the Manson criteria, thereby leading to a dismissal of the suggestiveness concern. We will call this latter process, in which suggestiveness causes inflated status on the Manson factors, which in turn causes courts to discount the suggestiveness, the suggestiveness augmentation effect. We believe that the suggestiveness augmentation effect is a very serious problem for the two-prong totality approach guiding Manson. We believe that the suggestiveness augmentation effect accounts at least in part for the rarity of suppressing identifications obtained from highly suggestive procedures, and we believe this effect creates a disincentive for police and prosecutors to jettison suggestive procedures.")

[4] Ibid., p. 12.

CHAPTER 45

[1] Written notes from interviews of jurors by Juana Gillispie.

CHAPTER 46

[1] Wagner and Dutton, "Out of Time," *Columbus Dispatch*, January 28, 2008 (Marx quote verbatim and "out of confidence in and respect for the jury, the appeals court and the victim").

[2] Ibid. (Landefeld quote verbatim).

[3] Dutton and Wagner, "Lost Hope" (governor's quote verbatim).

[4] Innocence Project, News and Information, "Facts of Postconviction DNA Exonerations," www.innocenceproject.org/Content/351.php.

[5] Innocence Project, News and Information, "Reevaluating Lineups: Why Witnesses Make Mistakes," www.innocenceproject.org/Content/2080.php (quoted material verbatim).

CHAPTER 47

[1] *Petitioners v. William G. Osborne*, Justice David Souter (dissenting), 557 U.S._(2009) .

[2] Gershman, "Misuse of Scientific Evidence," p. 19. (Regarding the role of the prosecutor: "A prosecuting attorney occupies two distinct but simultaneous roles in the criminal justice system—an adversarial role and a quasi-judicial role. A prosecutor in her adversarial role is the attorney for the government and may vigorously seek to convict persons charged with crimes. A prosecutor in her quasi-judicial role, however, has a different mission, namely, a constitutional and ethical duty not merely to win a conviction, but also to seek justice.") Gershman notes these, among other references: *Berger v. United States*, 295 U.S. 78, 88 (1935) ("[The prosecutor's] interest, therefore, in a criminal prosecution is not that it shall win a case, but that justice shall be done"); also, Model Rules of Professional Responsibility EC 7-13 (1981) ("A prosecutor has the responsibility of a minister of justice and not simply of an advocate"). Also, ABA Standards of Criminal Justice: Prosecution Function 2d Def. Function § 3-1.2(c), The Prosecution Function, standard 3-1.2(c) (American Bar Association 3d.ed.) ("The duty of the prosecutor is to seek justice, not merely to convict.")

[3] *Berger*, 295 U.S.

EPILOGUE

[1] Eric Ferreror, director of communications, Innocence Project, press release, March 16, 2010 (Rebecca Brown quotes verbatim).

Index